Understanding THE GOSPEL Culture and Environment:

Essays in Honour of Allison Mary Howell

Edited by Ini Dorcas Dah,
Ebenezer Yaw Blasu and Rudolf K. Gaisie

First published in March 2022

ISBN: 978 – 9988 – 3 – 3481 – 9

Typeset & Printed by University of Ghana Printing Press,
Legon P. O. Box LG 1181 Legon, Accra, Ghana
Email: ugpress@ug.edu.gh

Table of Contents

ACKNOWLEDGEMENTS

We are grateful to the Lord Almighty for answering our prayers through the fulfilment of this project.

Many thanks to all contributors listed in this volume. You bore with us until the completion of this volume. May the Lord always remember you for your collaboration and patience.

Our thanks also go to the copy editors, Ms. Morgan Wolf and Dr. Sara Fretheim, who helped to prepare the essays for publication. We really appreciate your service despite your busy schedules. May the good Lord be with you all.

Ini Dorcas Dah
Ebenezer Yaw Blasu
Rudolf K. Gaisie
27 September 2021

PREFACE

A Selfless, God-fearing Teacher and Friend, Who Can Find?

It is with great privilege and delight to have worked together with other colleagues to bring this collection of essays in honour of a lecturer and friend. The idea of this festschrift originally belongs to Dorcas Ini Dah. We do share in her sentiments leading to the initial planning and organisation.

On the 25th of December 2020, as I (Dorcas) was desperately looking for something to buy for my children, I contacted a friend from ACI, who told me I could get something in his shop. He picked me and the children up on 26th December 2020. At the shop, I met his wife, another "daughter" of Professor Allison Mary Howell, from Navrongo, Northern Ghana. I eventually mentioned my daughter's name (Namwin-Noumana Leonie Allisson Dah) to her, and my friend's wife responded by looking upwards and prayed 'O God give me a daughter that I can name after Auntie Allison'! Sometimes you left Prof. Howell's office wondering if you have said thanks enough. I first met Prof Howell at the Akrofi-Christaller Institute of Theology, Mission and Culture in 2008, when God led me to pursue an MA in Theology. She became instrumental in my progress through the Master of Theology programme and eventually supervising my doctoral research. Though she could not attend my graduation (in December 2015) due to health issues, she still sent someone to come and take photos for her because she really wanted to be with me. The idea of a festschrift began on my graduation day, as I pondered how I can best honour such an influential mentor. Travelling with Prof. Howell, and staying with her in Chiana in November 2018, gave me the opportunity to see how her stay in that area had positively impacted the community. Indeed, Prof Howell's contributions go beyond the classroom! It is, therefore, fitting that we honour her while she is still with us on earth, and we pray the Lord continues to keep her here longer! Though I had hoped this book, together with two other personal ones being worked on, would have been completed earlier before the year 2021, ill-health, and the eventual blessing of the birth of Allisson Dah in 2020, meant that my rhythm and pace of work slowed down. I decided to focus all my time and energy on this volume, and I am grateful to God that my colleagues Drs Blasu and Gaisie agreed to come along as co-editors to bring the work to this point.

Almost all the contributors met Prof. Howell in the context of undertaking theological training and research and thus we have endeavoured to produce essays that reflect the areas in which she has trained us or researched in, namely, Christian/Mission History; Gospel, Culture, and Spirituality; Theology, Human Need, and Environment; and Bible Translation and Interpretation. We trust that the essays on these topics will truly honour Prof. Howell.

We began with the question, "A selfless, God-fearing teacher and friend, who can find?" We can say that those who have studied under auntie, mother, and Professor Allison Mary Howell have found her! We are delighted to have met and share fellowship with one who teaches with such humility, and out of the depths of love for the Lord and for others, as she has. We, therefore, are celebrating you from Aberdeen, Burkina Faso, Canada, Ghana, Ethiopia, Kenya, Nigeria, Rwanda, Sierra Leone, South Africa, USA and all the corners of the world.

MAY THE GOOD LORD BLESS AND KEEP OUR SISTER, AUNTIE, MOTHER, FRIEND, MENTOR, COLLEAGUE, and PROFESSOR, ALLISON MARY HOWELL!
NAMWIN O BE NI FO!
NYAME NHYIRA WO!
BAŊA WƐ SWƐ NMO SWOLIM!
MERCI BEAUCOUP!
DANKE SHÖN!
MAWU NA YRA WO!

Ini Dorcas Dah
Ebenezer Yaw Blasu
Rudolf K. Gaisie
29 September 2021

FOREWORD

There was a moment very early in a young missionary's life in northern Ghana where she had to make a decision. Should she listen to the inner voice that said the event taking place before her was "something to do with witchcraft", or should she consider more carefully and try to discern the meaning that was behind the event. She decided to do the latter. Thus, was born one of the fundamental principles that guided Allison Howell's research for the next thirty eight years in Ghana – that hidden behind form there is meaning, and that meaning is what we need to understand.

There was, of course, an even more important principle that guided her then, as it does now: her love for God and the people who God gave her to serve. Howell loved not only with her words, but with her life; travelling for sixteen years with the Kasena: listening to them, learning from them, and speaking with them in their own language. Thus, was born *The Religious Itinerary of a Ghanaian People*, a text that must surely be one of the most seminal peregrinations of the gospel and culture dialectic. Except the words "gospel" and "culture" actually very seldom appear in the text. What does appear so many times in its 401 pages that it becomes utterly ubiquitous in the Kasena story, are the words *wɛ choŋa*, literally meaning "God's way". This is profoundly significant. While scholars tend to discuss one entity called the "gospel" and another called "culture", the Kasena talk about a single entity - "God's way", the synthesis of the thesis of the gospel and the antithesis of culture. A more startling expression of what happens when gospel meets culture one can hardly find. And it was for the Kasena, not Howell, to create the synthesis. Unlike the missionaries that had gone before her, she was as interested in what the recipients were doing to the message as she was in what the message was doing to the recipients. The paradigm had completely shifted. The teacher had become a learner. *The Religious Itinerary* simply documents the herculean struggles of the Kasena to find God's Way through all the vicissitudes of life that came with the meshwork of domains that make up the profoundly complex and fragile world of an African people. The result is a stunning piece of work that makes fascinating, compulsive, and demanding reading.

It would, of course, have been much easier for the Kasena (and for Howell) simply to reject their religion and culture and adopt the message and culture of the messenger, *tout court.* Many a missionary would have defined her task precisely in these terms and been more than happy with the result

– a mirror image of her own culture. But Howell not only repudiates this understanding of conversion but castigates those who perpetrate it because it "tore at the heart of family unity, undermined the authority of family heads and many other sanctions related to Kasena social control".[1] Instead she exhorts us to take seriously the proposition that the God who is behind the message of salvation is the same God who is behind the culture of those who receive the message of salvation.

Allison Howell's major work serves as a benchmark not only for missiological research in Africa but for how to do contextual theology; a popular term in progressive circles, but which often ends up becoming a synonym for legitimizing particular political ideologies. What *The Religious Itinerary* doesn't reflect, however, is Howell's latter passion for the environment. In her 2017 Kwame Bediako memorial lecture, inspired by Bediako's exhortation to discern the signs of the times, she focused specifically on the environment in the Ghanaian context, using the term "wicked problem", coined by scientists to identify complex and intractable problems that have multiple causes and solutions, to describe it. The lecture was another example of how to do contextual theology on the front burner issue of our time. This theme, as well as many of the others that have preoccupied her, and around which she has mentored scores of students, feature in this present volume of essays. The essays revolve around many of the themes that are central to her work in the field of gospel and culture, including translation of biblical texts into the vernacular; historical background that highlights the north/south encounter; in-depth description of particular issues surrounding gospel and culture; theoretical elucidation of the dynamics involved in the gospel and culture dialectic; the use of narrative or story-telling, and the inescapable politico-spiritual dimension of the church's mission. Most of the essays refer to her by name and reflect her influence in some way, one even theorizing the pedagogical importance of the mentor/student relationship, featuring Howell as exhibit A. Two of the contributors, Andrew Walls and Robert Addo-Fening, were her own mentors while all of the others, to one degree or another, were mentored by her.

There are three biblical images that come to mind as I read these essays. The first is from the book of Genesis where God brought all of His creation to "the man to see what he would name them; and whatever the man called each living creature, that was its name" (Genesis 2:19). The

1 Howell, *The Religious Itinerary of a Ghanaian People*, 134.

second is the image of the babe in a manger, who is also the incarnate God. The third is the image of the grain of wheat that has to fall into the ground and die before it can bring forth fruit. (John 12:24) The first speaks to the extraordinary responsibility that God has given us in the care for His creation and to His curiosity as to exactly how we would do this. He does the creating, we do the naming. Care and curiosity – the defining hallmarks not only of our stewardship of God's creation but of the scholarly enterprise that He has given us to undertake. The babe in the manger speaks to the profound vulnerability that lies at the heart of the gospel, God's project of salvation. Here indeed is a form that requires meaning. Just as God was curious to know what we might do with His creation, He is curious to know what we might do with the Son that He has given us; how we will understand him; "translate" him, believe in him and follow him. The third image of the grain of wheat that needs to fall into the ground and die before it bears fruit is offered by Jesus and speaks of His death, burial, and resurrection. In all of these images, God is giving something of Himself away. He gives away His power to name. He gives away his power to rule. He gives away His power to live. It is in this truth that the unique mystery of God's kingdom lies. It is a kingdom based not on getting power, but on giving it away. In the great transaction that God makes with the world He has only one requirement of us – that we give ourselves to Him as unconditionally as He gives Himself to us.

The principle of letting go of control is directly applicable to the translation principle in the gospel and culture dialectic. The significance of translation, as people such as Lamin Sanneh have been at great pains to explain, lies in the fact that when the message is translated the power to interpret it in a particular way is surrendered. If it were not translatable, the power to interpret it differently would not be granted. The fact that it is, multiplies exponentially the number of agencies and interpretations that will follow. This results in a challenging loss of control by the sender in which one becomes little more than a spectator to what ensues. And, when the risk is taken, and the power relinquished, the consequences are not always to the liking of the sender. Indeed, the infinite translatability of the gospel message, especially at the cultural interface, means transfer of agency to the receiving community and a whole new set of responsibilities, priorities, and meanings emerge under the guidance of the Holy Spirit. The rather benign sounding notion of the search for "keys to conduct" belies a far more serious kind of "nervous conditions" scenario somewhat reminiscent of what Chinua Achebe describes in *Things Fall Apart.* The expression was coined to describe the intense concern of the receiving communities to adjust to an entirely new set of circumstances that ensues as a consequence of embracing the gospel. This was not just to do with hearing and receiving the message; it was to do with a change of regime beginning in the spiritual realm and reverberating through the entire socio-cultural matrix. And while the receivers are busy searching for God's Way, the senders wring their hands, roll their eyes, and tear at their garments, while they watch their soteriology, Christology, pneumatology, and eschatology, get a makeover.

There were, no doubt, many moments in Allison Howell's career when she was hard pressed to understand what was happening in the mission field. We can be profoundly grateful that early in that career she decided not to respond in the default mode of most missionaries and consign to hell what was taking place before her because she interpreted it as witchcraft. Instead, she decided to become a listener, a learner, a fellow traveller with the Kasena on their journey of faith. In doing so she not only won the love and confidence of the Kasena but many others who joined her on the journey of faith and the journey of academic scholarship. It has been a long journey and one that has taken its toll on her body. But she is an extraordinarily strong woman that has become an extraordinarily capable, caring, and consistent mentor for scores of people. We thank God for her and for what she means to us all.

Anthony O. Balcomb (PhD)
27 October 2020

INTRODUCTION

Professor Allison Mary Howell's contribution to the development and growth of Akrofi-Christaller Institute (ACI) is immense. This is true of the total life of the institute but especially of its academic programmes and research efforts. Given ACI's position in the development of theological education in the world, especially Africa, this translates into far-reaching impact. A rare person and academic, she is always up to date in her endeavours even as she looks to and explores new ways that would improve the present.

As a member of the ACI family, Allison Howell dealt first and foremost with students, and it is little wonder that most of the contributors to this festschrift are her former students. To her students, she was not only a teacher and supervisor whose detailed remarks flooded their papers, both hard and soft, but also one who became a counsellor, friend, and mentor; always ready to welcome as colleagues those who chose a calling like hers. She has always been tough on her students to get the best out of them, but she has always accompanied them in all aspects of their lives as needed. ACI offered her the opportunity to serve students, but she served ACI at many other levels as well.

As the pioneer Dean of Accredited Studies Allison Howell laid many of the major foundations for the running of ACI's academic programmes – the development and periodic reviews of policies, the building of needed academic structures, routine review of courses, running of seminars and so on. Also, as pioneer Dean of Research, Howell spearheaded research activities, as well as the organisation of workshops and academic conferences, such as the International "Cocoa Conference" of 2015 that the Institute mounted to celebrate the centenary anniversary of the establishment of the Basel Mission. This resulted in the publication of *The 'Golden Pod': Its Religious, Socio-Economic and Political Impact on Gold Coast and Ghana* (Akropong: Regnum Africa, 2018), jointly edited by her and Professor Robert Addo-Fening.

These roles of faculty member (which involved the development of new courses and being the lead teacher in Research Methods), and Dean of Accredited Studies and later of Research, were all official responsibilities, but Howell unofficially played some other key roles to advance the work of ACI. She was always helping to recruit students. Many came to study at ACI because of her advocacy. Moreover, Howell has been an extraordinary fund-raiser for ACI. Unequivocally, she has been the focal point for major financial support for ACI. Many, including family, friends, associates and even strangers have supported the Institute simply because of her, or through her advocacy. In all these roles, official and unofficial, I have counted her a personal friend, advisor/consultant on many matters and one with whom I have also had the delight to co-supervise some students.

In this work undertaken to honour Allison Mary Howell, we encounter contributions by many of her students, some of whom have become colleagues in the academy. It is, however, also significant that two contributors are her own teacher and obvious role model, Andrew Walls, and her highly respected colleague, collaborator and friend, historian Robert Addo-Fening.

Divided into four parts, the essays in this work focus on Christian/Mission History; Gospel, Culture, and Spirituality; Theology, Human Need and Environment; and Bible Translation and Interpretation. All these areas have been pertinent to Howell's scholarship. Typical of the ACI approach, Howell sat in courses in Christian and Mission history taught by Andrew Walls and then co-taught with him before taking sole teaching responsibility. She would lead others through a similar mentorship exercise later on.

James Walton, one such mentee, uses Andrew Walls' indigenizing and pilgrim principles of cross-cultural transmission of the Christian faith to pursue a case study of Semisi Nau, a South Pacific missionary. This study validates Walls' position as Walton uses Nau's autobiography to exemplify these twin principles. Walton successfully places Nau in the context of an overview of the Christianisation of the South Pacific Islands.

In his contribution, Robert Addo-Fening, dilates on the encounter between the Basel Missionaries and the kingdom of Akyem Abuakwa, recounting the fascinating clash of two worlds. A conflict that precipitated missionary connivance with the British colonial government in order to extend the latter's authority into the Akyem Abuakwa kingdom in the name of freedom of worship, "civilisation" and progress. Prominent in this story is the figure of Amoako Atta I and his efforts to preserve his traditional religion against Christianity.

Angela Dwamena-Aboagye revisits the debate over the Western Missionary Movement's impact in Africa – whether it was negative in promoting colonialism or positive in preaching the gospel and bringing liberation and wholeness to Africans. In her case study of two missionaries – Mary Slessor of Calabar, Nigeria, and Johannes Christaller of the Gold Coast — Dwamena-Aboagye demonstrates the positive impact some missionaries made, having identified with the intertwining factors of culture, thought and language of the people among whom they worked. In her view, Allison Howell could be in this class without doubt.

Beyond Christian/Mission History, Howell also worked much in matters pertaining to the engagement of gospel, culture, and spirituality. The ongoing engagement between gospel and culture generates many potential pitfalls. In his contribution, Rudolf K. Gaisie reflects on the nature of these pitfalls and how they could be avoided while dialoguing with Allison Howell's article on the subject. Gaisie emphasizes the need to move beyond the "form" of various cultural activities, — the knowledge of which is important — in order to get to the "meaning" of such cultural activities. In the end, the affirmation of life in Christ in given cultural contexts is what matters.

Similarly, Ini Dorcas Dah examines the clan system among the Birifor and the power that the clans hold over their members. Dah discusses the origins of the four clans and how they function in their socio-cultural organisation. She articulates the challenges the system poses to Christians, and proposes how Christian engagement with the clan system could lead to transformation that enables greater allegiance on the part of Birifor Christians to Christ, rather than a person's clan.

The only contribution made by a team in this volume is that by John Kwotuah and Judith Bawa. They undertake a qualitative study of traditional funeral celebrations of elderly women among the Kasena. While Kasena Christians may legitimately distance themselves from certain aspects of this celebration which are at variance with their Christian faith, Kwotuah and Bawa argue that there are many other aspects of the celebration that are simply social in character and thus any wholesale rejection of the practice would be counter-productive to the spreading of the gospel and cultural engagement among the Kasena. The recommendation is for the Church to engage rather than disengage.

Another piece of qualitative research deals with the interplay of faith and daily life among Ethiopian Christians. This contribution by Seblewengel Daniel picks up on a variety of issues of everyday life including relationships; spirituality; violence; prosperity and health. Perspectives from Orthodox Christian, Evangelical and Muslim constituencies are tapped to enrich this study.

Victor Zizer advocates for theological education; the adoption of relational pedagogy with focus on dialogue. Faculty in theological institutions should play shepherding and counselling roles in their teaching ministry to offer the needed support to their students and thereby help to transform them into good Christian leaders. In this contribution, Zizer offers a personal testimony of his journey as a student at ACI and the major role that Allison Howell played in that journey. Apart from impacting individual students like Zizer, Howell, as noted earlier, also impacted ACI as a whole. Howell's first degree in geography no doubt served her well in the development of new courses in theology, human need, and the environment.

Contributions in this volume under theology, human need, and environment begin with one from Howell's teacher and mentor, Andrew F. Walls. In his piece, Walls takes a fresh look at the Great Commission (Mt. 28:17-20) and its implications for structural and systemic evil. Walls links this mandate of the Great Commission to Paul's dilation on the resurrection in 1 Corinthians 15. He demonstrates that Jesus' followers, having been commissioned to go and make disciples of all nations are also inextricably mandated in the authority of the risen Lord to help to dismantle evil in all its forms, taking account of the spiritual roots of evil as reflected in primal societies. He casts in a new light how current followers of Jesus Christ can fulfil he Great Commission by helping to demolish political and economic structures that perpetuate evil.

Ebenezer Y. Blasu's focus on Muslims' commitment to Islamic environmentalism in the Sokpoe-Sogakope Ecological Area of the Volta Region underscores the need for all religious segments of society to be marshalled towards creation care. Urbanisation has contributed to undermine creation care. Blasu illustrates that there are enough Islamic resources to tap to empower Muslims, especially those in urban areas, to pursue the preservation of the environment. But to do so, even the more in conjunction with people of other religious traditions in resolving a common task, African theocology is one such major and worthy resource.

In his contribution on creation care, Joshua D. Settles juxtaposes the exponential Christian activity in Africa with the dominant evidence of a lack of creation care. From a primal perspective, he articulates the unbreakable link that should exist between holistic mission and creation care. He calls on the Church to focus on relationships and live out in mission her identity as a reconciled and reconciling community that includes all of creation.

A final piece in creation care comes from Kehinde Olabimtan in which he laments the environmental degradation going on in Nigeria; the West African sub-region; and other parts of Africa and the challenge that all this poses for the future of our planet. He also examines the post-independence African Christian scene; from African indigenous churches, to the current situation in which many churches are rather western in their outlook, language, media usage and the international networks they cultivate and maintain. Olabimtan sets an agenda for the future and argues for the utilisation of available African primal resources for the care of the environment. He outlines steps that can be taken to sensitize African Christians to their responsibility for God's creation centering on pneumatology, soteriology, and eschatology.

The final section of the work focuses on Bible Translation and Interpretation with two contributions. Vellah Ngaina undertakes a case study of Lydia (Acts 16:14) to highlight the nuances of the multiple identities that women like Lydia had in the cosmopolitan setting of the first century Graeco-Roman world. Using her Sabaot mother tongue translation in addition to the Greek text — as well as engaging with many commentators — Ngaina paints a complex portrait of Lydia that should inspire Christian women involved in mission in our time.

Finally, Gabriel Akimana highlights the need for contextual translation in his contribution which addresses the Kinyarwanda translation of the phrase, "Visiting the iniquity of fathers upon sons ..." in the second commandment (Ex. 20:5). He examines and rejects the four existing Kinyarwanda translations that all suggest that in this commandment God claims, "to punish" or "to revenge". Instead, Akimana proposes the translation, "to investigate" as the best possibility for the Kinyarwanda context.

The essays in this volume remind the reader of a dedicated scholar and genuine human being in the academy serving Jesus Christ by serving others and advancing knowledge. Allison Howell taught many aspects of the research methods utilised by her former students in their contributions. Some of the essays involved field work; some, her approaches to research — especially as it relates to gospel and cultural issues—; and still others, reflect her interest in the use of primary and archival resources.

Many of these contributions also underscore Howell's priority for scholarship to serve people. Whether in terms of lessons history offers for the betterment of individual lives; the genuine engagement between the gospel and culture in resolving the problems of real people, or how an understanding of theology, human need, and environment can translate into practical care of God's creation, Howell emphasized that scholarship should serve, rather than be served. On this score, Howell lived out what she researched, wrote, and taught. It is noteworthy that Howell grounded her scholarship in the Word of God. She did not overlook the biblical foundations of her academic pursuits and, in this regard, the mother tongue scriptures were always in focus. The essays of Walls, Ngaina and Akimana similarly reflect this interest in scripture. Additionally, the upcoming commentary on John's Gospel in Kasena being produced under Howell's leadership will be of great benefit to her Kasena brothers and sisters.

Allison Howell's academic journey has proceeded in the face of many personal challenges, but she is first to attest to the faithfulness of God. This rich piece of work presents a testimony of how God has used Allison Howell to bless many people and through these essays, many more will be served.

B. Y. Quarshie (PhD)
Rector, ACI

PART ONE

CHRISTIAN / MISSION HISTORY

The 'Indigenising' and 'Pilgrim' Principles of Cross-Cultural Transmission of the Christian Faith: The Case of Semisi Nau, the South Pacific Missionary

James K. Walton

ABSTRACT

The paper sets out to illustrate the pilgrim and indigenising principles of cross-cultural transmission of Christian faith espoused by Andrew Walls and others. These principles which appear a reality in Christian communities across Christian history are played out in the Christianisation process of the South Pacific Islands. The paper thus attempts to use aspects of the life of Semisi Nau, a South Pacific Islander missionary to provide data which supports the observation. It is contributed because it arose out of Professor Howell's teaching in a course on Aspects of World Christian History, and the interest it generated in the Christianisation of the South Pacific Islands.

The work is a literary one, using established authorities in South Pacific Islander historiography to demonstrate the issues at hand. Of natural extensive use is the translated autobiography of Semisi Nau, pioneer Christian worker on Ontong Java, Solomon Islands to provide primary source material.

The essay thus shows that the ministry of Reverend Semisi Nau abundantly exemplifies the pilgrim and indigenising principles of cross-cultural transmission of Christian faith. It goes further to show that it was a pattern in the Christianisation process of the South Pacific Islands. Andrew Walls' observation thus appears validated – for the South Pacific.

Introduction

The 'indigenising' principle[2] of cross-cultural mission, espoused by Professor Andrew F. Walls, calls attention to the impress that is made on the Christian faith when it enters a particular culture. Even though at the outset it may take on characteristics of the culture of the missionary, in time the faith begins to express itself in the forms of the recipient culture.

First Century Christianity which had a Jewish impress or flavour was very different from Fourth Century Christianity, which had a dominant Greek impress. The process of incarnation into the culture of recipient communities has continued over Christian history to date. So that Christianity in Africa today largely bears the stamp of Africa and may be differentiated from European Christianity, from which the bulk of Africa's missionizing communities descended. The indigenizing principle enables one 'to live as a Christian and yet as a member of one's own society, to make the Church "A Place to Feel at Home."'[3]

The one great factor which promotes this occurrence is the infinite translatability of the Christian scriptures,[4] which is itself occasioned by the fact of the Incarnation, that historic event in which God became human. In the Incarnation, God translated himself from the transcendent realm to the realm of humanity. Just as in linguistic translation a person in one linguistic medium can tell a person in another medium, 'This is exactly what I mean', so also in the Incarnation Jesus was able to declare, 'This is what God is like!' As a result, the translated Christian scriptures enables recipient communities to hear the gospel, 'the wonders of God in their own languages'[5] making it easier for them to respond in their own culturally authentic ways.

The 'pilgrim principle'[6], on the other hand, emphasises the universality of the Christian faith. Although it is true that the Christian gospel has that quality which allows itself to be impressed with the culture of the recipient community, it still retains certain qualities which hold true for Christianity across the ages. So that even though the manifestation of the faith may vary from culture to culture, there are certain similarities that

2 This term was coined by Andrew Walls. See Andrew F. Walls, *The Missionary Movement in Christian History: Studies in the Transmission of Faith*, (Maryknoll: Orbis Books, 1996), 7-8.
3 Walls, *The Missionary Movement in Christian History*, 7.
4 Walls, *The Missionary Movement in Christian History*, 22, 25.
5 *Acts of the Apostles* 2:6, 8, 11.
6 Walls, *The Missionary Movement in Christian History*, 8-9.

mark out Christian practice, wherever it manifests itself, as belonging to the same family.

Andrew Walls has identified these "coherent... signposts of historic Christianity"[7] as:

a. "the worship of the God of Israel" – this links Gentile Christians with the history of Israel and gives them a point of reference.
b. "the ultimate significance of Jesus of Nazareth" – Jesus becomes the ultimate in every cultural vocabulary.
c. the conviction "that God is active where believers are."
d. the conviction "that believers constitute a people of God transcending time and space."
e. the observation of the following institutions: the reading of common Scriptures and the special use of bread and wine and water.

These signposts "whispers to ... [the Christian] ... that he has no abiding city and warns him that to be faithful to Christ will put him out of step with his society; for that society never existed, in East or West, ancient time or modern, which could absorb the word of Christ painlessly into its system ... the result of the transformation of the mind towards Christ."[8]

The Reverend Semisi Nau, a Tongan born Methodist Christian missionary to Ontong Java in the Solomon Islands, exemplifies the indigenising and pilgrim principles in his life and ministry. This comes out in the autobiography which was written at the instance of his lifelong friend Rev. William Leembruggen in the Roviana language, which was spoken in the western Solomon Islands, his field of mission work. A missionary nursing sister, Miss Mary Gartrell translated it into English. Alan Davidson published the original text together with an introductory section.[9] This essay will use the autobiography to show that the two principles were applicable in the Rev. Nau's life and ministry. Contemporary missionaries may yet learn from this, that these principles need to be applied for effective ministry. Indeed, they are values that Professor Allison Howell, in whose honour this festschrift is being written, embodied so beautifully. Truly, the article arose out of a course she taught which generated in me an interest in the Christianisation of the South Pacific Islands.

---

7 Walls, *The Missionary Movement in Christian History*, 23-24.
8 Walls, *The Missionary Movement in Christian History*, 8.
9 Alan K. Davidson (ed.), *Semisi Nau: The Story of my Life – A Tongan Missionary at Ontong Java*, (Suva, Fiji: The University of the South Pacific, 1996), 1,3,83,119. To distinguish between the Autobiography and the Introduction, the Autobiography will be designated as: Semisi Nau, *The Story of my Life*.

The Rev. Semisi Nau belonged to a long line of South Pacific Islander missionaries who sometimes, at the risk of their lives, left their own homes to go and share their new-found faith in Christ with peoples of other islands, languages and cultures. It is necessary to examine how and why this came about, beginning with how the gospel found a home in the Pacific Islands in the first place.

Historical Background

Beginnings of Missionary Work in the South Pacific Islands

By the 16th Century, Spain had crossed the Pacific with banners, crosses and incense following the Patronato real, the authority given it by the Pope in 1493 to propagate the gospel across the world west of a dividing line in Brazil. Portugal was to do the same in the east. The Philippines and the Mariana Islands were consequently introduced to the Christian faith.[10]

Formal mission work, however, did not begin till 1668 when Father Diego Luis de Sanvitores landed on the island of Guam, east of the Philippines. Unfortunately, misunderstanding between the people and the missionaries resulted in the mission closing down.

A century went by before Protestants of the London Missionary Society (LMS) permanently resumed formal missions. On 5th March 1797 a party of 18 missionaries landed on the island of Tahiti, part of a larger group made up of 30 men, 6 women and 3 children who were bound for different parts of Polynesia, the eastern section of the South Sea Islands. It appeared that the establishment of churches and thus a complete entry into the religious life of the community depended upon the king giving permission. Unfortunately, there was no community-accepted king, but rather a struggle between candidates for the monarch of the Society Islands group; the main island of which was Tahiti. In 1812, Pomare, one of the candidates, who had been friendly towards the missionaries, declared himself converted. To be really certain, the missionaries waited till 1819 before his baptism; they reasoned that as a royal with indigenous sanction for dalliance with both sexes, they needed to see the conversion lived out in practice.

10 John Garrett, *To Live among the Stars: Christian Origins in Oceania,* (Geneva: WCC Publications, 1982), 1.

Meanwhile, since the evangelical tradition of the LMS emphasised literacy in the Scriptures, the missionaries had managed to master and reduce the language to writing. They then set up a school for this purpose at Papetoai, on the island of Moorea, also in the Society Islands group. The task of Bible translation was also tackled seriously by Rev. Henry Nott. As time went on, more and more 'inquirers into Christianity' attended the 'Christian School', where training in spiritual issues and Bible knowledge were combined with literacy in vernacular reading and writing.

The king's conversion influenced a number of Tahitians who had had some contact with the missionaries, especially those who had attended the school. They began to hold secret prayer meetings in the bush. When the missionaries found this out, they started worship services on Sundays on Moorea.[11]

In 1815, Pomare succeeded in regaining his authority over Tahiti. He and his supporters (bure atua – praying people) had been attacked whilst at worship. But they had repulsed the attack and won a victory. This was seen as possession of a superior mana (divine power). Consequently, large numbers, which now entered the church, resulted in Tahiti and Moorea becoming nominally Christian. Thereupon, scholars from the school, haapii parau (learners of the Word) who had been converted, spread out all over the other islands of the Society group sharing (teaching) their newfound faith as well as literacy. Some of these early evangelists were later officially sent out as missionaries or 'native teachers' to other parts of the South Sea Islands; for on Raiatea, an auxiliary society was set up to recruit members to serve this purpose. Schools were also introduced on some of the other islands.[12]

The depressive lean years of Christian expansion now appeared over. Within 20 years, 'Ma'ohi[13] Christians had grasped Christianity firmly as an extension of their traditional religious ideas and were even ready to share their insights with other people.'[14] This they did to several islands, including Tonga, under the supervision of white missionaries.

---

11 Garrett, *To Live among the Stars*, 21-22.
12 Garrett, To Live among the Stars, 23,26,30. Raeburn Lange, Island Ministers-Indigenous Leadership in Nineteenth Century Pacific Islands Christianity, (Christchurch, N. Z.: Macmillan Brown Centre for Pacific Studies, University of Canterbury, 2005), 39.
13 The Ma'ohi are made up of the people of Tahiti and nearby islands.
14 Ian Breward, *A History of the Churches in Australasia*, (Oxford: Oxford University Press, 2001), 29.

Beginnings of Missionary Work in Tonga and the Solomon Islands

The Duff, the ship that transported the first group of missionaries to Tahiti also landed a party of ten on Tongatapu, the southern section of the island group of Tonga in 1797. The work received setbacks until gradually it was stabilised through the ministry of the Rev. John Thomas and Pacific Islanders from the Tahitian group. The ministry resulted in the Christianization of the greater majority of the population by 1850.[15]

In 1845, Methodist local preacher, George Tupou I came to the throne of the Tongan Island group. He helped the cause of Christ by promoting the sending of missionaries to the islands of Samoa and Fiji.[16] He was also very instrumental in the setting up of Tupou College in 1866. The founding headmaster, the Rev. Dr. J. E. Moulton, was unequalled for his leadership in education.[17] The College was in a class of its own and aimed for high academic attainments. It served both church and state well, producing well-trained church workers and civil servants, among the latter being young chiefs for public positions. In addition, all tuition was in mother tongue.[18] It was here that the Rev. Semisi Nau received the early and crowning stages of his preparation for mission work, first on his own island of Tonga and then on the Solomon Islands.

The Solomon Islands first exposure to Christian faith was in 1595 when Spanish navigators landed in a ship with Roman Catholic priests on board. No successful Catholic mission work could be established, however, until 1898 when another batch of Marist fathers, brothers and catechists arrived and began a more permanent and successful ministry.[19]

Protestant missions began from 1851 with the Anglican Church and gradually grew in the South and Central Solomons. The work was made difficult by the influence of local Big Men, the power of secret societies and traditional systems of amassing wealth all connected with non-Christian spirits.[20] The Christian message of liberation was a natural threat to these oppressive elements of Solomon Islander life.

15 G. Stringer Rowe, *A Pioneer: A Memoir of the Rev. John Thomas, Missionary to the Friendly Islands,* (London: T. Woolmer, 1885), 136 cited by K. S. Latourette, *A History of the Expansion of Christianity: The Great Century 1800-1914* (Grand Rapids: Zondervan, 1943), 211.
16 Garrett, *To Live among the Stars*, 75-79.
17 Latourette, *A History of the Expansion of Christianity*, 211.
18 Lange, *Island Ministers,* 105.
19 Garrett, *To Live among the Stars*, 179-182,297.
20 Garrett, *To Live among the Stars*, 182-185.

Methodist Missions to the Solomon Islands began when in 1902, the Rev. Dr. George Brown arrived in New Georgia together with the Rev. John F. Goldie, leader of an industrial mission to Munda in the Roviana Lagoon. The mission was the result of an earlier visit by the Rev. Brown, Secretary of the Australasian Wesleyan Mission Board, to the head-hunters of Roviana. Under Goldie, the work prospered through the establishment of technical and farming schools, resulting in the winning of several converts. Pacific Islander missionaries from Fiji, Tonga and Samoa, together with others from Australia and New Zealand, fanned the work to flame in this western part of the Solomon Islands (and also in adjoining Buka and Bougainville in Papua New Guinea).[21] The Rev. Semisi Nau was one of the first Tongan missionaries to labour in this regard.

Nature of Mission Work

Islander missionaries did receive some amount of training before they were stationed. But often they were thrown into their work with hardly any experience except their natural talents, their training, and of course the help of the Holy Spirit. For some of them, especially those from Samoa, there was a tendency to operate with a superiority complex and intolerance towards other cultures. Sione Latukefu, who reports this, reflects that this was the result of a similar attitude projected by some Europeans during the period of training[22]

At the initial stages, many of these stations were pioneer fields where the gospel was not known. The pattern of operation, therefore, was to seek the permission of the chief of a village or community for the establishment of a *lotu* (Christian faith or church). The authority of a ruling chief was crucial to the establishment of the lotu since his word directed the course of life of the community. Garrett notes that Taufa'ahau of Tonga, in referring to his influence on his people claimed, "When I turn, they all turn".[23] Similarly, on Luangiua, Ontong Java, Solomon Islands, Semisi Nau had a very difficult time at the beginning of his missionary work. The chief, Keapea, would not countenance a missionary in his village. For three months, Semisi and his family had to live in a boat anchored some distance from the shore. They almost died from thirst as they ran out of water. Finally, in a miraculous way, Keapea agreed to their stay. Only then, could Semisi's work begin.[24]

21 Garrett, *To Live among the Stars*, 300.
22 Sione Latukefu, 'Pacific Islander Missionaries' in Doug Munro and Andrew Thornley (eds.), *The Covenant Makers: Islander Missionaries in the Pacific*, (Suva: Pacific Theological College, 1996), 23.
23 Garrett, *To Live among the Stars*, 74.
24 Semisi Nau, *The Story of my Life*, 95,97-99,102,104.

Once the traditional authority had granted permission, the next step was to establish a home either by building one from scratch or occupying one which was often offered by the chief. Then began the business of the mission proper. Worship services were organised, together with a school, often during the weekdays. Not only children attended school; adults also participated in the lessons which were limited to either morning or afternoon.[25] For industrial missions, there was also practical work to be done either on a farm, or in other spheres.

As worship and instruction proceeded, a batch of baptismal candidates were formed who were willing to accept the full discipline of the Christian faith. In this way, the lotu was gradually built up. Request for baptism would mean that the person had been converted. Like today, therefore, it appears that there were many others at church who had not come to the point of requesting baptism. This should be expected since there were often mass people movements into the church,[26] often following after their chief.

Since the mission was part of the community, the missionary was sometimes consulted on traditional custom and its relation to the new faith.[27] Where the majority of people, including the chief, moved into the church, the missionary had to formulate a new social code of discipline as well as new, or transformed social institutions. Missionaries would also defend local people who were being cheated by white traders.[28] It was this kind of work that the Rev. Nau, together with his wife, was involved in most of his life.

Semisi Nau, Servant of God, Missionary:

Life Before Missionary Service on Ontong Java

Semisi Nau was born on the island of Fiji about the year 1866. His father, the Rev. Sioeli Nau, although serving in Fiji, was Tongan. Together with his mother, Mrs. Akosita Nau, they had eight children, four of whom worked for the church. Akosita was Fijian and was native to the island of Kadavu. In 1877, Semisi's father was re-stationed in Tonga.[29]

25 Semisi Nau, *The Story of my Life*, 92,94.
26 Latourette, *A History of the Expansion of Christianity*, 259
27 Davidson (ed.), *Semisi Nau*, 33,64.
28 Davidson (ed.), *Semisi Nau*, 58.
29 Davidson (ed.), *Semisi Nau*, 9.

When Semisi was 16 years old, he gained admission to the prestigious Tupou College in Tonga. It was while he was in school here that the Wesleyan Methodist Church entered into the troubled times which led to the imprisonment of some clergy and members. The Rev. Shirley W. Baker, who had served previously as Chairman of the Tongan District of the Wesleyan Methodist Church, but was now Prime Minister of Tonga, encouraged the King to break away and form the Free Church of Tonga. This new church was only different in name; its internal structure and operation was fully Methodist. It appears that the Prime Minister was motivated by political as well as personal selfish interests for leading the king in this direction. There seemed to be the possibility of a British take-over of government, and there were personality conflicts between

Dr. Moulton, the current Chairman of the Tongan District of the Wesleyan Methodist Church and the Prime Minister, Rev. Baker divesting the country of any British connections appeared to be a wise path of protest.

Customarily, it was required for Tongans to obey their king in all things. Consequently, large numbers followed him into the Free Church. The Rev. Sioeli Nau and his son Semisi were among a small minority who remained faithful to the Wesleyan Methodist Church. For the Rev. Nau, his ordination vows prevented him from changing camps.[30]

Since Tupou College under Rev. Dr. Moulton was fully Wesleyan, a plan to disband it resulted in an order for all students to enrol in the militia and to swear an oath of obedience. Semisi was among a number of students who refused to swear the oath since they were not sure of what they were committing themselves to. They were consequently imprisoned in 1886 until 1887, when as a result of an intervention by the British government, a general amnesty was granted. Both Semisi and his father sailed with other Wesleyans to Fiji where they were stationed in the Rewa District under the Rev. William E. Bromilow. They had both showed the strength of character that should mark out all true servants of God. In his later ministry on the Solomon Islands, Semisi would again exhibit this strength of character in the different crises which hit his family.

While in Fiji, Semisi sat under the ministry of the Rev. Bromilow who preached a sermon that won his whole heart for Jesus. The Reverend had

30 Davidson (ed.), *Semisi Nau*, 14.

challenged his hearers to throw in their lot with Moses who rejected the pleasures and glory of Egypt for the difficult life of walking in the will of God. Strong conviction and sorrow for sin was followed by an assurance of sins forgiven when Semisi surrendered his whole heart to the Lord. Says Semisi, "...my heart was soon full of pain & heaviness through conviction of sin. I was not long in this state when ... a word of peace came to me spoken by the Holy Spirit, 'My Son I have cast away all thy sin.' When I heard that a great joy filled my heart..."[31]

The pattern of events in Semisi's conversion was typically Methodist. It fitted the 'heart strangely warmed' experience of John Wesley and Methodism. Here there was an emphasis on a clean heart and a life of holiness. Already, in his personal life, Semisi was beginning to exemplify marks that were characteristic of several other Christians in other places. He would bequeath his 'pilgrim' experience of conversion to his mission communities, for they also became 'the people of God' among whom 'God was active', with Jesus as ultimate.

Semisi continued in school in Fiji until 1890 when the records suggest that he returned with his father to Tonga upon a request for stationing on his home island. Semisi was thus readmitted to Tupou College, his alma mater, where he completed his studies in two years. He reports that it was during these completing years at the College that he began to feel stirrings towards missionary service. "I knew that God had called me to be a worker in His vineyard, but though I knew that He had called me I knew not to what place God intended me to go."[32]

At his first teaching station, Niuafo'ou, an appeal was made for workers to New Guinea. Semisi offered to go but was turned down on account of his unmarried status. Soon, Semisi was praying for a wife; if this was what it took to become a missionary, then he would be married. Matelita Tuliakiono was the girl who became Semisi's life-long partner in his missionary career. In 1895, a request came from Folaha, Tongapatu and Mr. and Mrs. Semisi Nau were stationed there as missionaries in response. Semisi's father died on 18th December 1895 in a tragic sleep-walking accident. Possibly as a result of this, his extended family requested him to re-join them, presumably for a while. In June 1896, Semisi received permission.

31 Semisi Nau, *The Story of my Life*, 86.
32 Davidson (ed.), *Semisi Nau*, 11,18,86.

In this first missionary experience, Semisi's resolve to "take hold of my cross to follow Christ anywhere, that I might bring forth fruit unto everlasting life" seems to have proved successful. The people of the Wesleyan Methodist Church in Folaha began to love him "with a great love" and he "became greatly attached to the people" even though there appears to have been some harassment from members of the Free Church.[33] This attachment to a man of God, and commitment during a time of persecution, is a natural mark that the people had accepted the message of Jesus Christ as all true Christians have done across the ages; a mark of family likeness and an indicator of the success of Semisi's ministry.

Back home in Vava'u, Tonga, Semisi began to feel restless even though surrounded by family and friends. He felt he was neglecting his call to ministry. Jesus had all the joys of heaven, yet he came down to the sufferings of earth in order to uplift humankind to similar glory. Semisi, therefore, felt that if he would be true to the faith he would have to follow after him. He confessed, "Surrounded as we are by earthly goods I am afraid lest they take hold of my heart & I forget that God has called me."[34] He accepted an appointment to Fatai, Tongupatu; but barely seven months later he was asking permission "to rest a while". He was thus sent to 'Utulau. It is not clear why there was this break in missionary service. Whilst in 'Utulau, Semisi and Matelita lost three children, a very heavy blow to the young couple.[35]

In 1902, the Rev. Dr. Brown, General Secretary to the Australasian Wesleyan Methodist Missionary Society visited Tonga to recruit missionary teachers. After a wait for about three years, the Nau family made up of Semisi, Matelita and Akosita, their only surviving daughter, sailed for the Solomon Islands, the arena for their major missionary engagement in 1906.[36]

It has already been noted that the Rev. Semisi Nau exemplifies the indigenising and pilgrim principles of cross-cultural transmission of the gospel.

33 Davidson (ed.), *Semisi Nau,* 11,87.
34 Semisi Nau, *The Story of my Life,* 88.
35 Semisi Nau, *The Story of my Life* 88.
36 Davidson (ed.), *Semisi Nau,* 20,89.

Pilgrim Principle

To recapitulate, this principle manifests the universalising nature of Christian faith. As noted in the introduction of this work, Andrew Walls has identified five major marks which together summarise this principle as a characteristic notable of Christians across the world and in Christian history. How do the marks of this principle manifest in the life of the Rev. Semisi Nau as inferable from his autobiography?

Commitment and Devotion

Semisi Nau had a very clear understanding of his call to ministry as a missionary; an understanding that has characterised all true and successful missionaries down through the years. In my view, his commitment and devotion to his calling reflects his belief in the ultimate significance of Jesus and how God's activity among believers is ubiquitous. When asked by Dr. Moulton, his College Principal, whether he was "ready to go as a missionary to take the Light to some dark land", he replied, "Dr. Moulton if it is only to chop wood or carry water in the service of God I want to go; whether the way be difficult or easy; if I live or die I have given all my life to God."[37] Matelita Nau was similarly convinced, so when Dr. Moulton interviewed her later, she said, "I know that Jesus loves me & has brought me from death unto life & my only wish now is to do His bidding & follow His will. I have taken up my cross & am willing to go wherever you decide to send me."[38]

Here was a wife who was as committed to the cause of Christ as her husband. Unfortunately, the identity of many of such missionary women gets lost for the simple reason that they were only designated with their husbands in the records as '...pastor's name *and wife*'.[39] Together, the Naus became a strong force for the work of the Kingdom.

Dr. Bogue, one of the directors of the LMS, said in 1795, "A missionary must be a burning and a shining light. The rays of divine knowledge must shine forth brightly from his mind, and the fire of divine zeal burn with a pure flame in his heart."[40] Indeed, the missionary societies were careful about the motives of their candidates.

37 Semisi Nau, *The Story of my Life*, 89.
38 Semisi Nau, *The Story of my Life*, 89.
39 Munro et al, *The Covenant Makers*, 210.
40 Neil Gunson, *Messengers of Grace: Evangelical Missionaries in the South Seas, 1797-1860* (New York: Oxford University Press, 1978), 48.

They accepted only those whom they were sure truly wanted to obey Christ's command to save the lost and were concerned for the glory of God.[41]

In Semisi Nau, the commitment to the calling of God was exemplified in several areas of his life and ministry. In the Solomons, he had several opportunities of making money even though it was mission policy for missionaries not to engage in business. Semisi writes,

> I did not want to fix my affections upon earthly things, my friends, worldly possessions, comforts or family ... I had many opportunities of making money, but I knew that as God had chosen my father & mother to take the Gospel to Fiji, so He had chosen me & wished me to keep myself separate & apart from other things. [42]

Even if it meant the loss of personal comfort, Semisi was willing.

The Luanuia people lived chiefly on fish & cocoanuts (sic) ... It was not a place of much food but if God wanted me to be hungry it did not matter. His will only I wanted to do ... At Tonga, Jesus was in every place ... [But] I knew that the pathway here was different – a pathway known by blood – but still my heart coveted it, whether difficult or not difficult, I would strive to follow. If it led to life, well; or if it led to death it would be well; as long as Jesus was there I would walk in it.[43]

But above all Semisi yearned for the conversion of the souls of the people who had been put in his charge:

> I gave all my strength & all my heart so that many might be led into the kingdom of Jesus Christ ... I prayed to God & asked Him to turn many into His kingdom & when God did hear & turn them & I saw many of them coming to school & Lotu my heart was satisfied & I gave God my praise & hallelujah because He Himself had caused His own work to grow.[44]

It is clear then, that for both Semisi and his wife, the joy of life was in pleasing Jesus. Jesus of Nazareth was indeed ultimate. Semisi also discerned that God was active in his Solomon Islands church. He had drawn the people into his Kingdom and given them a love for His business.

41 Gunson, *Messengers of Grace*, 58.
42 Semisi Nau, *The Story of my Life*, 88,92,93.
43 Semisi Nau, *The Story of my Life*, 105,93.
44 Semisi Nau, *The Story of my Life*, 94-95.

All these are signs of the pilgrim principle of commitment and devotion at work.

Prayer Life

Semisi had a very vibrant prayer life. It was interwoven and bound to his devotion and commitment to be a missionary. Thus, as demonstrated above, in this he was once again reflecting the marks of the ultimate significance of Jesus of Nazareth and the conviction that God is active where believers are; — the group who constitute the people of God. Take, for example, when first Semisi was looking for a suitable partner, he had prayed, "Father send someone to me who, when she knows that thou dost want me to go away to a foreign land, will not refuse but will be glad to do Thy will."[45] And as shown above, God willingly did it.

Also, when during the interview for mission work in the Solomon Islands, Dr. Moulton wanted to know the mind of his wife, says Semisi, "Matelita was not with me … Dr. Moulton sent someone to bring her & for the remainder of all that & all the following night I prayed & asked God that if it was His will for me to go He would remove all the darkness & allow no obstacle to remain in my path."[46]

On the way to the Solomons, when they had called at Suva, Fiji, they "held a service & prayed very earnestly that God would make us zealous & strong to go forth & fight for Him."[47] Together with others who were convinced that they were the people of God, they had banded together and prayed concerning their missionary task like the early disciples had done[48]; once again exhibiting the pilgrim principle, of prayer. Additionally, when tasked with the duty of beginning a new work in another community called Dudi; upon arrival at Roviana, Solomon Islands, Semisi "prayed earnestly that God would make the chiefs & people love me. He answered my prayer…"[49] And in his more permanent place of labour, Ontong Java, Semisi reveals,

> I asked God to teach me so that I would be able to lift the people up & cause them to stand in His kingdom. I knew that God had given me the thing which I had asked for (sic) numbers of people came to Lotu on Sunday; the church was always full & the day school was good & I knew that it was God who had done it all.[50]

---

45 Semisi Nau, *The Story of my Life*, 86.
46 Semisi Nau, *The Story of my Life*, 89.
47 Semisi Nau, *The Story of my Life*, 90.
48 *Acts of the Apostles* 4:23-31.
49 Semisi Nau, *The Story of my Life*, 92.
50 Semisi Nau, *The Story of my Life*, 105.

Further, when very sick and near death, he prayed,

> Oh God Thou hast sent a great sickness upon me & there are so many people who do not know the name of Jesus, Him whom Thou didst send to me so that I would come to these Islands & tell the Gospel & Thy name to those who do not know Thee. Oh God what did I come for? Let me go & do Thy will so that these people will know & follow Thee. That they may know the Blood of Jesus in order that their sins might be washed away & their souls received into Heaven.[51]

In all this, Semisi was following after what many an ardent disciple of Christ had done. David Brainerd, missionary to the Indians of North America, for example, was known for his challenging prayer life.[52] Similarly, Paul in his letter to the Ephesians exhorts, "Pray in the Spirit on all occasions with all kinds of prayers and requests. With this in mind, be alert and always keep on praying for all the saints"[53] Semisi Nau was thus a typically good missionary, for like others elsewhere, his actions show that he believed that God was with him and would, through his Son, Jesus Christ, hear him as he prayed. In addition, when needful, he could band together with other people of God for communication to the God of Israel. He was exhibiting the coherent signs of historic Christianity – the pilgrim principle.

Love for Family - Christian Families - God's People

The pilgrim principle of recognising believers as God's people may be observed in Semisi's relationship with his family. Semisi had a big place in his heart for his family, which according to Paul is inferably the first congregation of God's people for a pastor to care for (1 Tim. 3:2, 4-5). He was sensitive about subjecting them to the harsh realities of mission life. In the choice of Matelita as wife, he had put before her the possibilities of missionary life, to which she had answered in the affirmative.[54] Upon reaching Ontong Java, when faced with the opposition of a chief to the establishment of a mission, Semisi had to decide between retreating, or persevering until permission was given. Immediately, he brought his wife into consideration; asking for her opinion, "I will go & see my wife & hear what she has to say." Her response was for them to stay even if it meant death.[55]

---

51 Semisi Nau, *The Story of my Life,* 104,105

52 An *ordinary* record in David Brainerd's diary reads "…and God again enabled me to wrestle for numbers of souls and had much fervency in the sweet duty of intercession." Again, "This morning I spent about two hours in secret duties and was enabled more than ordinarily to agonize for immortal souls…"(Fred Barlow, *David Brainerd: Missionary, Accessed* 26 April 2007, www.wholesomewords.org/biography/biorpbrainerd.html,).

53 *Ephesians* 6:18.

54 Semisi Nau, *The Story of my Life,* 87.

55 Semisi Nau, *The Story of my Life,* 95,97.

Matelita was a strong woman and must have given a lot of good Christian support to her husband.

On another occasion, when their daughter Akosita fell ill, Semisi desired to take her back to the head mission station for better treatment. However, the Head Missionary, the Rev. Goldie, felt that the work would suffer with his absence. Semisi, who was by then a probationary minister of the Methodist Church, reports, "…my heart was weak for I loved my child & I said to Mr. Goldie that we would have a talk to Matelita about it. Matelita thought it would be best for me to remain & look after the work at Luanuia while she took Akosita …"[56]

The loss of their three children in the early part of their marriage probably contributed to Semisi's intense affection for his family. He writes, "the loss of my children was like three storms in my life when my vessel was threatened with shipwreck."[57] Later he reminisced, "I understood too that He had taken my children from me in order to lighten my burden & leave me free to work for Him."[58] So when Akosita grew seriously ill, he prayed passionately for her,

> Jehovah Thou art a God of love & didst send Thy Son to shed His Blood to wash away our sins & be our path to Thee; if we want to ask Thee for something we ask through Jesus. Here, oh God, is my daughter very ill; death is near to her. This child Thou didst give to me; have mercy upon me & leave her here for me to care for. Jesus I am clinging to thy Word. Thou didst say, 'Ask & it shall be given thee; seek, & ye shall find; knock & it shall be opened unto you.' Jehovah, give to me for I am asking; open the door of Thy love for I am knocking; come & give to me for I am seeking life for my child. Do not take her away Jehovah, leave her with me. Father do not weigh me down with sorrow but in love and mercy lift up my head.[59]

Obviously, Semisi considered his daughter one of God's people whom "Thou gave to me." As a pastor he was to care for God's people, including his daughter who God should "leave here for [him] to take care of." In the same way he saw the God of Israel, Jehovah, as his own God; for he used His name in passionate prayer as he related to Him. Though Semisi Nau was not a Jew, by faith he joined in a heritage that reached back to Abraham. He had become a member of the people of God, now called Christians, who based their prayers upon the common Scriptures. Akosita

56 Semisi Nau, *The Story of my Life,* 112.
57 Semisi Nau, *The Story of my Life,* 88.
58 Semisi Nau, *The Story of my Life,* 92.
59 Semisi Nau, *The Story of my Life,* 111.

recovered slowly. Seven months later, Semisi requested to take her back to Tonga "as she was getting too old to be in the Solomon Islands"[60] and it was also time for their furlough. Semisi's love for his family was perhaps simply an act of obedience to Scripture, "Husbands, love your wives, just as Christ loved the church [God's people] and gave himself up for her…"[61] Here was a missionary who took God's word seriously and thus exhibited the characteristics of a true missionary Christian; as other soldiers of Christ over the ages have done.

He walked the way of Jesus in loving and caring for not only his family as God's people, but also the people among whom he worked. Indeed, his family life shows that Semisi reflected the pilgrim principle of Christian expansion.

Indigenising Principle

Use of Language

The Rev. Semisi Nau exemplified not only the pilgrim principle by living as a true Christian, but also the indigenising principle of cross-cultural communication of the gospel. His love and concern for their better lot was exhibited in self-inculturation by learning their language in order to promote clearer and more effective communication of the gospel. On Ontong Java, and indeed across the South Pacific, English was hardly used as the official medium of communication in mission work. The early missionaries have to their credit that they painstakingly acquired the local language and put it into writing. In both church and school, mother tongue was used. This should have contributed to the wonder that most of the South Sea Islands became Christian in a relatively short period of time, albeit nominally in some cases. Kenneth Latourette observes,

> The nineteenth century record in the spread of Christianity among the Pacific Islanders is one of the most spectacular in the history of that or of any other faith. Within the course of a hundred years, often within a generation, Christianity displaced the native cults, eliminated some of the social practices most contradictory to its tenets, and contributed to the construction of new societies … In none was a more extensive change wrought in so brief a span of time.[62]

60 Semisi Nau, *The Story of my Life*, 114.
61 *Ephesians* 5:25.
62 Latourette, *A History of the Expansion of Christianity*, 263.

The translation of the Scriptures, as well as the use of mother tongue, helped the South Sea Islanders to own the Christian faith for themselves. The God whose *mana* (divine power) and values seemed superior to that of their own gods and religious systems could speak their language. No obstacle could thus stand in the way of His worship and to the acquisition of some of His *mana*; so necessary for a happy and fulfilled life.

On the Western Solomon Islands, the Rev. Dr. George Brown had recommended Polynesian missionaries from Tonga, Samoa and the Niue Islands because the Ontong Javanese language was similar to theirs.[63] It would not have been too difficult for the Rev. Nau to learn the language as a result. Initially, Semisi used an interpreter on Ontong Java. Later, however, he acquired the language himself, for he could discuss local customs using local words.[64] The God of Israel could now become the God of the people of Ontong Java. They could relate to Him in their own way; sharing with Him their most intimate concerns which were expressed not only in speech or language, but also enacted in local customs according to their religious self-understanding or theology.

Use of Local Custom and Theologising

With the language well in hand, the Rev. Nau studied local customs and beliefs and their affinity with the Christian faith. He noted that the people worshipped spirits and so learnt their names; the chief spirit was *Puemakua*. He observed their roles in the lives of the local people, as well as the role of sacred men in their worship. Further, he must have acquired some knowledge of their funeral and marriage customs, as the Rev. Benjamin Danks refers to them in an article he wrote after a visit to Semisi in Ontong Java.[65] For the Rev. Nau, local belief was useless in arresting the destruction of life. The sacred men only told lies, perpetuating the religious system for their personal gain. It was Semisi, rather, who, in times of sickness, stood in persistent prayer until it was abated.[66]

The Rev. Nau used the knowledge of local culture in his ministry. As opposed to the confrontational style adopted by the Rev. Shackell, his main successor after his initial stay on Ontong Java, the Rev. Nau preferred to win the confidence of the people through the use of tact and patience.[67]

63 Davidson (ed.), *Semisi Nau,* 25,27.

64 Davidson (ed.), *Semisi Nau,* 70.

65 Davidson (ed.), *Semisi Nau,* 69,102. The article was published in the *Australian Methodist Missionary Review,* 4th November 1909, 17; 4th December, 1909, 15-17.

66 Semisi Nau, *The Story of my Life,* 110,111.

67 Davidson (ed.), *Semisi Nau,* 36,60.

As a result, it is little wonder that he was much loved. Upon his departure after his first stay, the chief who had been vehemently opposed to the establishment of the mission at the beginning, wept bitterly.[68]

This knowledge of local customs prompted the Rev. Semisi Nau to make a keen analogy from his observations. A bird, 'kikia' was trapped simply by beating with a specific rhythm on a special local drum made from a young coconut. The Rev. Nau observed,

> I went with my Gospel drum & beat at Luanuia. I hit straight with Jesus Christ; beat, beat, & the chiefs of the place began to come, beat, beat, & all the chiefs started. I did not cease beating & all the head men began to hop; then all the people & the children came to hear the Gospel. This was only if I hit straight with Jesus Christ; if I hit the wrong way no one came but they all stayed in their own place by themselves. Another thing that came to my mind was this. All the blessings of God are with Him in Heaven; the blessings of Light, Life, Peace, Wisdom, Happiness. If we take hold of Christ & strike with Him in our Lotu all the blessings will come (hop) from Heaven. If, however we are not faithful this will not be so; if we have not a firm hold of Christ we will strike wrongly & the blessings of God will not come to us.[69]

This illustrates how Semisi engaged local thought forms in communicating the gospel and as an effort to indigenize the faith. In this way, the Rev. Nau brought the message of Jesus Christ to the Ontong Javanese in familiar ways.

In reality, what the Rev. Nau was doing was theologising, for "theology springs out of practical situations, it is therefore *occasional* and *local* in character."[70] And since the sourcebook of all valid theology is the Christian Scriptures, one may say that it is an effort to apply or reflect on Scripture as it relates to an existential situation. This is what Semisi was doing, illustrating what Latin American theologian Gustavo Gutierrez has defined as "critical reflection on Christian praxis in the light of the word."[71] Indeed, true theology may only be said to be valid because of the indigenising principle.

---

68 Semisi Nau, *The Story of my Life,* 108.

69 Semisi Nau, *The Story of my Life,* 106-107.

70 Gustavo Gutierrez, *A Theology of Liberation,* rev ed. (Maryknoll: Orbis Books, 1988), 6-15 cited by Walls, *The Missionary Movement in Christian History,* 10.

71 Walls, *The Missionary Movement in Christian History,* 10

South Sea Islanders are culturally known for the celebration of feasts. By the time the Rev. Semisi Nau was nearing the end of his second main assignment on Ontong Java, it appears that this celebratory custom had been introduced into the church and was promulgating social cohesion.

"For the first time in the memory of living men" two neighbouring villages, Luangiua and Pelau, who were not friendly, were coming together for their "festivities". This potentially resulted because both kings, and a majority of the people, were now Christian.[72] The church was receiving a Pacific Islands impress. In addition, there must have been a recognition that, as Christians, the two communities were now one people of God transcending space; —tribal and cultural divisions were no longer ultimate. In this particular instance, the indigenising principle is seen to be working hand in hand with the pilgrim principle.

That the church on Ontong Java was receiving a South Islander indigenous impress is illustrated further by the gift of 10,000 coconuts that was made to the Mission by the people of Pelau.[73] The effort is significant because South Pacific Islanders are known for the giving of gifts. Local culture is thus seen to be in use in living out the implications of their association with Christ. The South Pacific characteristic of giving gifts had been harnessed to the advantage of the church. Within five decades of the establishment of the Wesleyan Methodist Church in Tonga, it was self-supporting.[74]

This indigenisation of church life was not new in the South Pacific. In *A History of the Churches in Australasia*, Ian Breward observes that, "Polynesians ... rapidly created a form of Christianity with a European overlay, but deeply rooted in village life and culture."[75] Again, the "partnership with converted chiefs who often doubled as deacons was vital in grooming Christianity in village life ... Each island has retained distinctive forms of culture and discipleship, though family prayers, Bible reading and keeping the Sabbath were universal."[76] The same may be said of Melanesia and Micronesia, the other parts of the South Pacific. Semisi Nau helped in this process in Melanesia.

---

72 Davidson (ed.), *Semisi Nau,* 60,100.
73 Davidson (ed.), *Semisi Nau,* 36.
74 Davidson (ed.), *Semisi Nau,* 13.
75 Breward, *A History of the Churches in Australasia*, 38.
76 Breward, *A History of the Churches in Australasia*, 54.

Conclusion

John S. Mbiti relates the indigenising and pilgrim principles of cross-cultural transmission of the Christian faith as follows:

> If Christ identifies Himself with man's culture in order to redeem man within that culture, we have to develop a Christology which makes it possible to interpret Christ in terms that are relevant to the cultural expressions of our peoples. Yet, Jesus Christ resists being made into a Jew, a Greek, an American, a Chinese or an African. In another sense His being the expression of man, His being universalised by the Ascension, makes it possible for Christians of all places, cultures and times, to 'localize' Him within their meaningful terms ... His universality reaffirms our different cultures, and calls for a kind of cultural plurality as we march into the Church.[77]

The two principles belong together; they manifest the nature of Christian faith. The faith does take a local impress when it crosses cultural boundaries. It can only cross the boundaries, however, because it has universal characteristics.

It should not be a wonder that the Rev. Semisi Nau embodied the two principles in his life and ministry. They belong to any effective Christian missionary activity. In this, Africa can be said to have been short served in the missionary transmission of the gospel, for the indigenising element was largely left out. The faith was presented in the clothing of a so-called superior Western culture. To be effectively Christian therefore, was to be Western. It is gratifying to note, however, that with the maturing of the African Church, several adjustments have been made to correct the shortfall.

The Rev. Nau, however, was different. He returned home to Tonga in 1919 after approximately eleven years[78] as a missionary to the western Solomon Islands. Alan Davidson observes of him that "his whole life was understood and viewed within a Christian framework..."[79] In this, he followed in the footsteps of the long line of soldiers of the cross who lived and died for the cause of Christ across human existence. As a worker for Christ, he shared these life values with the flock put under his charge. There is evidence that his shepherding had borne fruit, as some local

77 John S. Mbiti, 'African Indigenous Culture In Relation To Evangelism And Church Development' in R. Pierce Beaver (ed.), *The Gospel and Frontier Peoples – A Report of a Consultation: December, 1972,* South Pasadena: William Carey Library, 1973, 91.
78 Rev Nau had two terms of missionary service: 1906-1909, 1911-1919.
79 Davidson (ed.), *Semisi Nau,* 67.

church members had been willing to suffer persecution for their faith.[80] One month before his death, the Rev. Nau could write to his friend Rev. William H. Leembruggen, "I am very sick and weak. I'm still following Christ as my personal Saviour. Believe and trust in Him so that he would bless you as well as our people here in Tonga. We will meet each other in heaven"[81]

Again, that the testimony about Rev. Semisi Nau was that "he was an able observer of the culture, beliefs and practices of the people among whom he worked,"[82] showed that he cared about translating the gospel into forms that would be well assimilated by his flock. The evidence, as has been shown, is that he did this quite successfully and that consequently the Christian community on Ontong Java was truly western Solomon in character. Christ had found a home there. This may be said to be true of the South Sea Islands in general. In spite of the fact that, in its initial fervour to secure total commitment, the Church uprooted some religious aspects of local culture; it also helped to preserve large portions which

would have been eroded away with the arrival of the white man and the consequent political and commercial activity. Such aspects of culture as language, feasting, the giving of gifts and music have made the local church manifestly South Sea, a truly indigenous establishment, while at the same time a truly Christian one, bearing all the marks of historic Christianity; and Semisi Nau was part of this transformation.

80 Davidson (ed.), *Semisi Nau,* 53.
81 Davidson (ed.), *Semisi Nau,* 67,128.
82 Davidson (ed.), *Semisi Nau,* 69.

When Two Worlds Collide: The Story of the Basel Mission in Akyem Abuakwa (1852-87)

Robert Addo-Fening

Abstract

In 1852 the Basel Mission entered Akyem Abuakwa, one of the largest Akan kingdoms in southern Gold Coast. Missionaries believed it was a polytheistic society in which faith in the gods and ancestral spirits not only legitimized political power, but also defined cultural and social norms. The state authorities welcomed Christianity as an additional religion to the extent that it was prepared to co-exist peacefully with other existing forms of religious expression.

For 15 years the Basel Mission went about their work with cautious optimism. However, lack of progress, combined with the "Christian conscience" and race prejudice began to exhaust the patience of the European missionaries. As the practice of ancestor worship hampered Christian evangelism, the Basel Mission threw caution to the wind and became defiant. In turn, the traditional authorities responded with harassment of converts. They imposed a ban on street preaching; and the Asafo, (the traditional militia), hounded Christian converts out of their villages into exile.

Left with no other alternative, the Mission colluded with the British Administration of the forts and castles along the coast which had been looking for an excuse to extend British colonial territory inland. The result was the subversion of the political independence and sovereignty of Akyem Abuakwa in the name of freedom of worship, "civilisation" and progress.

Introduction

The first attempt at Christian conversion in the Gold Coast (now Ghana) was made by Portuguese Catholic monks at Elmina Castle. It was their custom to preach the gospel to African slaves and baptize them prior to their embarkation for Europe. In 1503, in what can only be described as an exercise in futility, they attempted to convert the *Omanhene* (King) and *ahenfo* (sub-chiefs) of nearby Fetu (Cape Coast).

The Moravian United Brethren Mission was the first Christian mission to attempt to plant Christianity in Ghana. A Danish chaplain at Christiansborg, Elias Svane, opened a school for mulatto children at the castle in 1722 with the backing of David Herrn, commandant of the castle. Four years later, in 1726, Svane took two of his pupils to Denmark for higher education. One of them, Frederick Pederson Svane, was his own son by an African woman; the other, was another mulatto called Christian Protten.[1] In 1737, Protten was sent back to Christiansborg with Henrich Huckuff to start mission work.

Five years after Protten's arrival at Christiansborg, that is in 1742, Jacobus Elisa Johannes Capitein arrived in Elmina as a missionary of the Holland Branch of the Moravian Mission. He was an Ivorian ex-slave; educated at Leyden University. Capitein opened two schools, one for mulattoes and the other for Africans. Capitein and Protten died in 1747 and 1769, respectively, without winning any souls.

The Church of England's Society for the Propagation of the Gospel (S.P.G.) was the second Christian mission to arrive in Ghana. Its first missionary, the Reverend Thomas Thompson, arrived in 1752 as Anglican Chaplain. After only five years in Cape Coast, he was invalided out of the country. Fortunately for the mission, two years earlier he had sent three Cape Coast boys to England to be trained as priests. The sole survivor, Philip Quacoe (1741-1816) returned home in 1766 to serve the mission for 50 years. In that period, he produced 52 converts and opened a school at Cape Coast which he kept going until his death in 1816. The SPG did not resume missionary work in Ghana for the next 75 years.

1 H.O.A Mc William & M.A. Kwamina-Poh, *The Development of Education in Ghana* (London: Longman, 1975), 18.

For over a century after the death of Philip Quacoe, there was hardly any sign of Christianity in Ghana until the arrival of the Evangelische Missionsgesellschaftzu Basel. Founded in Basel, Switzerland, and popularly known as the Basel Mission, it was the third Christian mission to send out missionaries to Ghana. Of the first four missionaries, three were Germans, namely, Johan Philip Henke, Karl Ferdinand Salbach and Gotlieb Holzwarth. The fourth, Gottlob Schmidt, was Swiss. They arrived at Christiansborg in December 1828.2 Within five months, three of them were dead, leaving Henke as the sole survivor. In 1831, he also died. In March of the same year, another batch of three missionaries, Andreas Riis, P Jaeger and Dr. Heinze arrived to replace the dead missionaries. Dr. Heinze died six weeks later, and Jaeger soon after;3 leaving Andreas Riis as the sole survivor.

Riis owed his survival to "a native herbalist" who healed him when he fell sick.4 After his recovery at the farm of a local trader called Georg Lutterodts, he conceived the idea of moving inland to a healthier climate to establish a mission station.

The Move to Akropong Akuapem (1835)

Accompanied by Lutterodts as interpreter, Riis travelled to Akropong in 1835 to see Okuapemhene (King) Addo Dankwa (1816-36) and negotiate for land. Oral Tradition has it that at the meeting with the Okuapemhene, Riis tried to convert him to the Christian faith; but he challenged Riis in these words:

> When God created the world, he made the Book [Bible] for the Whiteman and juju Fetish) for the Blackman. If you can show us some Blackman, who can read the Whiteman's Book, then we would surely follow you.[5]

Riis picked up the gauntlet and returned to Europe to recruit black missionaries from the Caribbean to convince the Okuapemhene that Africans "were not excluded from the Christian message of salvation."[6]

In 1836, two missionaries, I. Murdter and A. Stanger arrived at Akropong to join Riis. With them was Miss M.A. Wolter (later to become Mrs. Ann Riis). Stanger died in December 1837 followed by Murdter in November 1838.

---

2 Clifford Charles Campbell, *Full Circle: The Caribbean Presence in the making of Ghana*, 1843-1966. (PhD Thesis, University of Ghana, June 2012), 149.
3 Campbell, *Full Circle: The Caribbean Presence in the making of Ghana*, 150.
4 Campbell, *Full Circle: The Caribbean Presence in the making of Ghana*, 150.
5 Campbell, *Full Circle: The Caribbean Presence in the making of Ghana*, 151.
6 Campbell, *Full Circle: The Caribbean Presence in the making of Ghana*, 158.

In July 1840, Riis returned to Basel on sick leave never to return. In 1843, six black West Indian families he recruited with the help of J. C. Widmann, arrived at Akropong to lay a firm foundation for the Basel Mission in Ghana.

The Mission opened its first Boys' School at Akropong in 1843. It followed it up with a Girls' School which was transferred from Akropong to Aburi in 1847. In the latter year, J. G Dieterle, I. Stanger and J. Mohr arrived as new missionaries. From Aburi, the Basel Mission began its penetration into Akyem Abuakwa, Kwawu, Asante Akyem and Asante.

The Basel Mission in Akyem Abuakwa (1852-87)

In the middle of 1851, Basel missionary, I. Stanger dropped a hint that the Wesleyan Mission, headed by newly arrived T.B. Freeman, had intentions to open a mission station in Akyem Abuakwa.7 Based on that information, the Rev. Mr. Suss made a preliminary visit to Gyadam in January 1852. Gyadam was situated about twenty kilometres north of the Abuakwa capital of Kyebi. At the time, it was a "fugitive" Kotoku state established on Abuakwa soil. Its ruler was Kofi Agyeman.

From Gyadam, the Rev. Suss continued his reconnaissance of Akyem Abuakwa to Kyebi, where he met with Okyenhene Atta Panin (1835 - 1859). The Okyenhene "had been to a Wesleyan School himself"[8] and expressed three wishes: a wish for Suss to teach him "to read"; a wish for the mission to build a school at Kyebi; and a wish for two of his sons, Gyekye and Asrifi, to be admitted to the school at Akropong to learn English.[9]

In June of the same year, while in Accra in connection with the Poll Tax Ordinance, the Okyenhene granted audience to the Rev. Zimmerman and accepted three gifts: an English Bible with gold letters on the binding, an English spoon, and a hatchet. He also attended a church service with the missionaries and pressed for a mission station "in his territory".[10]

On September 4, 1852, the Rev. Suss returned to Akyem Abuakwa to found a mission station at Gyadam. The following year the two *ahenemma*

---

7 R. Addo-Fening, *Akyem Abuakwa 1700-1943 from Ofori Panin to Sir Ofori Atta*, (Faculty of Arts, No 19Trondheim Studies in History, African Series No.1, Department of History, Norwegian University of Science and Technology NTNU,1997, 2000), 55-56.
8 Addo-Fening, *Akyem Abuakwa 1700-1943 from Ofori Panin to Sir Ofori Atta*, 56.
9 Addo-Fening, *Akyem Abuakwa 1700-1943 from Ofori Panin to Sir Ofori Atta*, 56.
10 Addo-Fening, *Akyem Abuakwa 1700-1943 from Ofori Panin to Sir Ofori Atta*, 56.

(princes) were duly enrolled at the Akropong Catechists Institute.[11] The Kotoku State abandoned Gyadam in 1860 after a war with its host and re-established itself near Akyem Swedru near Akyem Oda. As a result, the Basel Mission relocated; first to Kukurantumi in 1860, and then to Kyebi, in 1861.

Abuakwa's Pre-European Religious Culture

It is a common fallacy that suggests that the African had no knowledge of God prior to the arrival of Christian missionaries in Africa.

Akyem Abuakwa does not fit that description. As far as knowledge of God was concerned, Abuakwa was certainly not a religious *tabula rasa.* Several immemorial Akan aphorisms point to that fact:

- *Obi Nkyere abofra Nyame*, to wit, no one points out God to a child; he knows him by instinct or intuition;
- *Obi rekra ne Nyame no na obi nnyina ho*, literally, one's destiny is a function of one's parting conversation with God before one enters the world;
- *Nkrabea nni Kwatibea*, to wit, one's destiny is foreclosed or sealed at the moment of birth.

These aphorisms show that the Akan were not only aware of God from the mysteries of creation; they acknowledged his omnipresence and awesomeness as well. That the Akan people recognised the omnipresence of God is also self-evident in the language of libation pouring; an act of invocation and worship that forms an essential ingredient of religious rites performed at the shrines and at the courts of Chiefs. On those occasions, the first name on the roll of spiritual powers invoked is that of God, described variously as:

- *Onyankopon*, to wit, The One and only Mighty God;
- *Twediampong* (a corruption of *Tweredua mpan*) to wit, when one leans against the dependable and faithful tree, one does not fall;
- *Odomankoma* (a corruption of *Adom a nenko ma*), to wit, He who alone gives grace.

A keen observer cannot fail to notice that religion informed the Akan people's social, political and cultural expressions; be it at festivals, funerals, burial rites, naming ceremonies, etc. The Akan World view taught that humans were surrounded on earth by a host of spirits, some benevolent

11 Addo-Fening, *Akyem Abuakwa 1700-1943 from Ofori Panin to Sir Ofori Atta*, p. 56; Also, *Research Review* Vol. 1 No 2, July 1985, 129.

and others malevolent. Of the evil spirits, the most fearsome and hated was witchcraft known as *bayie* among the Twi speakers, and *ayen* among the Fante. Witchcraft was conceived as a supernatural force which human beings used to perpetrate evil. Illness, infertility and death were invariably blamed on witches. Witchcraft needed to be countered by benevolent spirits; and among them were the spirits of dead ancestors.

Departed ancestors who—in life—ruled their people well, had their stools (the equivalent of thrones in Europe) ritually blackened and deposited permanently in a stool room called *Nkonwafieso.* Once every forty days, the elders of the state entered the stool room to pour libation, pray to the ancestors to prosper their community, and protect it from evil spirits. As already mentioned, the first name on the "libation roll" was God, followed by good spirits and ancestors.

We need to examine an important norm of Akan cultural practice in order to understand why; notwithstanding their recognition of God's omnipotence and omnipresence; the Akan people did not seek to engage Him directly. Akan cultural practice frowned upon an ordinary citizen walking directly into a Chief's palace for an audience with him. Such an encounter needed to be mediated; usually by an intermediary called *Okyeame*, (the so-called Linguist). It is in this light that the Akan person's pre-Christian relationship with God must be viewed. He considered God to be too distant and exalted to be approached directly for help in times of trouble. Hence, he sought to reach Him through the intermediation of good spirits and the spirits of dead ancestors.

Religion was the Akan person's way of cultivating and supplicating the good spirits; using them to provide him with greater leverage in his struggle with malevolent spirits on Earth. Akan festivals such as *Odwira* and *Adae* were therefore both social and religious occasions. The main focus of attention at these festivals was supplication, veneration, and adulation of God, the Earth, water bodies and ancestors.

The Period of Entente (1861-1868)

The period up to 1868 may be described as a period of *entente* between the Basel Mission and the Akyem Abuakwa state. The entente established between the Mission and Okyenhene Atta Panin (1835-1859), continued under his younger brother and successor, Okyenhene Obuom (1859-1867). The new Okyenhene readily provided the Mission with land to construct a church building and mission station at Kyebi. On two occasions he listened to sermons from the Rev. Suss on the difference between right and wrong.[12]

Obuom counted the Basel missionaries among his political advisors. On 15 March 1863, he invited the Rev. Eisenschmid and the Rev. Stromberg to sit with the Kyebi executive council to participate in decisions of great political import. Two weeks later, the two missionaries were with the Okyenhene again at his audience with an Asante envoy.[13]

In 1865, the Mission offered Okyenhene Obuom assistance in resolving an acrimonious land dispute between two Abuakwa towns; namely Kukurantumi and Asafo.

Obuom took keen interest in the affairs of the Kyebi Primary School and enrolled his own son, Apeanyo. He did not object when the Mission baptised him alongside other children during the third quarter of 1866.[14] At the time of his death in 1867, the good will toward the Mission was still strong. The Kyebi Community still admired the Basel Mission for introducing formal education which was a novelty. They also showed enthusiasm for its attendant prospects of social recognition and opportunities for skilled employment. Among the new skills introduced by the Mission were carpentry, masonry, and baking. Additionally, the introduction of new and profitable crops such as coffee, mango, and later cocoa, caught the fancy of farmers. Nonetheless, it took only one year into the reign of the next Okyenhene for the fund of goodwill towards the Mission to dissipate.

The Period of Confrontation (1867-1887)

Obuom's nephew and successor was Okyenhene Amoako Atta I, (1867-1887). The new Okyenhene was, before his enstoolment, a pupil of the Basel Mission Primary School at Kyebi. He liked the Christian message, used to attend religious service every Sunday, and contributed to the offering.[15] By 1867, when he became Okyenhene, the Basel Mission had become frustrated and was losing its patience with the lack of progress. Missionaries believed that Akyem Abuakwa, like other Akan states, was a polytheistic society that teemed with shrines. Nearly every village had a

12 Addo-Fening, *Akyem Abuakwa 1700-1943 from Ofori Panin to Sir Ofori Atta*, 56.
13 Addo-Fening, *Akyem Abuakwa 1700-1943 from Ofori Panin to Sir Ofori Atta*, 56.
14 Addo-Fening, *Akyem Abuakwa 1700-1943 from Ofori Panin to Sir Ofori Atta*, 57.
15 Addo-Fening, *Akyem Abuakwa 1700-1943 from Ofori Panin to Sir Ofori Atta*, 57.

shrine that exercised a stranglehold on the community. Shrines were the sole providers of cure for ailments and for emotional and psychological problems. In addition, family heads and parents exercised strict control over their kinsmen in a way that left little room for individual initiative, discretion, and choice.

The early Christian missionaries found this culture repugnant but tolerated it and acted with caution and discretion. During this period, few freeborn Abuakwa citizens showed enthusiasm for the Christian message despite several preaching tours of villages; and in the meantime, the Mission pinned their hopes on pupils of the Kyebi Primary school and on non-indigenous slaves. Irregularity of attendance and instability of enrolment militated against the success of the first strategy; while recruitment by purchase and emancipation of slaves required a larger sum than was available in the Mission's Slave Emancipation Fund.

With little to show for fifteen years' investment in time, money, and effort, the Mission grew increasingly impatient; and sought to cast their evangelical net wider and more indiscriminately; even into "forbidden waters" in defiance of the traditional order. As the Mission's frustrations boiled over, it adopted several strategies for winning souls that lent credence to the hint in missionary Stromberg's Report of 1863, that there was a lingering suspicion on the part of the people that the missionaries were out to "to set up a state within a State—withdrawing people from their normal allegiance."[16]

From 1868 onward, the Mission began to act with increasing impunity. In that year, a scuffle occurred in the Okyenhene's Court room during which the hand of a Christian convert, called Duko, accidentally struck the Okyenhene. This was a serious offence, and he was arraigned on a charge of assault. The Rev. Eisenschmid interfered with the trial and threatened to have the Okyenhene punished by the British governor at Cape Coast "if any harm should come to Duko."[17] About the same time, the Mission intensified its campaign of encouraging Christian coverts to abandon their homes in the native townships and villages and relocate to *Salems*; the nascent Christian villages known to the people as *Oburonikrom* (Whiteman's village). Furthermore, the Mission embarked on street preaching targeting free-born citizens, slaves, and state functionaries alike.

16 Paul Jenkins, *Abstracts from the Gold Coast Correspondence of the Basel Mission*, Stromberg's Report for the Kibi Station in the year 1862, 24 Jan 1863, No Akim 17 (Akrofi-Christaller Institute Library, Akropong Akuapem), 508.
17 Paul Jenkins's *Abstracts*, Eisenschmid's Report, 30 Oct 1868 (No Akim 10).

The new posture was unacceptable to the ruling elite because of its inherent threat to the stability of the traditional order which made no distinction between Church and State. For the Akan, religion was inseparably linked with management of state affairs. The Okyenhene's oath of office enjoined him to preserve all institutions and cultural practices bequeathed to him by his departed ancestors; and that included the traditional religious heritage. Therefore, at a meeting with the missionaries, he was emphatic and unequivocal in his opposition to the proselytization of royal functionaries. In a tone of indignation, he queried:

> Must I let my horn-blowers, my drummers, my pipers—my sword bearers and Executioners, my hammock-carriers etc. become Christians? If I do, then I can no longer carry out my—ceremonies, nor can I receive foreign Embassies worthily. Whoever has an obligation to serve me...will never be allowed to become a Christian.

Most of the Okyenhene's sub-chiefs spoke in like manner and insisted that the Mission should first seek their consent before it proselytised or baptised any of their pawns or slaves. The Rev. Lodholtz and the other missionaries would not accept any exemptions.

The traditional rulers resented the Basel Mission's seeming determination to turn Akyem Abuakwa into a European-style secular state with its tolerance of freedom of conscience and of worship for all citizens, including royal servants. Amoako Atta I was determined to prevent the Mission from having its way. He was unalterably opposed to the baptism of state functionaries whose roles were related to ancestor worship and propitiation of the gods.

For a culture that set great store on communal living and camaraderie as a source of strength and security, the idea of encouraging Christian converts to live in physical isolation from their communal homes was irksome. It had the potential to undermine family solidarity and introduce a dichotomy between religiosity and traditional rulership. This was the reasoning behind the condition set by Chief Kwaku Buabeng of Anyinam when in 1879, he reluctantly sold the Basel Mission a plot of land for the construction of a Mission Station; namely, that the Salem "should not be sited too far away from town as this might ruin the town."[18]

From the end of 1870 up to the eve of the proclamation of the Gold Coast Colony, hostility to missionary work in Akyem Abuakwa intensified. At Tafo, the local god banned preaching in the village in 1871. *Asafo*

18 Paul Jenkins's *Abstracts* p 116; Mohr to Basel, 29 October 1879 (No 1579).

(warrior) groups followed in 1872 with a "systematic attempt to prevent anyone, slave or free, becoming a Christian." Within the same period, the Okyenhene and his Elders turned deaf ears to appeals for more pupils for the Mission's boarding school.[19] As a deterrent, a freeman who showed interest in becoming a Christian was fined "enough sheep to put him into serious debt."[20]

Proclamation of the Gold Coast Colony

On 6 August 1874, the British proclaimed the southern part of modern Ghana as the Gold Coast Colony and Protectorate. The portion designated the Gold Coast Colony was limited to four miles radius of the coastal strip of land on which the British forts and castles actually stood. Beyond that, lay the "Protectorate" which consisted of independent native kingdoms allied to the British in their long struggle with the powerful Asante Empire in the interior.

Prior to the proclamation, Lord Carnarvon, Secretary of State for the Colonies, wrote to Captain Strahan, Governor of the Gold Coast specifically on "the subject of slavery and slave dealing in the Protected Territories of the Gold Coast". For the avoidance of doubt, he stressed that

> Her Majesty's territorial dominion [extended] merely to the forts, or at most to so much of the lands immediately adjacent [as might be required for] defensive, sanitary or other purposes essential to the maintenance of the British position on the Coast.[21]

Lord Carnarvon considered all lands

> beyond that [as] foreign territory divided amongst native Chiefs and rulers standing in no relation of allegiance to Her Majesty, independent of one another and each presumably sovereign within the limits of his own dominion.[22]

While acknowledging the sovereignty of the Protected Chiefs, the Secretary of State expressed the wish that they would accept "the immediate abolition of slave-dealing and the importation of slaves [in] deference and conformity" to the wishes of Britain to whom they owed their deliverance from the Asante yoke. Strahan was urged to proceed in a manner that would "excite no needless fears" on the part of the Chiefs but reassure

19 Addo-Fening, *Akyem Abuakwa 1700-1943 from Ofori Panin to Sir Ofori Atta*, 61.
20 Addo-Fening, *Akyem Abuakwa 1700-1943 from Ofori Panin to Sir Ofori Atta*, 61.
21 Addo-Fening, *Akyem Abuakwa 1700-1943 from Ofori Panin to Sir Ofori Atta*, 62.; Carnavon to Srahan, 21 August 1874, c1139, in G.E. Metcalfe: *Great Britain and Ghana; Documents of Ghana History 1807-1957*, (Accra: Nelson and Sons, Limited 1964), 371.
22 Addo-Fening, *Akyem Abuakwa 1700-1943 from Ofori Panin to Sir Ofori Atta*, 62.

them that no "sudden and ruinous subversion of the existing social relations depending on upon slavery"[23] was intended.

This was the limited extent to which, "for the first time", the British Government sought to exercise power in the so-called "Protected Territories" through the Gold Coast Legislative Council. Contrary to instruction, the Colonial Administration sought to abrogate the sovereignty of the Protectorate Chiefs altogether.

Events leading to the Church-State Confrontation

The two Ordinances concerning slavery were enacted on 17 December 1874 by Governor Strachan's Administration. The first declared "all selling, buying, or dealing in slaves" unlawful and "absolutely and forever abolished." Clause 3 of the Second Ordinance, titled "An Ordinance to Provide for the abolition of Slavery in the Protected Territories" fell short of complete abolition. It did, however, declare all persons born in the Gold Coast Protectorate after November 5, 1874, as free persons.[24]

> Before the passage of the Ordinance, Governor Strachan met with the Protectorate Chiefs and assured them that the Emancipation Ordinance was not intended forcibly to separate households to disturb the old relations whilst the members themselves desired to no change.[25]

He told the Chiefs that every emancipated slave was free to leave his former master's household if he so desired; but he was not to be forced to do so if he was happy and contended to remain in the service of his former service. [26]

The Ordinances provided the Basel Mission with an opportunity to revive the fortunes of Christianity which had been on the wane since 1870 when the traditional authorities imposed a ban on conversion and street preaching. The Mission needed no prompting to assume the role of self-appointed agents of enforcement.

By coincidence, the Head of the Kyebi Mission was the Rev. David Asante, son of Odehyee Owusu Akyem, described by the Mission as "cousin and heir" of Okuapemhene Adum (1836-1845). As such, Asante and Amoako Atta I were near kin. Asante had returned home after his education in

23 Addo-Fening, *Akyem Abuakwa 1700-1943 from Ofori Panin to Sir Ofori Atta*, p. 62.
24 Addo-Fening, *Akyem Abuakwa 1700-1943 from Ofori Panin to Sir Ofori Atta*, p. 62.
25 Addo-Fening, *Akyem Abuakwa 1700-1943 from Ofori Panin to Sir Ofori Atta*, p. 62.
26 Addo-Fening, *Akyem Abuakwa 1700-1943 from Ofori Panin to Sir Ofori Atta*, p. 62.

Basel (1857-1862) and had been ordained a minister and posted to Kyebi in 1874. Okyenhene Amoako Atta I expected Asante, as someone raised in the ambience of Akan palace culture to be sympathetic to his cause. Events soon proved him wrong as Asante became the main instrument of the Mission in its confrontation with the Okyenhene.

As Head of the Kyebi Mission, Asante undertook certain measures that were bound to antagonise the Okyenhene and his Court. Between 1875 and 1877 he gave wide publicity to the Slave Emancipation Ordinances and explained their implications to slaves who visited the mission station. He instigated them to assert their freedom and sever their ties with their masters. He assured them that they no longer required the permission of their masters to become Christians. He promised employment, refuge, and protection at the mission station to those who took his advice. When in February of 1875, a government official, Dr. Gouldsbury, made a stop-over at Kyebi on his way to present-day Bono, David Asante asked to be granted "definite powers" to report breaches of the Emancipation Ordinance for prosecution.

In the spirit of the conditions set out in the Emancipation Ordinance, the Okyenhene visited the Mission on several occasions to seek the return of royal slaves who had taken refuge there, but Asante would not oblige him. Instead, he flaunted the "definite powers" he had obtained from Dr. Gouldsbury and upheld the right of royal slaves to leave the palace. He even wrote to the civil Commandant of Christiansburg to request police protection for ex-slaves at Kyebi, alleging molestation by their former masters.[27]

By 1876, David Asante had succeeded in baptising several of the royal slaves and functionaries including sword-bearers, executioners, drummers, and horn-blowers. Most painful to the Okyenhene was the loss of the services of Emmanuel Yaw Boakye, his boyhood friend and chief state drummer. Apart from seducing the Okyenhene's slaves, Asante also interfered in his jurisdiction. Acting on his own authority, he arbitrated disputes between Christians, offered advice to persons indicted before the king's court for violation of his oath, and wrote letters of introduction for persons desirous of appealing to the Supreme Court against judgements of the Okyenhene's court.[28]

---

27 Addo-Fening, *Akyem Abuakwa 1700-1943 from Ofori Panin to Sir Ofori Atta*, 64.
28 Addo-Fening, *Akyem Abuakwa 1700-1943 from Ofori Panin to Sir Ofori Atta*, 64-65.

The Confrontation

Unable to endure Asante's defiance any longer, the Okyenhene summoned him before his court on 20 September 1877. After recounting Asante's acts of provocation, he issued a banning order against him and had a gong-gong beaten around the town to announce it. He stressed that he had "no palaver with any [Christian] only Assanti." Asante refused to leave town, and in the commotion that ensued, palace guards seized him and forcibly expelled him. He went to Accra and filed a suit against the Okyenhene personally, for unlawful banishment.[29]

The case against the Okyenhene was heard before Chief Justice David Chalmers between 17 and 21 December 1877. The Court found as a fact that David Asante had acted injudiciously and provocatively towards the Okyenhene; that his quarrel with the king was essentially a political one; that Amoako Atta had no intention of destroying the work of the Basel Mission in his State; that the traditional authorities at Kyebi had suffered provocation "from the injudicious, swaggering and unconciliatory demeanour and conduct of Mr Assanti."

Accordingly, Governor Freeling recommended Asante's removal "at once to another District not under King Attah."[30] He warned the Mission that they would bear full responsibility for any future trouble arising from Asante's indiscretion if it kept him at Kyebi. Fearing the loss of the colonial government's goodwill and protection; and possibly, withdrawal of its annual subvention of £100 to the Church, the Local Committee transferred Asante to Akuapem in March 1878.[31]

Having regained the political initiative, Okyenhene Amoako Atta I, in a mood of vindictiveness, put the lives of the Christian community in Akyem Abuakwa at risk. First to suffer was Emmanuel Yaw Boakye, his former Chief State Drummer, and a key witness for David Asante in his suit against the Okyenhene. Amoako Atta 1 had Boakye's property—his entire furniture, clothes, farm and his 16-room house—sold by public auction to defray his indebtedness to him.[32] Fear of the Okyenhene caused people of Kyebi to boycott street preaching; and required former palace

29 Addo-Fening, *Akyem Abuakwa 1700-1943 from Ofori Panin to Sir Ofori Atta*, 67.
30 Addo-Fening, *Akyem Abuakwa 1700-1943 from Ofori Panin to Sir Ofori Atta*, 67.
31 Addo-Fening, *Akyem Abuakwa 1700-1943 from Ofori Panin to Sir Ofori Atta*, 67-68.
32 Addo-Fening, *Akyem Abuakwa 1700-1943 from Ofori Panin to Sir Ofori Atta*, 68.

functionaries to swear an oath abjuring the Christian faith. Elsewhere, Christians were assaulted by local Asafo (warrior) groups. They were denied the right to smoke pipes and forbidden to fell Odum trees for building houses.[33]

Government Intervention and Exile of Amoako Atta I

The Mission now sought to use the colonial power as a shield to fight the Okyenhene and resolve the Church-State imbroglio in its favour. In July 1879, the Rev. Buck, head of the Kyebi Mission, travelled to Accra to seek a government guarantee of protection for the Basel missionaries. He told the governor about the persistence of slavery in Akyem Abuakwa and the sale of "a whole row of people" at Anyinam. This report, followed by another by a widow, that Amoako Atta's Court had "caused her sisters, sons, daughters, nieces to be sold" to satisfy a fine of £144, outraged the government.

Amoako Atta's case was made worse by a letter he wrote to the governor on 29 December 1879. In it, he hinted at preparations he was making, to secure by force, if necessary, the repatriation of members of Abuakwa Royal family still living in Adanse, and the retrieval of the famous Adanse god, Bona. Ussher became exasperated by Amoako Atta's tenacity of purpose, conservatism, and spirit of independence. The last thing the governor wanted was Asante intrusion into the Colony and Protectorate. Amoako Atta's removal now became an option for British policy to realize the separate ambitions of both the government and the Mission.

Earlier, Ussher had asked Amoako Atta to send his messengers with the persons he was alleged to have sold into slavery to Accra; warning that if the reports "proved true, it will be very hard for you."[34] He now gave him up to the 15th February 1880 to go to Accra to explain his "proceedings in that and other matters" which formed the subject matter of complaints against him.[35] After an initial show of defiance, Amoako Atta arrived in Accra and was indicted on three charges before the May Assizes. The first was arson, for allegedly burning down the house of a widow of his predecessor in a fit of anger; the second was two counts of slave-dealing by receiving 2 pawns; and the third was ritual murder.[36]

33 Addo-Fening, *Akyem Abuakwa 1700-1943 from Ofori Panin to Sir Ofori Atta*, 68-69.
34 Addo-Fening, *Akyem Abuakwa 1700-1943 from Ofori Panin to Sir Ofori Atta*, 70-71.
35 Addo-Fening, *Akyem Abuakwa 1700-1943 from Ofori Panin to Sir Ofori Atta*, 71.
36 Addo-Fening, *Akyem Abuakwa 1700-1943 from Ofori Panin to Sir Ofori Atta*, 72.

The all-African jury that tried him dismissed the first two counts, convicting him only on the third count. His death sentence was commuted to five years penal servitude. On 14 May 1880, the Okyenhene was put on a warship bound for Lagos where he remained in exile from 14 May 1880 until late December, 1884.[37]

The main beneficiary of Amoako Atta's exile was the Basel Mission. In the four and a half years of the king's exile, congregations in Akyem Abuakwa increased their membership by leaps and bounds. The Kyebi District congregation had over 600 members while the local congregation of Kyebi had 204 members. These figures increased to 703 and 260 respectively, by the end of 1881. The number of houses in the salem at Kyebi, excluding those of missionaries and teachers, increased from 12 at the end of 1879 to 21 at the end of 1880. A new chapel was begun in 1880; and in the following year, a two-storey mission house was completed by Huppenbauer and Munz. At the Asiakwa outstation nearby, founded in 1877; membership increased by 130 percent at the end of 1882. School enrolment equally went up during the king's exile. By the beginning of 1882, existing schools at Kukurantumi (1860), Kyebi (1861), Begoro (1876), Apapam (1881), Asiakwa and Abomosu (1881) were attracting more pupils. A provisional Girls' School was started at Kyebi with 16 pupils; and shortly after, another was established at Begoro with girls recruited from Kukurantumi[38].

The gains made by the Basel Mission in the period of the Okyenhene's exile were limited to the eastern half of Akyem Abuakwa. In the western half, the people maintained their hostility to Christian influence. At Asuom, the home of the powerful god, *Apaam*, the local *akomfoo* (so-called fetish priests) were "annoyed and embittered" by the Christian presence. In 1882, Ramseyer, Mohr and Muller found no one at Asuom willing to become a Christian.

The baptismal candidates recruited in the period of the king's exile fell into two broad categories. The first comprised those who considered membership in the church as granting them immunity from the jurisdiction of the traditional courts. Such potential converts were attracted by the perceived immunity of the salems from political interference. The other category comprised ex-slaves, ex-pawns and other poor and needy people who were attracted by largesse from the Poor Relief Fund of the Church.[39]

37 Addo-Fening, *Akyem Abuakwa 1700-1943 from Ofori Panin to Sir Ofori Atta*, 73.
38 Addo-Fening, *Akyem Abuakwa 1700-1943 from Ofori Panin to Sir Ofori Atta*, pp. 76-77.
39 Addo-Fening, *Akyem Abuakwa 1700-1943 from Ofori Panin to Sir Ofori Atta*, p. 78.

The relatively high rate of growth of church membership in the period of the Okyenhene's exile lulled the missionaries into a false sense of success and security and led to an underestimation of the Abuakwa people's loyalty to their king and attachment to their socio-cultural institutions. Behind the facade of political disarray and atrophy of faith in the divinities lurked a fund of goodwill and loyalty towards Amoako Atta personally, and reverence for the ancestral spirits. Throughout the Okyenhene's exile, the people not only ignored the government's call for them to elect a new Okyenhene; they avoided the British courts and saved their complaints for his return. According to missionary Huppenbauer, Amoako Atta I received an estimated 15,000 francs in complaint money from "innumerable people who brought cases before him" in the first three weeks of his return from exile.[40]

Amoako Atta's Return and the Final Showdown

Governor Young brought Amoako Atta I back from exile by steamboat at the end of December 1884. As the Assembly of Chiefs and people desired "that he should be restored to his throne"; the governor sent him down to Kyebi to be reinstated after one week's rest in Accra. He was accompanied by a high government official, C.D Turton.

Before leaving Accra, he was fully briefed about the situation at Kyebi; which irritated him greatly. He learned that his court was in shambles. Strangers had been making frivolous use of his oath. Several of his wives had been seduced by Christians and non-Christians alike; and one had died of an abortion. Joseph Bosompem, the leader of the Christian congregation whose testimony had contributed to his conviction, now occupied the high traditional office of *Gyasehene* (comptroller of the royal household). Several members of the royal family had adopted the Christian faith; and there was widespread violation of customary taboos that undergirded ancestor worship which provided the sanction behind his "chiefly" authority. He entered Kyebi in an angry mood determined to end the pretensions of the Basel Mission and reverse its gains.[41]

When Amoako Atta rose to address his people at the durbar held to welcome him, he did not mince his words. In the presence of Turton, and to his hearing, Amoako Atta re-imposed the ban on farming, fishing and gold-digging on the sacred days of his ancestors and warned that whoever violated the ban would be severely punished. When Emmanuel

40 Addo-Fening, *Akyem Abuakwa 1700-1943 from Ofori Panin to Sir Ofori Atta*, p. 78.
41 Addo-Fening, *Akyem Abuakwa 1700-1943 from Ofori Panin to Sir Ofori Atta*, 79.

Yaw Boakye, his former State drummer-turned Christian, rose to protest he silenced him. He refused to be cowed by threats from Huppenbauer and Weimer to report him to the governor; and threw down the gauntlet with these words:

> The Christians do not honour and fear me. When I as king to whom all the lands which your eye see belong, who can do and order what he wants, when I order that the Christians should celebrate those days which to our ancestors from olden times were sacred, they say no; that we do not do! Isn't that disobedience?

He reminded the missionaries that he was a sovereign ruler and would insist on the ban against working on sacred days. He continued:

> These days belong to my stool... so I cannot allow the Christians to work on the mentioned days. Whoever wants to work on such days should buy himself his land.

A few hours after the meeting ended, he appeared on the street and swore by his late sister's name that he would "discipline the Christians" till they respected the laws of the land or quit his state. He would rather risk being sent back to Lagos than allow the Basel Mission to dishonour the memory of his ancestors.[42]

Amoako Atta spent 1885 trying to re-establish his authority. Apart from the ban on work on sacred days, he forbade his subjects to take cases to the Supreme Court. Thirdly, he made an example of those found guilty of seducing his wives by imposing ruinous fines on them. When catechist Emmanuel Yaw Boakye attempted to preach the gospel at Asuom, he was forcibly expelled. He subsequently went to court to apply for criminal summons against his assailants.

From August 1886, the Christians took to preaching on the street outside the salem during which they said unkind things about former Akyem rulers killed in wars with Asante. The resentment against Christians reached a crescendo on 14 December 1886 when the Rev. Mohr visited Kyebi accompanied by several Christian carriers from Begoro. A riot broke out the next day between Mohr's carriers and *nhenkwaa* (Palace servants). The riot degenerated into "a general assault" upon all Christians.

---

42 Addo-Fening, *Akyem Abuakwa 1700-1943 from Ofori Panin to Sir Ofori Atta*, 81.

Pandemonium broke out at Kyebi the next day when Amoako Atta announced the theft of gold dust, velvet cloths, and some trinkets. The theft was blamed on Christians and their leaders, such as Joseph Bosompem; a former *Gyasehene (*Chief of Staff*)* of Amoako Atta and now the first leader of the Kyebi congregation. The arrested persons were subjected to indignities, and by the end of January 1887, there was "not a single Christian at Kyebi." Throughout the state, Christians abandoned their homes and sought refuge, particularly at the Abetifi Mission Station, in the neighbouring State of Kwahu, some 40 miles away.[43]

Intervention of Government and the Death of Amoako Atta. The use of violence against the Christian community at Kyebi led directly to the colonial government's intervention in the domestic affairs of the "Protected" State. The Colonial Secretary, Charles D. Turton, described the Okyenhene in a minute on 20 December 1877 as having "reverted to what he was before he was transported to Lagos, e.i (sic) a savage barbarian";[44] and urged the governor to stand firmly behind the Basel Mission and exploit the connection to subsume the "Protected Territory" of Akyem Abuakwa into the Gold Coast Colony. Turton's minute urged:

> Apart from the complaints which have been received of the manner in which this native King administers justice, and of the arbitrary way in which he treats his subjects there is a great political question at issue and that is the struggle between Christianity and [heathenism] which shall prevail. … Matters have now come to a crisis and it is for this Government to say whether Christianity with its many blessings is to be suppressed by the persecution of those who belong to the Christian Churches.[45]

Within a few hours of Turton's minute an executive meeting approved the arrest of Amoako Atta I. In lieu of an Officer of the Constabulary, the task was entrusted to the Registrar in the Secretariat, Jacob Simons. He was to be accompanied by "a Corporal and three constables by way of adding weight to his mission." Jacobs's instruction was to bring the Okyenhene and the persons he accused of the theft of his valuables.

43 Addo-Fening, *Akyem Abuakwa 1700-1943 from Ofori Panin to Sir Ofori Atta*, 84-5.
44 Addo-Fening, *Akyem Abuakwa 1700-1943 from Ofori Panin to Sir Ofori Atta*, 85.
45 45 Addo-Fening, *Akyem Abuakwa 1700-1943 from Ofori Panin to Sir Ofori Atta*, 85.

Irritated by the government's continual intervention in the domestic affairs of their state, the *Amantoomiensa* (soldiers of the Ofori Stool) contemplated armed resistance. Men were sent secretly to Saltpond to buy ammunition. Their intentions were leaked by some Christians, and the government realized that Amoako Atta would not obey it "unless force [was] used." Accordingly, a force of Hausa troops, waiting at Aburi, was instructed to get ready to take the Okyenhene by force, if that became necessary.[46]

On 8 January 1887, Amoako Atta was escorted to Accra accompanied by six of his principal Chiefs and Amantoomiensa. On the 20th of January, the government set up a three-man Commission of Enquiry to enquire into Church-State relations since 1874. Its members were W.H. Qualye-Jones, Queen's Advocate, (President); Honourable George Frank Cleland, Justice of the Peace and Member of the Legislative Council; and Mr. Sunter Clark, Inspector of Schools. Before the first meeting could be convened, the Acting Chief Medical Officer reported the death of Amoako Atta at 6:20 a.m. on 2 February 1887, from double pneumonia[47]. The news of the Okyenhene's death in Accra touched off another round of persecution of Christians. Church buildings were destroyed; and Christians sought refuge in nearby states. The colonial government sent troops to occupy the state and forcibly integrated it into the Gold Coast Colony.

Conclusion

The death of Amoako Atta I ended Akyem Abuakwa's dogged struggle to hold on to its cherished ancestral religious culture against the combined force of Euro-Christian culture and British colonialism. Amoako Atta did not hate Christianity. Like his predecessors, he appreciated the benefits of formal education and the socio-economic change that it introduced. He was disposed to tolerate Christianity in his state but only as one of the forms of religious expression, and on terms that did not seek to undermine and obliterate the spiritual foundations of Abuakwa society. Amoako Atta's faith in, and respect for, the beliefs and usages of his ancestors was too strong to allow an alien faith, with adherents constituting only about 0.5 percent of his state's population, to impose its dogma and social norms on the rest of Abuakwa society. It was typically, a case of two worlds colliding

46 Addo-Fening, *Akyem Abuakwa 1700-1943 from Ofori Panin to Sir Ofori Atta*, 86.
47 Addo-Fening, *Akyem Abuakwa 1700-1943 from Ofori Panin to Sir Ofori Atta*, 87.

Western Missionaries who made a Difference: The Legacies of Mary Slessor of Calabar, and Johannes G. Christaller of Gold Coast

Angela Dwamena-Aboagye

ABSTRACT

The Western Missionary Movement evokes mixed feelings about its motives, methods and impacts, particularly in Africa. There are historians and scholars who believe that missionaries furthered the European colonial agenda in Africa, serving also as civilizing agents for 'the heathen'. Others believe that missionaries came to do what they felt called to do: to spread the gospel of Jesus Christ. This article examines the work of two missionaries: Mary Slessor of Calabar, Nigeria, and Johannes Christaller of the Gold Coast. It concludes that although these missionaries may not have been completely devoid of the Europeanisation agenda and the ideas of Christendom, they were indeed "missionaries who made a difference" to Africa because of their commitment to engage in the culture, language and thought forms of the people they served. By doing so, they left visible and credible legacies for mission which cannot be ignored.

Introduction

Following the Evangelical Revival at the end of the 18th century was the Western Missionary Movement. Many Western missionaries came to Africa in the 19th century to win souls for Christ. However, most of them saw almost nothing good in the "heathen" African. The following statement in the 1910 Edinburgh Report is instructive regarding the attitudes and thinking that accompanied missionaries then:

> With regard to the personal demeanour of the missionary towards the native, Dr. Nassau writes some weighty words: "I have known missionaries who seemed to have come with only a feeling of hard duty to bring the Gospel to dirty, degraded, fellow-members of the human race. They felt a personal antipathy to colour, dirt, vermin and ugly faces. Unintentionally, they showed that antipathy in their manners. The alert-eyed natives saw it...Some of them, by their hard words or curt manner, brought only evil to the missionary name.[1]

Kwame Bediako asserts that it will be hard to prove any charge of outright racism against the missionary movement.[2] Yet he acknowledges also that the missionaries "participated in the general European outlook more intimately than [they] would probably have realized."[3] Consequently, it is not difficult to conclude that Western missionaries that came to Africa generally viewed the African race as belonging to a low place and status.

Nonetheless, I intend to argue in this article that missionaries Mary Slessor and Johannes Gotlieb Christaller, to a large extent, despite their Eurocentric cultural self-understanding, were different. There are plausible observations to aver that these two missionaries belonged to a more culturally sensitive and respectful class of missionaries than their counterparts; they, by the very evidence of their work, lives, and engagement with Africans, demonstrated a significantly different approach to mission. They chose to engage with the African culture, religious traditions, thought and ways. Like Dr. David Livingstone, who believed that the duty of missionaries was to make Africans "gentlemen, civilized and Christian", Slessor and Christaller credited the African with enough intelligence to work with them, genuinely befriend them, and employ methods that "absorbed concepts of inculturation and contextualisation."[4] These observations motivated this article, because they remind me of Professor Allison Howell, an Australian missionary, who in her approximately thirty-eight years sojourn in Ghana, presented a different face of mission work; perhaps like those of Slessor and Christaller. How different were Mary Slessor and Johannes Gotlieb Christaller from their contemporary missionaries?

---

1 Jonathan Hill, *Zondervan Handbook of the History of Christianity* (England: Lion Publishing, Mayfield House, 2006) 274.

2 Kwame Bediako, *Theology and Identity: The Impact of Culture on Christian Thought in the Second Century and Modern Africa* (Oxford: Regnum Books, 1992) 233.

3 Bediako, *Theology and Identity*, 233.

4 A phrase used to describe Johannes Christaller (which I believe is also true of Mary Slessor). See, Thomas Bearth, 'J.G Christaller: A holistic view of language and culture – and C.C. Reindorf's *History*', in Paul Jenkins (ed.), *The Recovery of the West African Past-African Pastors and African History in the Nineteenth Century* (Basel: Basler Afrika Bibliographien, 1998): 91. See also A.E. Orobator *Theology Brewed in the African Pot*, (Maryknoll, New York: Orbis Books, 2008): 127-136 for a discussion on the concepts of *inculturation* and *contextualisation*, which resonates with what Slessor and Christaller did in their work in and for Africa.

Western Missionaries, Christendom and Europeanization

Missionaries Mary Slessor and Johannes G. Christaller, both Europeans, came into West Africa in the second half of the 19th Century, as part of the evangelical enterprise. At the time they came, the image that Europeans had of Africa, formed long before the modern missionary movement ventured into Africa was very negative.[5] This image of the continent, gleaned mostly from reports of explorers, earlier missionaries, and traders was one of darkness; a continent without religion or morals; ignorant, pitiful and in a condition made worse by the vicissitudes of the Slave Trade.[6]

Europe was the missionary-sending continent, whose historical associations with threats from the Muslim world and its experience with the Crusades had brought about an emergence of self-consciousness and identification as Christian Europe; a territorial concept that sought to conquer 'enemy' lands and "Christianize" them. Thus, Europe became associated with the concept of Christendom which had as its primary quest the "Europeanisation" of lesser civilized peoples in the non-Christian world; whether through territorial conquests and colonization, or more benignly, through the missionary enterprise. In this enterprise, Christianity was to be utilized as the agent to bring about civilization. Adrian Hastings writes:

> [E]vangelisation was seen as liberation from a state of absolute awfulness and the picture of unredeemed Africa was often painted in colours – as gruesome as possible the better – to encourage missionary zeal at home.[7]

It appeared, that the 'Europe as Christendom' concept was unchallenged even by the Protestant Reformation,[8] and this concept held sway for a long time, as evidenced by the 1910 Report of the World Missionary Conference in Edinburgh.[9]

Missionaries who made a Difference?

The modern Western Missionary Movement was steeped in the prevailing Eurocentric ideas of the time; and it was in this context and prevailing circumstances that missionaries Mary Slessor and Johannes Christaller

5 Kwame Bediako, *Theology and Identity: The Impact of Culture on Christian Thought in the Second Century and Modern Africa* (Oxford: Regnum Books, 1992) 228.
6 Bediako, *Theology and Identity*, 226.
7 Bediako, *Theology and Identity*, 225, quoting Adrian Hastings, *Church and Mission in Modern Africa* (London: Burns and Oates, 1967) 60.
8 Bediako, *Theology and Identity*: 229.
9 *The Missionary Message in Relation to non-Christian Religions: The World Missionary Conference, 1910, Report of Commission IV*, (Edinburgh and London: Oliphant, Anderson and Ferrier, 1910).

came, lived, and worked in Africa. The purpose of this paper is to demonstrate that despite Europe's civilising agenda for Africa, there were European missionaries who in their lives and work, appeared to have significantly departed, in a sense, from that agenda. In other words, the missionary movement had remarkable people who, though not completely divorced from the baggage of the prevailing Eurocentric worldview about the non-Christian world, did live differently from the mainstream of missionaries Africa received. These remarkable personalities achieved notable feats and legacies worth learning and applying to mission – for all time. They were missionaries who made a difference.

Mary Slessor, Scottish Missionary to Calabar, Nigeria

Mary Slessor was born in 1848 in Aberdeen, Scotland. She was the second of seven children, most of whom predeceased her before reaching their teen years. Her father was a shoemaker with an alcoholic and temper problem; her mother, a sweet-natured Christian homemaker who raised her children with strong Christian virtues. Mary's family was Presbyterian, and one day, she had a conversion experience; repented and believed in Jesus as her Saviour. She grew up in poverty, but from a young age her heart was set on becoming a missionary to Calabar. The hardships of her upbringing appear to have prepared her for the work ahead. In 1875, she offered her services to the Foreign Mission Board and in 1876, aged 26, sailed for Calabar, in the eastern part of modern Nigeria.[10] In typical missionary-style writing at the time, this was how Calabar was described:

> Calabar exhibited the worst side of nature and of man. While much of it was beautiful, it was one of the most unhealthy spots in the world - sickness, disease, and swift death attacking the Europeans who ventured there. The natives were considered to be the most degraded of any in Africa. They were, in reality, the slum-dwellers of negro-land...a people without a history, with only a past of confused movement, oppression and terror... to the horrors of the internal slave-trade was added the horror of the traffic for the markets of the West Indies and America. [11]

Because of the long period of lawlessness and the effects of the slave raids and trade, missionaries who went there are said to have had a hard time selecting the applicable epithets. Words such as "bloody", "savage", "treacherous", "devilish", "cannibals", "fetish-worshippers", "murderers," were used.[12]

---

10 Mary Slessor's life story is taken mainly from the biographical book by W.P Livingstone, *Mary Slessor of Calabar: Pioneer Missionary* (London: Hodder and Stoughton, 4th Edition, MCMXVI). There are several internet sites that have her life story.

11 Livingstone, *Mary Slessor of Calabar: Pioneer Missionary*, 15.

12 Livingstone, *Mary Slessor of Calabar*, 16. One cannot deny that a people so affected by war and slavery would not have had characteristics such as those described; as well as customs that were corrupted. War and slavery of that magnitude occurring in any place would result in marked degradation in the quality of life of the affected people. As a result, the words used by the missionaries who preceded Slessor are not that surprising, since the generally held European view was that native Africans did not have

In spite of the conditions, Slessor, "who shrank from nothing which she thought her Master would have done,"[13] considered it an honour, and started as a teacher in the Calabar Mission. However, her heart lay towards going into the hinterlands to do real missionary work. She had her prayer answered, and that move further inland into Igbo territory began for her an extraordinary life of intense service and sacrifice; earning her a place in both British and Nigerian annals as an indomitable personality who laid down her life so others might live. Thus, for almost forty years she lived most of her life in the Calabar region until her death in 1915, in a hut at Itu, aged sixty-six. She never married.

Johannes Gottlieb Christaller: A Basel Mission Missionary to the Gold Coast

In 1828, the first mission from Basel, Switzerland, arrived on the Gold Coast. The mission worked in the Ga and Akuapem areas. The Basel Mission Committee was of the strong conviction that "...the African was to hear the Gospel, to read the Bible and worship and be taught in his own tongue."[14] The Basel Mission therefore emphasized use of local languages in its activities. Being Christian meant being literate and vested with the capacity to read the religious literature produced for converted Africans. It was the Basel Mission that sent Christaller to the Gold Coast, to devote himself entirely to the Twi language, the most widely spoken in the country.[15]

Christaller was born in Winnenden, Germany, in 1827. The son of a tailor, he took interest as a young boy in reading the many books that his father had, and thereby developed his philological and linguistics skills. He decided very early in life to become a missionary. After schooling at the Basel Mission Training School in Switzerland, he underwent the four-year missionary course, and was sent to the Gold Coast. Christaller's linguistics skill was remarkable. He knew Greek, Latin, English, Hebrew and German, and became one of the leading linguists of his century.[16]

---

anything of real value in their heritage; and that outlook still held sway until much later in the 20th Century.

13 Livingstone, *Mary Slessor of Calabar*: 26. It was written of Mary, that "[A]s she observed and assimilated, she came to a clearer view of the people and the problems confronting the missionaries. She realised that the raw negroes, though savage enough, were not destitute of religious beliefs: their "theology," indeed, seemed somewhat too complicated for comprehension. Nor were their lives unregulated by principles and laws; they were ruled by canons and conventions as powerful as those of Europe, as merciless as the caste code of India; their social life was rooted in a tangle of relationships and customs as intricate as any in the world." This observation set Slessor apart as a European missionary who came to understand quite early that the long-held views about the African having no religion or culture that contained anything of religious worth or value was untrue. See also, Murimi, 'The Impact of Christendom on Western Missionary Practice': 52. Based on Slessor's observation, she decided to carefully study the Africans, so as to appreciate and understand them as best as she could.

14 Noel Smith, *The History of the Presbyterian Church of Ghana: 1835 – 1966* (Accra: Ghana Universities Press, 1965) 54.

15 Smith, *The History of the Presbyterian Church of Ghana*, 54.

16 L. H. Ofosu-Appiah, *Dictionary of African Christian Bibliography* 'Christaller Johann Gottlieb, 1827 to 1895, Basel Mission, Ghana' https://dacb.org/stories/ghana/christaller-j/, accessed 15th February 2020. See also, Kwame Bediako, https://dacb.org/stories/ghana/christaller-johannes/ accessed 15th February 2020.

According to Thomas Bearth, the *Lexikon der Afrikanistik* calls Christaller the "founder of the scientific study of West African languages."[17]

Christaller taught at the Basel Mission Seminary at Akropong. He stayed in the Gold Coast from 1853 till 1858, went to Basel for four years because of illness, returned in 1862 and stayed till 1868. Christaller married a fellow missionary, Emilie, who died while they sojourned in Kyebi, in the Gold Coast.[18] Within this period and till his death in 1895, Christaller worked on Twi translations of the Bible, a scientific grammar of the Twi language, the publication of a *Dictionary of Asante and Fante Language - called Tshi (Twi)*, a collection of 3,600 Twi proverbs, Twi translations of Christian doctrinal works, Twi periodicals and a Twi hymn book.[19]

Christaller lived primarily in Akropong and Kyebi, both towns in a part of the Gold Coast that had Akan as their language. The two towns, linked by a common ancestral history of the ruling houses of their traditional leaders, had been areas of focus for the Basel Mission's work. The Akan religious heritage includes a belief in the existence of the Supreme Being, "Onyankopon" who is the Creator and Sustainer of the universe, a variety of deities, and the world of the ancestors, that is, the living dead of the clans or families.[20] Christaller engaged so deeply in the study of Akan thought that, according to Kwame Bediako, he was able to come to the conclusion that the Akan, who were presumed polytheistic were 'to a great extent, rather monotheists, as they apply the term God only to one Supreme Being.'[21]

Mary Slessor's Work

When Slessor landed in Calabar, she was assigned as a teacher at the mission school at Duke Town. After the novelty of her surroundings wore off, she began to see the problems confronting the "natives" and missionary work. It was here that she resolved to "acquire a thorough mastery of the language in order to enter completely into the life and thought of the natives."[22] This decision was an important one; undergirding her influence and effectiveness throughout her missionary career since language is the expression of a people's culture, and "... the means for assuming the

17 Bearth, "Recovery in the West African Past," 83.

18 Described as a deeply devoted wife, it is said that her death affected him deeply. Soon after, he moved back to Akropong and a year later, he left the Gold-Coast for good. See, Ofosu-Appiah, *Dictionary of African Christian Bibliography* 'Christaller, Johann Gottlieb'.

19 Bediako, *Christianity in Africa*, 52.

20 Kwame Bediako, "Jesus in African Culture: A Ghanaian Perspective," in *Jesus in Africa: The Christian Gospel in African History and Experience*, ed. Kwame Bediako (UK: Regnum Africa, 2000), 22-23.

21 Bediako, *Christianity in Africa*, 213.

22 Livingstone *Mary Slessor of Calabar*, 28.

weight of a culture."[23] She identified herself with the life and thought of the community in which she worked as a missionary by being able to speak and understand their language, Efik. This must have enabled her to effectively relate her "theological reflection and construction to the actual vernacular articulation of faith in African Christian experience."[24] For it is "only through the vernacular that a genuine and lasting theological dialogue with culture can take place."[25]

Slessor was given charge as missionary to Old Town and its surrounding areas. A difficult post, but one she tackled with zest as she was practically free to implement her own ideas and methods. It was here that she came into contact with the cultural practice of infanticide through twin-murdering,26 and the abandonment of infants born by slave women when the mother died. Slessor so passionately set about working against this cultural practice that rescuing children from infanticide became her life-long, and a significantly acknowledged, mission activity.

Her next post, Okoyong, was so dreaded by both "natives" and Europeans that many had little hope of her surviving. With strong reliance on God, she preached, engaged the rulers and made friends out of many, saved twin and orphaned babies, engaged with sorcerers, and opposed the traffic in European rum and slave trading. She also triumphed in stopping human sacrifices which were done when notable men and chiefs died. She practically changed the face of Okoyong, socially, economically and politically.

It is worthy to note, that Slessor's push inward was of her own initiative and willingness to go 'where angels fear to tread.' She had a resolute spirit, and went on, after her 'conquest of Okoyong',[27] to the Enyong Creek area. She was then 55 years old and went there accompanied by her seven adopted children. Finally penetrating further into the hinterlands, she continued her work until her death at Itu in 1915.

---

23 Bediako, *Christianity in Africa*, quoting John Pobee, 72.
24 Bediako, *Christianity in Africa*, 72.
25 Bediako, *Christianity in Africa*, 72.
26 In this custom, a woman who gave birth to twins was regarded with horror. Not only were the twins crushed into pots and left in a bush to die, but the mother was also banished into a bush. It was believed that the father of one of the twins was an evil spirit, and the mother had also committed a great sin, hence the twins. Slessor perceived that the custom held sway because of "... superstition and fear, and she could see how, from the native point of view, it was essentially for the safety of the House..." (i.e., the households or families). On the throwing away of infants whose slave mothers died, she understood that no slave woman had the time to take care of another woman's child, who would grow up only to become the property of the master. See Livingstone, *Mary Slessor of Calabar,* 36.
27 J.H. Proctor, "Serving God and Empire: Mary Slessor in South-Eastern Nigeria, 1876 – 1915," Journal *of Religion in Africa*, Vol. 30, Facs. (1 February, 2000): 45-61. It is reported by Mary Kingsley, a famous 19th century traveller and writer who was not enthused with the missionary aims of conversion and civilizing non-Christian peoples; after meeting Slessor in Calabar; that she (Slessor), was "...ruling as a veritable white chief over the entire Okoyon district. Her knowledge of the natives was extraordinary, and she had won profound esteem and exercising an influence and power among negroes unmatched in its way by that of any other white." See Livingstone, *Mary Slessor of Calabar,* 48.

Religious Work and Life

From the day she arrived in Calabar, almost to her dying day, Slessor held services for her family at the mission churches and from village to village, preaching Christ. Though much grieved about the depth of 'heathenism' of the Africans she worked for, she perceived many times that the God she had come to serve had actually "preceded... her in the field...and that... to discover His true identity, the missionary would have to delve deep into the local culture."[28] She was 'mission in action', by the manner in which she reached out to people, studied their culture, and tried to convince them to believe in Christ. Many times she was frustrated by the seeming small number of conversions made.[29] However, she reached many more people, especially women, who, though coming from their own religious tradition and having a primal apprehension of the transcendent, would rather not publicly declare a stance for the saviour for fear of societal penalization.[30] As a pioneer missionary, Slessor often walked barefooted; a remarkable demonstration of identification with the bare-foot Africans.

Through her work, she opened up the hinterlands so other missionaries could come later. She made their work easier because she had gone ahead of them. In her time, many mission posts were established in the creek towns; and she trained many indigenes, including her adopted children, who assisted her in teaching and managing the churches. Slessor entrusted herself absolutely into God's providential care, power and protection through much prayer. W. P. Livingstone said of her:

> She had deliberately given up everything for her Master, and she accepted all the consequences this renunciation involved. What she did was for Him...as she was not her own...[31]

28 Lamin Sanneh, "The Horizontal and the Vertical in Mission: An African Perspective," *International Bulletin of Missionary Research*, Vol. 7 No. 4 (October, 1983): 166.

29 Livingstone writes: "...her chief aim was to win the people (of Okoyong) to Christ and all her efforts were directed to that end. It was for souls she was always hungering, and the lack of conversions were her greatest sorrow. Nevertheless, she was making progress. The people were becoming familiar with the name of God and Christ...whilst some in their hearts believed." See Livingstone, *Mary Slessor of Calabar*, 145.

30 Slessor perceived that this was the case especially with women. It is reported that: "...Mary saw behind the veil; she knew quiet women whose souls looked out of their eyes, and who were more in touch with the unseen than they dared tell; women who prayed and communed with God even while condemned to heathen practices. There was one blind woman whom she placed far before herself in the Christian race..." See Livingstone, *Mary Slessor of Calabar*: 54.

31 Livingstone, *Mary Slessor of Calabar*, 132.

Social and Socio-Cultural Work

Slessor did not divorce the sharing of the gospel from social action.[32] She trudged miles through tropical forests to heal sick chiefs and ordinary persons alike. She also established several schools and vocational training for girls, and through innovative means undertook peace initiatives between warring tribes. Slessor saved people from trial by ordeal and encouraged substitution of customs such as slaughtering goats instead of humans as sacrifice.

Perhaps Slessor's best-known work was her unrelenting fight against cruel customs, particularly against women and children. She tackled twin-murders with single-minded fierceness. As explained earlier, it was customary to regard twins as evil, an aberration and therefore not to be kept alive. The tribes believed that their Supreme God, Chukwu, abhorred twins because he created only one male and one female; only lower animals like cats, dogs, sheep etc., could have multiple births. Parents of the twins were also stigmatized and ostracized.33 Slessor adopted several methods to rescue the baby twins. According to J. Theodore Mueller,

> Each day she scoured the woods to find babes exposed and mothers beaten and expelled from the tribal town. These she would bring to the compound, and though by doing this blessed work, she violated every tribal custom, no one dared to interfere with her or molest those whom she sheltered in the compound.[34]

She preached against the practice, pleaded with tribal chiefs to help her put an end to it and also took care of the babies she rescued so well that after a while, the local people, including chiefs, became enthralled by them, and would come into her compound and touch them.[35]

---

32 Slessor's remarkable social activities were so many and so varied that space may not permit a good summary of them in this paper. "She was a missionary after their own heart; they found her different from other missionaries. She would enter their townships as one of themselves; show them in a moment that she was mistress of their thought and ways and get right into their confidence." Livingstone, *Mary Slessor of Calabar*, 38.

33 See http://www.thenigerianvoice.com/nynews/26137/1/arochukwu-twins-before-mary-slessor, for the article "Arochukwu Twins before Mary Slessor to be Accepted: Twins expected to Undergo Cleansing." Posted Monday, 7th June 2010, accessed 15th February 2020.

34 See http://www.wholesomewords.org/missions/bioslessor10.html, accessed 15th February 2020, for an article by J. Theodore Mueller, "Mary Slessor, 1848 – 1915, Missionary Biographies."

35 See "Dictionary of African Biographies," at https://dacb.org/stories/nigeria/slessor-mary , accessed 15th February 2020. As to whether Slessor succeeded on completely erasing fear of twins from among the people with whom she worked is the subject of the article at http://www.thenigerianvoice.com/nynews/26137/1/arochukwu-twins-before-mary-slessor, "Arochukwu Twins before Mary Slessor to be Accepted; Twins expected to Undergo Cleansing." It is reported that years after Slessor, twins are still stigmatised and suffer discrimination among the Aros and Arochukwus, although they are not openly killed as in the past. This has implications for gospel-culture engagement, especially in the necessity for using the gospel to address such customs from the worldview of the people, and finding credible alternative or acceptable customs. Obviously, Slessor succeeded in getting goats and sheep used instead of human sacrifice at the burial of chiefs, but for twin murders, there is no indication a replacement rite or custom was found.

As mentioned earlier, Slessor helped stop human sacrifice in many parts of Calabar.[36] She also helped to save many slaves[37] from being stripped and flogged to death for the slightest offences. She also provided shelter in her own home for orphaned children[38]; personally adopting many of them.

Slessor's social work and struggle against some African customs that were cruel in nature and degrading to the dignity of the poor and vulnerable served many who would otherwise have had no protection. Many commendable customs exist in the African cultural heritage which must be continued, but those that point away from Christ need to be addressed with all seriousness; abolished, converted, or adapted. Slessor's work typified one who humanly illustrated the work of Jesus in reaching out to the outcasts, poor, and sick.[39]

Influencing the Economy

Slessor's peace-making initiatives among the tribal chiefs encouraged trade among tribes, and between the hinterlands and the coast.

Added to this was opposing traffic in rum, in which she achieved success.[40] She argued passionately for the establishment of industrial training for young people because she believed the native was capable of learning useful skills that would grow the local economy.

Political and Judicial work

Slessor cooperated with British colonial officials at many levels, seeing herself not only as a missionary, but also as one in service to the Empire.

---

36 In the primal cultures of West African people, important people such as chiefs had to be served in this world and the next, so when they died, ordinary members of the society and slaves were killed to accompany them to the next world to render service. The more important the dead person was, the higher the number of slaves sacrificed (reference?).

37 See, Ogbu U. Kalu, "Poverty in Pre-colonial and Colonial West Africa," in *Themes in West Africa's History* ed. Emmanuel K. Akyeampong, (Ghana: James Curry Ltd/Woeli Publishing Services, 2006): 163-185. (173). Slessor's anti-slavery efforts were significant especially in an era when after the abolition of the Slave Trade, slave raiding and kidnapping in the interior had produced an excess of slaves who could not be utilized in plantation farming, and therefore became victims of cultic blood sacrifices. Because of their slave status they were stigmatised; discriminated against; denied means of production, human rights and political freedom.

38 In some West African societies, orphaned children whose parents died of inexplicable diseases were regarded with fear and suspicion. The Igbo called such children 'Ogbanje,' and usually abandoned them to die. See Kalu, "Poverty in Pre-Colonial West Africa," 173.

39 Louis Luzbetak, *The Church and Cultures: New Perspectives in Missiological Anthropology* (Maryknoll, New York: Orbis Books, 2000),. 374., tells of the complaint of a Jesuit Indian to a group of missionaries about their methods: "'You say that you bring Jesus and new humanity to us. But what is this "new humanity" you are proclaiming? We would like to see it, touch it, taste it, feel it. Jesus must not be just a name, but a reality. Jesus must be illustrated humanly.'"

40 Slessor said: "Perhaps the greatest obstacle to Christian truth and progress is not superstition or custom, but drink." Livingstone, *Mary Slessor of Calabar*. 86. Her success in stemming the rum trade in Okoyong paved the way for other goods to come in; opening up the enclosed Okoyong to Calabar and other places for travel and trade. The people began to make oil; bought and sold kernels to be taken to the factories and were kept busy enough to lose their inclination for drinking European rum, quarrelling and fighting. See Livingstone, *Mary Slessor of Calabar*, 88-90.

Nevertheless, she was not altogether uncritical and acquiescent to all government policies and officials.[41]

She acted as go-between for the government and the natives; explaining new policies, and how best to have these implemented. In fact, her work as a missionary facilitated, to a great extent, the expansion of colonial authority into the hinterland, wittingly or otherwise.

The colonial authority was so impressed by her knowledge of the customs and the people that they made her vice-president of the native court at Okoyong, and also at Ikot Obong. She served with dedication and enterprise, and it was said that "the natives got justice – unhampered by legal technicalities."[42]

Personal Life and Modelling

Slessor's remarkable life and service is worth telling and emulating. Often susceptible to sicknesses of all kinds; facing loneliness; bereavement; tropical storms; and leopard-inhabited forests; —she never gave up. Because of her love and concern for people she raised many to believe in themselves, especially women; many of whom became economically viable and lived in freedom from abuse. In her churches, it was said that some women would "die for Jesus" no matter the persecution they faced.

From all accounts, she was a woman of modesty and strength, prayer, gratitude and praise. She was everyone's 'Ma'; so called with fondness by chiefs, officials, slaves, women and children. She worked for little or no remuneration and gave up many basic comforts for the sake of the gospel.

Kwame Bediako[43] gives a model for a new African theological and Christian formation for mission.[44] It would not be out of place to say that before this circular model was conceptualized and expressed, Slessor was

41 Slessor was often distressed at the authorities resorting to the use of military measures to deal with disorder in the localities; and she was heard to refer to some of the colonial officials as 'pompous', 'foolish', 'superficial' and so on. On occasion, she had sharp differences with some of the officials because of their insensitivity and ignorance concerning the needs of the Africans. See Proctor, "Serving God and Empire: Mary Slessor in South-Eastern Nigeria, 1876 – 1915," 45-61.

42 Proctor, 'Serving God and Empire': 48-50. She presided over land matters, inheritance, unjust customs, assault, theft, debts; won freedoms for women and wives and settled conflicts between chiefs and tribes, among other cases. Her judgements were highly respected, as she tempered justice with mercy and also used the Gospel to influence people's behaviour in her rulings.

43 See Kwame Bediako, "The African Renaissance and Theological Reconstruction: The Challenge of the Twenty-first Century," *Journal of African Christian Thought*, Vol. 4. No. 2 (December 2001): 30.

44 Emphasis on the words used by Bediako in the model he describes are mine. Although the focus of Kwame Bediako's article cited above is that of a contemporary African Theologian raising critical questions for the African Church for theological formation relevant to the African context and the worldwide Church, I see Slessor's life and work as reflective of this model, in spite of her Eurocentric background and 'baggage.'

already working in it to a considerable extent. Keeping a central focus on *the Living God*, the *Bible* and her *faith and spirituality*, Slessor came into Africa with a mind for *mission* and to *transform* the lives of many – which she did. She may not have *discerned the times* enough in terms of theological engagement with the religious thought forms of the Igbo people but was relevant enough in her methods to change the generality of their socio-cultural and economic circumstances positively.

No doubt she thoroughly entered into, and lived in the *traditions* of the people, even if not their *history*, and worked to convert, adapt, — or eliminate as necessary— cruel customs. And, who knew better than Slessor the *context* within which she worked for nearly forty years, even if she did not entirely lose her Europeanizing tendencies? Perhaps the people who assembled for the 1910 Edinburgh Conference would have benefitted greatly from her insights and experience if she had been invited.[45]

Johannes G. Christaller's Work

Not much is found on Christaller as a preacher who went about converting Africans; he concentrated on making the Twi language come alive as literary language. Bearth asserts that Christaller "... became the scholar he was by pursuing his primary calling as a missionary. Being a missionary also meant being an educator. What he felt called to do to as a missionary and an educator is what led him to develop his capacities and objectives as a pioneer of the study of African languages and cultures, as a scholar and a mediator between cultures."[46]

Kwame Bediako gives a glimpse into the significance of Christaller's work when he says of Carl Reindorf's stay at the Akropong Seminary, that he (Reindorf) was:

> ...[b]rought into contact with the meticulous study of language, culture and historical investigation and writing that grew up around Johannes Christaller and his African associates, David Asante and Jonathan Bekoe Palmer.[47]

45 Proctor, "Serving God and Empire," 54. "She had a deeper understanding of and a more tolerant respect for African beliefs and practices than her colleagues... she did not think a thoroughgoing repudiation of their way was a pre-requisite to the acceptance of Christianity." In this sense, she reflects to some extent St. Paul's way of identifying with the gentile people as human and as one of them, which was how Slessor got into the confidence of the people before inviting them to come to Christ. It may be said though, that it appears St. Paul was more successful with engaging with the religious thought forms of the gentile Greeks than perhaps Slessor was with the Igbos.
46 Bearth, "J.G Christaller: A Holistic view of Language and Culture – and C.C. Reindorf's 'History'," in *The Recovery of the West African Past*, ed. Paul Jenkins (Basel: Basler Afrika Bibliographien, 1998) 85.
47 Bediako, *Christianity in Africa*: 46.

Christaller was a believer in teamwork and the capability of his local associates. He consistently worked with them, training them to take detailed notes of local religious activities and the traditions.

Christaller worked in his study, making sure that as far as possible, a Twi term was found for every item of thought. Kwame Bediako writes that Christaller did this:

> …[b]y painstaking interaction with students, chiefs and traditional language experts, the chief's spokesman (and) visiting the king's palace regularly.[48]

Christaller was an expert and passionate communicator. Bearth not only acknowledges this but sees it at the heart of his well-noted scholarship.[49]

Having learnt some Twi from Rev. H.N Riis, Christaller started practicing it the moment he stepped on Gold Coast soil. He also took advantage of the communicative resources of the people with whom he worked. By this method, he:

> …[w]ould explain a portion of text to his two assistants, each of whom then produced his own version. These versions were discussed and evaluated by all three of them before Christaller proposed his own version based on this hermeneutic-interactional process.[50]

The practical objectives for Christaller's work, which derive from being commissioned by the Basel Mission and also as his own career demanded, were:

> [T]o enable Europeans to communicate in African languages, and to enable Africans – all Africans, not just the elite – to have access to knowledge…not limited to the Bible – through the written medium of their own languages.[51]

Embarking on work of such monumental proportions was not without challenges. Christaller had to decide which particular Akan dialect was to be chosen for his work. After carefully considering Asante, Fante, Akyem and Akuapem, he settled on the Akuapem dialect as the most suitable.

Kwame Bediako quotes Odamtten regarding Christaller's work in Bible translation, that: "… using the vernacular was based on the principle of helping the people to get a clear understanding of the teaching of the Bible…"[52] This finds resonance in John Mbiti's insistence that:

48 Bediako, *Christianity in Africa*, 46.
49 Bearth, "J. G. Christaller," 83.
50 Bearth, "J. G. Christaller," 84.
51 Bearth, "J. G. Christaller," 84.
52 Bediako, *Christianity in Africa*, 50.

> For most people in… Africa, an African language is still the mother tongue, and forms the psychological background for their thinking and understanding. Great emphasis should be given to the use of African languages in communicating the gospel, and in making Christian concepts assimilated in the life of the Church… This is no mean task, and calls for much research and experimentation. The gospel has to sink into the thinking process, the attitude, and the vocabulary of the people…[53]

The significance of Christaller's work in translation is perhaps captured by what Lamin Sanneh asserts about missionaries according priority to the work of translation and the impact this had on the missionary enterprise:

> …that the local languages … could serve as adequate bearers of the divine revelation… God was not so disdainful of Africans to be incommunicable in their language…[54]

Sanneh commended missionaries for unwittingly contributing to the success of local adaptation of the gospel, over which "Africans presided with effective authority."[55] Yet he made a comment which, I believe may not be truly reflective of the kind of missionary Christaller was, judging from the depth of his work and engagement in the culture and religious thought of the Akan. Sanneh writes:

> Whatever their degree of competence, missionaries remained outside the local culture. The language into which they translated the Scriptures remained the mother tongue of Africans. In the Christian setting of Scripture and liturgy this language resonated with familiar religious notions to which the missionary would be oblivious.[56]

Certainly, this may be true of the generality of missionary translators, but not for Christaller in particular. I am of the opinion that one only has to examine his attitude and methods he brought to the work of translation, as well as the high degree of respect he gained for his works from personalities like Joseph Boakye Danquah, the great Akan philosopher, historian Carl Reindorf, and theologians like John Pobee and Kwame Bediako. Danquah, for example, thought Christaller's work went beyond ethnographic significance, and asserted that it demonstrated that, "'[t]he Spirit of God is abroad even in the Akan of the Gold Coast.'"[57] For his

53 John Mbiti, "The Ways and Means of Communicating the Gospel," in *Christianity in Tropical Africa*, ed. C.G. Baeta (London: Oxford University Press for International African Institute, 1968) 331.

54 Sanneh, "The Horizontal and Vertical in Mission," 166.

55 Sanneh, "The Horizontal and Vertical in Mission," 166.

56 Sanneh, "The Horizontal and Vertical in Mission," 167.

57 Joseph Boakye Danquah, quoted in Bediako, *Christianity in Africa*: 78. Danquah thought so highly of Christaller's work that he wrote: "'…[b]ut for Christaller's foresight in recording in permanent and highly intelligible form the scattered elements of the beliefs and hopes and fears of the Akan people…when European ideas in the form of new learning, a new religion and a new economic life were sweeping the country, the Akan… would today have failed to bring their indigenous contribution to the spiritual achievements of mankind.'"

own work, *The Akan Doctrine of God,* Danquah actually accorded Christaller the status of an ancestor, claiming that he was:

> …[i]n the higher sense of that attribute, the ancestor of thought that informs these pages with one lived memory and imagination. In that sense, the spiritual sense, this book must be taken as having been written by him, or not to be unnecessarily mysterious, with his spiritual co-operation.[58]

While the objectives stated for his work were not unique to Christaller as a missionary linguist, Bearth asserts that what distinguishes him from other missionary translation efforts was his:

> …[p]erception of otherwise neglected phenomena of language and the methodological thoroughness with which he pursued his enquiry into them, far beyond what the immediate practical objectives would have required. Christaller united in his person…the passion of the communicator but also the pioneering spirit of the discoverer and the meticulous mind of a philologist.[59]

Perhaps what gives this writer the best impression about the man Christaller is found in the preface he wrote for his *Dictionary of The Asante and Fante Language called Tshi.* His language exudes his passion, deep empathy and the respect he had for his subject and the people from whose thought life he did his work. He writes:

> And so the author concludes with the fervent wish and prayer that his work may contribute to a thorough knowledge of this important language, so that it may more and more become the vehicle of true knowledge and spiritual light to the numerous tribes to which it has been assigned.[60]

Notable Impacts of Christaller's work

Having raised the Akan language to one imbued with a transcendent range of thought, Christaller paved the way for others to follow. Books like *Kan me Hwe*[61] followed suit in the Scottish missionary era. Dr. Ephraim Amu and Otto Boateng experimented with local music forms and became famous for their works. The Akropong Theological Seminary became a research institution for theology, mission and culture and was rechristened in honour of Christaller and Dr. Clement A. Akrofi.[62] Dr. C. A. Akrofi's

58 Bediako, *Christianity in Africa*, 78.

59 Bearth, "J. G. Christaller", 84.

60 J.G Christaller, *A Dictionary of The Asante and Fante Language called Tshi (Chwee, Twi).* (Basel: Printed for the Evangelical Missionary Society, 1881): xii.

61 Authored by Scottish missionary Elspeth Elder. See, https://allafrica.com/stories/200401290661.html , accessed 15th February 2020.

62 See https://aci.edu.gh , *the website of the Akrofi-Christaller Institute of Theology, Mission and Culture.*

works in translation, such as *Twi Kasa Mmara: A Twi Grammar in Twi*[63] in the following century made him a worthy successor of Christaller. Basel missionary education methods, especially the use of local language, became so successful that it is still spoken of with great nostalgia in contemporary Ghanaian society.

Legacy and Lessons for Contemporary Mission

In fulfilling Christ's commission to "go and make disciples of the nations,"[64] European missionaries Mary Slessor and Johannes Christaller made their homes in the languages and culture of the African people. In this, they demonstrated their conviction that the gospel was translatable; that God speaks the languages of Africans. Considering their passion and commitment in the face of several daunting challenges, it is not difficult to infer they were convinced that Christianity was, after all, not merely a Western religion. In their work, both Slessor and Christaller evidenced their belief and hope that the gospel could find a home among African peoples through the grace of God.

For Slessor, I describe her as "theology in action,"[65] for her life spoke what she believed. While Christaller spoke through the language of the people; expressing their mother tongue in his translation and thereby contributed to the quest of Africans to be both African and Christian. As "treasures in earthenware vessels"[66] they may not have made thousands of converts in their time, but who can measure the lasting impacts of the legacies they left? They gave their best as they knew how, in spite of their Eurocentric self-understanding. They fulfilled mission in creative ways, even if imperfectly. Andrew Walls asserts that "as for the missionaries, they achieved – sometimes in spite of themselves – exactly what they believed they had been sent to do. After all, they had not gone to transmit evangelicalism to Africa, but the gospel."[67] This is true in the light of the shift in the centre of gravity that has revealed the non-Western character of Christianity and its blossoming in Africa. However, it is a worthwhile enquiry to delve into the missionary past to examine the lives of individual women and men who generously gave their service and time to bequeath to the African continent the greatest gift, the gospel, who is Jesus,[68] the self-revelation of God to humankind.

63 See https://dacb.org/stories/ghana/akrofi-clement/, accessed 15th February 2020.

64 Matthew 28:19-20.

65 A statement from Bishops at a Dar es Salaam Conference in August 1976; in Bediako, *Christianity in Africa*, 160, reads in part: "[W]e reject as irrelevant an academic type of theology that is divorced from action…" I believe that Mary Slessor's life and work showed that this is her self-understanding of God and His relationship with humanity; that she could not help but be actively involved in the very lives of the people she had sworn to serve.

66 2 Corinthians 4:7.

67 Walls, *The Missionary Movement in Christian History*, 101.

68 Bediako, *Christianity in Africa*, 57, quotes Dr. C. A Akrofi who, at being honoured by the Johannes Gutenberg University, Maine, for his work, said: "….and in view of the tendency to regard Christianity as a foreign religion, I will remind my fellow Africans that although Christianity is Europe's greatest gift to Africa, it is not exclusively the white man's religion…Christianity is a world religion because Jesus Christ is the Lord and King of the universe."

PART TWO

GOSPEL, CULTURE, AND SPIRITUALITY

Gospel Misunderstood, Culture Mislabelled: A Reappraisal of some Avoidable Pitfalls in Issues of Gospel and Culture

Rudolf K. Gaisie

Abstract

Though issues of gospel and culture are perennial, they are not always insurmountable. Some of the pitfalls are avoidable. The root cause of most of the difficulties in addressing issues of gospel and culture are quite clearly a misunderstanding of the nature and dynamism of two narratives. The gospel is a story, a narrative of God's unfolding purpose for his created world. Culture is also a story; a narrative of the responses of humans to the reality (both physical and spiritual) around them. This article reappraises Allison M. Howell's contribution to understanding issues of gospel and culture, as well as her suggestions at avoiding some of the pitfalls. It takes as point of departure an article by Howell titled, "Avoiding Mislabelling and Misnaming: Learning to Engage the Gospel of Christ with Culture", in which, among others, she highlighted the *form* and *meaning* of every cultural practice and the need to be mindful of the role of Scripture in interpreting the meaning of cultural forms.

Introduction

In her article, "Avoiding Mislabelling and Misnaming: Learning to Engage the Gospel of Christ with Culture", Professor Allison M. Howell shares a story and some cross-cultural lessons in her experience as a young missionary in Northern Ghana among the Kasena.[1] She relates how the operation of a *voro* [pl. *vora*] (traditional diviner) eventually led her to a study of divination and God's communication with people in the Bible in order to appreciate the significance of the role of the *voro* among the

1 Allison M. Howell, "Avoiding Mislabelling and Misnaming: Learning to Engage the Gospel of Christ with Culture," *Serving Together* (October 2014): 4-7.

Kasena. In Howell's view, such an understanding is to be the basis for any helpful engagement between the gospel and this aspect of Kasena traditional culture. What follows is a reappraisal of some of the pitfalls identified and addressed in issues of gospel and cultural engagement, especially in cross-cultural settings, shared in this story of the traditional diviner.

Culture Mislabelled

When two men presented a chicken to a voro early one morning, young Howell's reaction was to classify the scene as a "witchdoctor performing some ritual."[2] Kwame, the Christian son of the voro, ; and her interlocutor that morning, ; assured her that it was not an unusual event. In spite of her anxious trepidation, she managed to ask for an explanation of the voro's ritual. The earlier English designation, witchdoctor, Howell found out, was an inadequate word to describe the person and function of the voro. A diviner or soothsayer, was a close rendering. Among the Kasena, Howell notes, a voro is consulted for a variety of issues. "If you need guidance to respond to a problem such as a sick child or wife, or if you believe someone or a 'witch' has caught the soul of a person, the surest way to obtain guidance is to go to a voro."[3] Thus, unlike a witchdoctor who is essentially a traditional healer concerned with therapeutic remedies, the voro acted "like a guidance counsellor and a mediator as he or she mediated between the person [consulting] and the spiritual realm."[4] In fact, according to Howell, the voro is primarily concerned with yazura (health, well-being, peace).[5]

The connection between Jesus Christ and the *voro* became clearer for Howell some weeks after the experience with Kwame's father. Howell became nervous when she heard from the conversation of two old men under a shed one afternoon that the *voro* is *wɛ bu* (God's child).[6] Missionaries in the Kasena context have referred to Jesus as *wɛ bu*. Typical of her guarded curiosity, Howell asked the two old men what they thought when Christians proclaimed *Yezu ye Wɛ Bu* (Jesus is God's Child). One of the men responded, "*Yezu ye felsim voro*" (Jesus is the white person's diviner).[7] This demonstrates how, in most contexts, indigenes create a cultural space

2 Howell, "Avoiding Mislabelling and Misnaming," 5.
3 Howell, "Avoiding Mislabelling and Misnaming," 5-6.
4 Howell, "Avoiding Mislabelling and Misnaming," 6.
5 Allison M. Howell, *The Religious Itinerary of a Ghanaian People: The Kasena and the Christian Gospel* (Achimota: African Christian Press, 2001), 93.
6 Howell, "Avoiding Mislabelling and Misnaming," 6.
7 Howell, "Avoiding Mislabelling and Misnaming," 6.

for Jesus in their religious and spiritual universe after the initial missionary proclamation of Jesus in their context.[8]

Thus, it is only a matter of time before the meaning and significance of Jesus will assume full cultural weight. This invariably requires the work of more than one generation. The realisation that the *voro* was traditionally seen as *wɛ bu* led to a reimagining of Jesus in the Kasena religious universe in such a way to distinguish him in superiority to the *voro*. Already among the Kasena, the *vora* were never associated with *Baŋa Wɛ* (High Creator God). This indigenous resource, as it were, will aid Christian proclamation of Jesus as *Baŋa Wɛ*.[9]

Though most early missionaries saw the *voro* in negative terms, the Kasena "had a very high view of diviners whom they considered as a gift from God ... to guide them in life and to mediate between them and the spiritual realm."[10] It is not enough to stop at first impressions: the early missionary view of things. One invariably needs to probe further to discover the cultural or traditional view of things, which in most cases takes time and effort to fully comprehend.

It appears that there is an indigenous control mechanism for the activity of divination among the Kasena. These are mostly cultural efforts to protect people from being victims of what is otherwise a good indigenous service. Visits to, and reports or directions from, the voro are invariably concealed in conversations with some euphemism. Thus, one man was asked from his return from a voro, 'what did you roam and see?' He, in turn, prefaced his response in literal rendering 'he lied he said'. According to Howell,

> for the Kasena, this opening phrase was an acknowledgment of the humanity of the diviner and a form of rejoinder to ensure that, if you do what the diviner tells you to do and the problem is not resolved, or the sick person dies, you cannot be held personally responsible.[11]

In this way, both the *voro* and the client are somewhat protected. It also points to the apparent uncertainty in dealing with things in the spiritual realm.

8 When Jesus was proclaimed as Logos in the wider Graeco-Roman context, Christian converts eventually need to clarify some of the implications of this proclamation, such as the issue of origin, or generation in contradistinction to the manner of generation of divine-human beings in the Graeco-Roman world of thought. During an interview session with one traditional priest in Larteh— a town in the eastern region of Ghana— he remarked that the Supreme Being has given their tradition *nana* Akonnedi (local tutelary deity), just as He has given the Christians and Muslims, respectively, *nana* Jesus and *nana* Mohammad. Thus, for the priest there is a space for Jesus in his spiritual universe.

9 Howell, "Avoiding Mislabelling and Misnaming", 6. Perhaps it would further take Kasena Christians to explicate the Sonship of Jesus in the Godhead in say proclaiming also that Jesus is also Son of *Baŋa Wɛ*.

10 Howell, "Avoiding Mislabelling and Misnaming," 6.

11 Howell, "Avoiding Mislabelling and Misnaming," 6.

In dealing with the issue of divination as practiced by the *voro* among Kasena Christians, Howell would later realise that the typical Biblical prooftext approach was "inaccurate and inadequate".[12] This approach naturally led to the condemnation of people who consulted diviners as Leviticus 19:31 and Deuteronomy 18:10-11 would warrant. In her estimation, these texts were applied usually to "the externals or form - what we saw or thought we knew". In other words, "Christian engagement with the issue was not informed by an understanding of the meaning behind the ritual of divination."[13]

In his helpful application of anthropological insights in the theological discussion of gospel and culture, Charles H. Kraft, among other deduced models, highlighted "cultural forms and their functions, meanings, and usages."[14] According to this model, "any cultural element, whether material or nonmaterial" constitutes *forms* which serve certain *functions* as they are "developed and perpetuated" and as they are "used" serve as "vehicles of meaning from and to their users."[15] Kraft argues that "cultural forms" are conceptualizations of material (such as houses, clothing and dogs) and nonmaterial (such as marriage customs, family structures, words and sleeping) elements and that these are essentially static.[16] Though cultural forms are used to "serve particular functions", the people in that context may, or may not be aware of the specific functions that these serve, or may be aware of some and unaware of others.[17]

Kraft cautiously hints that while conveying meaning is an important function of a cultural form; they do not in themselves *contain* meaning because of the subjective nature in arriving at the essential meaning of any given cultural form.[18] According to Kraft, each cultural form is used to "convey impressions, values, attitudes and connotations from person to person and group to group."[19] Hence it is only through observation within its cultural context that the meaning of a given custom can be determined or discerned. Observation must involve a keen awareness of

12 Howell, 'Avoiding Mislabelling and Misnaming': 6.
13 Howell, 'Avoiding Mislabelling and Misnaming': 7.
14 Charles H. Kraft, *Christianity in Culture – A Study in Biblical Theologizing in Cross-Cultural Perspective* 25th anniversary ed. (Maryknoll: Orbis Books, 2005), 52-64.
15 Kraft, *Christianity in Culture*, 52.
16 Kraft, *Christianity in Culture*, 52.
17 Kraft, *Christianity in Culture*, 53.
18 Kraft, *Christianity in Culture*, 53.
19 Kraft, *Christianity in Culture*, 53.

"how a cultural form is used" since how a form functions, and what it means "are dependent on the way active human agents employ them."[20]

Indeed, it is the human who is at the heart of a culture and determines what *form* to use and what *meaning* to convey.[21] One prime pursuit of the human existence is the harnessing and preservation of life. Harold Turner's six-feature framework for analysing and understanding primal religions points to the primal quest for the sustenance of human life in an environment where there are invariably threats to life; whatever that may mean to the primal human.[22] It may be helpful to keep an eye on the overarching concern for life in the cultural forms that one encounters and the search for their functions and meanings.

Seeking to understand the "meaning behind a ritual" is both hard work and time-consuming. It should not be the work of the missionary alone; but rather extend beyond to first and second generation of indigenous Christian converts. The indigenous converts, in most cases, may be in a better position to explicate the meaning behind indigenous rituals and thus provide a helpful avenue for further engagement with the gospel.

Since the "search for guidance to resolve a problem, difficulty or crisis that people have encountered" was at the heart of divination for Howell, ; the quest to discover how Scripture addressed the issue of spiritual guidance became paramount.[23] As church leaders and missionaries began to "study Scripture and to discuss the various ways that God guided people,", and about mediation, some inroads were made in addressing the issue of divination.[24]

The Bible gives examples of God guiding His people through various means: directly to people such as Moses and Samuel; through dreams and visions; and through the use of the Urim and Thummin. Ultimately, God has spoken through Jesus Christ, the one mediator between God and humanity (1 Timothy 2:5).[25] The Holy Spirit, whom Jesus promised, leads believers in truth; unlike the *voro* whose limitation and possible deceit is conceded.

20 Kraft, *Christianity in Culture*, 53.
21 Kwame Bediako, 'Gospel and Culture: Some insights for our time from the experience of the earliest Church' in *Journal of African Christian Thought*, Vol.2, No.2, (December 1999): 8-9(8).
22 Harold W. Turner, "The Primal Religions of the World and their study, " in *Australian Essays in World Religions*, ed. Victor C. Hayes (Bedford Park, South Australia: AASR, 1977): 27-37.
23 Howell, "Avoiding Mislabelling and Misnaming", 7.
24 Howell, "Avoiding Mislabelling and Misnaming", 7.
25 Howell, 'Avoiding Mislabelling and Misnaming': 7.

The above approach proved helpful and points to the opportunity for an enduring impact in cross-cultural encounters on issues of gospel and culture. "For every practice and ritual", Howell observes, "there is an underlying meaning, and it is crucial to discover it in order to learn what Scripture affirms and what needs to be modified or purified."[26] Howell insists that there is a background to questions and issues that arise in each context as the gospel is presented and that "knowledge of this background provides a basis for theological input."[27] Theology indeed, is the fruit of gospel and cultural engagement. As Andrew F. Walls has taught us, "theology is about testing your actions by Scripture" and that it "arises out of situations that actually happened, and not from general principles."[28]

Howell gives the example of a woman accused of witchcraft who eventually went mad and disappeared from the community. This, for Howell, was one inadequate Christian response to the issue of witchcraft. She highlights Andrew F. Wall's view that witchcraft is "hatred objectified" and that if hatred is "acknowledged for what it is" then the forgiveness and reconciliation that are possible in Christ can be pursued afterwards.[29] Accordingly for Howell,

> If the lost Kasena woman had voluntarily confessed to being a *chero* (witch) and someone with spiritual gifts of discernment and healing had helped her voice her jealousy or hatred, she could have been taken through process of forgiveness, reconciliation and restoration. Instead of the torment that drove her mad and caused her disappearance, she could have discovered the transforming and liberating power of Christ and have been re-integrated at a new level with her family.[30]

In this way, a Kasena Christian theology about witchcraft could have developed in the process, where Christians are faced with a traditional issue that required a Christian response. Howell, from her study on the religious experience and itinerary of the Kasena, helpfully identified that theology does not begin with sermons, but rather with "questions and grappling with problems."[31] Academic theologies are tools and not monolithic solutions to be applied uncritically to problems or issues.

26 Howell, 'Avoiding Mislabelling and Misnaming': 7.
27 Howell, *The Religious Itinerary of a Ghanaian People*, 296.
28 Andrew F. Walls, *The Missionary Movement in Christian History: Studies in the Transmission of Faith* (Maryknoll: Orbis Books, 2004), 10-11.
29 Andrew F. Walls, The Significance of Christianity in Africa, Friends of St. Colm's Public Lecture, Church of Scotland, 1929 cited in Howell, *The Religious Itinerary of a Ghanaian People*, 297.
30 Howell, *The Religious Itinerary of a Ghanaian People*, 297.
31 Howell, *The Religious Itinerary of a Ghanaian People*, 299.

The crucial attitude is a willingness to fully explore the background of cultural questions and issues that Christians face in living out their faith in Jesus Christ in their given context. Theology, then, remains a process and not a destination. When the theological process is seen for what it is: "occasional and local in character";[32] that it is situational; — it prevents us from falling into the trap of misnaming cultural forms. Theology demands that we probe for the *meaning* behind cultural *forms*.

Culture is not inherently evil. It is a story of God's undeniable witness. As a product of human activities, it is crucial not to overlook the "manifestations and signs of the personal elements at the heart of culture." [33] Therefore, a sense that culture is inherently evil and in need of redemption can be problematic. It is inadequate to exclusively pursue that "culture is the pen of disobedience from which freedom is possible only through the gospel."[34] The gospel was etched in a cultural context. Jesus did not come to condemn everything in the cultural world that gave him a language, clothing, food, water as well as the intellectual and religious space.[35] Indeed, as Moses before Him demonstrated with the nascent Hebrew nation, failure to look solely to God eventually leads to corruption. Jesus's charge to the Pharisees and scribes in Mark 7 is that God's commandment is abandoned in preference to human teachings; the focus was not God, but humans.

What about demons or evil spirits and their operations in culture? The story of Jesus in the Gospels, and the early activities of the apostles in the wider Graeco-Roman context, points to the ubiquitous nature of the operations of demons. Demons oppress and take away the reality of a full life from people (Matthew 8:28-32; Luke 8:26-39; Acts 19:11-16). The good news is that Jesus has dealt with them and gives the authority to his disciples to do same. It is quite easy to demonise everything in our culture if we only focus on the *forms*. There is certainly the spiritual dimension (power encounter) in issues of gospel and culture, but we should not be quick to reduce everything to that. In seeking to bring every cultural thought to the obedience of Christ (2 Corinthians 10:4-5), we can rely on God's Spirit of truth and pray for God's leading in every situation. Kwame Bediako theorised that there are two strands in every tradition.

32 Walls, *The Missionary Movement in Christian History*, 10.
33 Niebuhr, *Christ and Culture*, 32-33; Kathryn Tanner, *Theories of Culture - A New Agenda for Theology*, (Minneapolis: Fortress Press, 1997), 28; Bediako, 'Gospel and Culture', 8.
34 Sherwood Lingenfelter, *Transforming Culture – A Challenge for Christian Mission* (Grand Rapids: Baker Book House, 1992), 18.
35 Cf. Lucien Legrand, *The Bible on Culture – Belonging or Dissenting?* (Maryknoll: Orbis Books, 2000), 77-83.

One strand which is indicative of the traditional response to the "reality of the Transcendent" that leads to Christ and another strand which points away from Him.[36] God's witness in every tradition is always good and points to Jesus Christ. Indeed, faith is required to recognise these strands as faith is a prerequisite to discern God's activities. One challenge in gospel and cultural engagement is discerning the witness of God in cultural contexts that have been overshadowed by human actions and teachings. The paradox remains that in the obscure teachings and actions of the culture's ancestors the witness of God could still be discerned if one is patient to recognise them. The indigenous cultural witness to the "reality of the Transcendent" is invariably imperative to the appropriation of the gospel and the working out of a Christian identity in any given cultural context.

Gospel Misunderstood

Sometimes it is not only a cultural element that is mislabelled. The gospel itself can be inadequately conceived, and this can be linked to an inadequate view of the nature of Scripture. Indeed, the Bible is more than just a record, or the product of various divine-human encounters at different periods separated by decades and centuries. As Jesus alluded to, the testimony of the Old Testament points to Him and leads to life (John 5:39-40). As God's creative Word in the world, through whom and for Him, is creation; the Son of God became human for the salvation of humanity and creation. That the Word became flesh, and that the life in Him is the light of humanity (John 1:4, 14) implies that the Bible is ultimately a witness to life.

Christianity is *not* the gospel. As God's *eternal gift*, nothing can be added to the gospel. However, Christianity, as John S. Mbiti puts it, "is always a beggar seeking food and drink, cover and shelter from the cultures it encounters in its never-ending journeys and wanderings."[37] Christianity remains a cultural response to the gospel and therefore invariably limited to its cultural home. Christianity, nonetheless, remains viable beyond the cultural world so long us it stays focused to its kernel, the gospel, Jesus Christ. Salvation is thus ultimately, not by Christianity, but by Jesus Christ Himself.[38] It is therefore helpful to keep the focus on Jesus Christ

36 Kwame Bediako, *Theology and Identity – The Impact of Culture upon Christian Thought in the Second Century and Modern Africa* (Oxford: Regnum Books, 1992), 436-438.

37 John S. Mbiti, 'Christianity and Traditional Religions in Africa' *International Review of Missions*, Vol. 59. No. 236 (October 1970): 438.

38 Walls, *The Missionary Movement in Christian History*, 67.

and not merely on a set of principles or teachings. As Bediako reminds us, the person of Christ, His life and work on earth, His death and resurrection, and how all these relate to humankind in their traditions, histories, and environment is what we should have in mind when we think of the gospel.[39] Hence even though human descriptions of the things concerning Jesus are inadequate in capturing His totality because they are culturally conditioned, as Niebuhr helpfully pointed out, they are nonetheless adequate in encountering Him: "Jesus Christ, who is the Christian's authority, can be described, though every description falls short of completeness and must fail to satisfy others who have encountered him".[40]

When the Bible is viewed merely as received text(s) to approve or disapprove cultural elements, it inhibits its life transforming witness and power. We recall the story of the office of the *voro*. It was when the local church leaders and missionaries devoted themselves to study the Bible for its witness to the practical life issue of seeking guidance and maintaining the needed link with the transcendent world that a proper appreciation of the Kasena quest for guidance was realised. The centrality of Scripture in researching issues of gospel and culture, according to Bediako, means that the nature of Scripture; particularly the Old Testament; in Christian understanding is vital.[41] More than just a body of texts, Scripture serves as the "hermeneutic or the interpreter of who we are in the specific concrete sense of who we are in our cultures and traditions."[42]

The Bible presents us with the model of the quest for full life through which we can understand and interpret different respective cultural quests for life. Thus, Scripture enables us to understand where we have come from; where we are; and where we aspire to go. It is our road-map; it defines our identity; it is our story and our world of participation.[43] Our natural or cultural tradition—an ongoing story—merges with Scripture, which, for Bediako, serves as "the control experiment" so that eventually we "recognise ourselves in Scripture and Scripture may become more and more recognisable as our story and our narrative."[44]

39 Bediako, 'Gospel and Culture': 8.
40 Niebuhr, *Christ and Culture*, 14.
41 Kwame Bediako, 'Scripture as Hermeneutic of Culture and Tradition' *Journal of African Christian Thought* Vol. 4 No. 1 (June 2001): 2-11.
42 Bediako, 'Scripture as Hermeneutic of Culture and Tradition': 2.
43 Bediako, 'Scripture as Hermeneutic of Culture and Tradition': 2-6.
44 Bediako, 'Scripture as Hermeneutic of Culture and Tradition': 6.

This is only possible, in my estimation, when the *life* in Scripture genuinely meets *life* in our cultural narrative.

Our encounter of Jesus, or better still, the impact of Jesus on our lives, confronts our past and present. If the truth is, or is in Jesus, (John 14:6; Ephesians 4:21) then the onus is on Christians "to discover how the pre-Christian conception of the reality of truth in their traditions enables them to hear more clearly the voice of Jesus and thus affirm Him as the Truth."[45] It is the gospel that enables us to maintain a positive view of culture. In this way, we can search for truth, for the witness of God's goodness in a cultural context. An inadequate view of the gospel invariably leads to a negative view of culture. There are witnesses to the truth in cultural traditions, and Jesus's charge to make the nations his disciples is also in the understanding that the nations are not *tabula rasa*. Christian conversion, understood as essentially turning to Jesus, as Andrew Walls has delineated, does not mean that one "starts or continues his [or her] life in a vacuum", but rather from the point where his or her culture and history has conditioned them.[46]

It is in the nature of the gospel (and the Bible) to make people at once at home within their culture as well as look beyond their cultural world. Walls shows how these two opposing tendencies or principles, 'indigenising' and 'pilgrim', have been at work in the course of Christian history.[47] While each has its origin in the gospel, it takes a balanced understanding of the gospel and of the nature of the Bible in order to keep both in creative tension. Based on Jesus's work alone God accepts us as conditioned by our past culture in order to transform us into the image of Jesus.[48] At the same time, the imperative of the "adoptive past", accessed intimately through the vernacular Scripture, particularly the Old Testament, according to Walls, brings "Christians of all cultures and ages together through a common inheritance, lest any of us make the Christian faith such a place to feel at home that no one else can live there; and bringing into everyone's

45 Rudolf K. Gaisie, '*Edeɛn ne nokorɛ* (What is truth?) (Jn 18:38): Exploring the Conception of Truth in Akan Thought and the Fourth Gospel' *Journal of African Christian Thought* Vol. 21 No. 1 (June 2018): 14-24(24).
46 Walls, *The Missionary Movement in Christian History*, 8.
47 Walls, *The Missionary Movement in Christian History*, 3-15. Walls highlights three significant discernible features in the history of the transmission of the Christian faith, namely, 'an essential continuity in Christianity', the 'indigenising' principle and the 'pilgrim' principle. He lays the foundation for discussing such features by the visit and observation of an imaginary 'long-living, scholarly space visitor – a Professor of Comparative Inter-Planetary Religions'. This professor visits earth at five different times at specific significant times in Christian history and to representative groups of Christians: Jerusalem Christians in 37 CE; Greek Christian leaders in 325 CE at the Council of Nicea; a group of Irish monks in 600 CE; a group of English Christian leaders in London's Exeter Hall in the 1840s and finally in 1980 to members of the Cherubim and Seraphim AIC in Lagos, Nigeria (Africa). Though there are visible differences in these groups of Christians, there is both a historical connection between them as well as 'other definite signs of continuity ...: continuity of thought about the final significance of Jesus, continuity of a certain consciousness about history, continuity in the use of the Scriptures [translated into the particular languages], of bread and wine, of water'. Despite these continuities, there are distinct characteristic features about these respective groups that are largely the product of their cultural environment. The two principles account for the continuities and distinct characteristics.
48 Walls, *The Missionary Movement in Christian History*, 7.

society some sort of outside reference."[49] The gospel, rightly grasped, enables us to look in both ways; the local and the universal.

The Enduring Case of Language – An Unavoidable Factor

The narratives of both the gospel and culture are mediated chiefly through language. In the history of the Christian faith, literacy— in most parts of the world and chiefly in Africa —has been under the auspices of Christian missionaries. Among the Kasena, Howell notes, for example, it was the Bible that largely 'rescued' the Kasem language from its demise.[50] Thus the role language plays in helping Christians formulate and articulate the problems and issues they face in their cultural world remains crucial. As an Australian missionary and a fluent speaker of Kasem, Howell maintains that 'where the language of the hearer is used in responding to questions and problems, it allows the speaker to enter the hearer's world and explore ideas and concepts with the hearer.'[51]

Language is a key channel into the heart of every culture and not merely a social convenience. As the "the fruit of culture", Legrand notes that language serves as "the vehicle of a world vision, of an implicit system of values, of a latent but living memory giving words their intensity and metaphorical potency."[52] It is language that helps us to experience the world. It is itself an "incipient theology", according to Aloysius Pieris, who also maintains that it is "the *experience* of reality and religion is its *expression*".[53] Culture, in this sense, remains the deposit of peoples experience of reality mediated via language.

Language and culture are thus "interrelated and inseparable" [54] and for Howell:

> If you try to learn one without the other, things can become quite distorted and you may misunderstand what people say or do. Besides, you can't learn a language or culture properly without socially interacting with the people and being in their environment. These are the things you need if you are to understand what life means to the people among whom you will live or work.[55]

A greater appreciation of and knowledge of people's language and culture enable us to sympathise with their fears and hopes in the quest for life. Scripture is culturally mediated, and it is meaningless without the

49 Walls, *The Missionary Movement in Christian History*, 9.
50 Howell, *The Religious Itinerary of a Ghanaian People*, 313.
51 Howell, *The Religious Itinerary of a Ghanaian People*, 300.
52 Legrand, *The Bible on Culture*, 9.
53 Aloysius Pieris, *An Asian Theology of Liberation* (Edinburgh/New York: T & T Clark/ Orbis Books, 1988), 70.
54 Allison M. Howell, *A Daily Guide for Culture and Language Learning* (Abokobi, Accra: AmaraZaane Consulting Services, 2014), 9.
55 Howell, *A Daily Guide for Culture and Language Learning*, 9.

context of culture and language. The translated Bible remains a veritable avenue for entering and engaging respective cultures. The translated or vernacular Scripture facilitates the impact of the gospel on cultures over generations. Indeed, for Bediako, it is fundamental in the engagement of gospel and culture because "it is as we take the experiences, the struggle, the engagement in one context, and funnel it through our own reading and experience of the Scripture in the mother tongue, that we find that other Christian stories do indeed illuminate our story."[56] In other words, it is the Scripture in the mother tongue that helps us to interpret our own cultures.

Life Meeting Life – The Gospel Transforming Culture

The primary goal of gospel and culture engagement is the transformation of cultures. It is Life transforming life; Jesus addressing the hopes and fears of people's quest for a life of which He is the source. The quest for life, in almost all primal contexts, has been pursued in relation to the physical environment. This life that Jesus brings as the "first born of creation" also relates to "the physical environment (including rocks, trees and rivers) and the way human beings relate to them."[57]

Howell is thus apt in pointing out that "the purpose of the gospel is to redeem people within their context and to bring substantial healing to the spiritual, psychological, sociological and ecological divisions."[58] It is important to constantly keep in mind the cosmic therapeutic function of the *Logos* made human. Faith in Christ leads to a life of healing, and restoration of the relationship between God and humans with all of God's creation.

The aim of gospel and cultural engagement is the realisation of the abundance of life that Jesus Christ brings. This life-giving perspective helps us to further appreciate the vital role of the translated Bible in issues of gospel and culture. If the witness to life is not mediated in the language of the cultural context, it is difficult for that culture to affirm the life that is in Jesus, which is light for humanity (John 1:4).

The various gospel-culture positions that Christians in the course of history have eventually approximated could also be a product of their view of Jesus and Scripture. The positions that H. Richard Niebuhr highlighted have Scripture texts to warrant them; yet, could it be that the

56 Bediako, 'Scripture as Hermeneutic of Culture and Tradition': 6.
57 Howell, *The Religious Itinerary of a Ghanaian People*, 299.
58 Howell, *The Religious Itinerary of a Ghanaian People*, 312.

inadequacies of these positions can be traced to the value placed on the life-giving essence of the gospel with respect to people and cultures?[59] The life-transforming perspective in the relationship between Christ and culture remains a helpful paradigm. The beauty of cross-cultural encounters is perhaps more revealing when various contexts, using respective indigenous resources, explicate and witness to this life-giving transformation that the gospel of Jesus brings.

The *conversionists* who fall under the "Christ the transformer of Culture" group, have a "more positive and hopeful attitude toward culture".[60] According to Niebuhr, the conversionists' "affirmative stand" is closely connected with three theological convictions; underscoring the "creative activity of God and of Christ-in-God",[61] that humanity fell from "His created goodness",[62] and that God is able to do all things in history seen as a "dramatic interaction" between God and humanity.[63] Therefore, human culture—for those in this group— can be "a transformed human life in and to the glory of God".[64]

The *meaning* of the gospel is *life* irrespective of the *form* it takes in its expression. The meaning of culture is the struggle for life, regardless of the form it takes in its realisation. When we lose sight of the quest for, and witness to, life in gospel and culture engagements; the quest for transformation can become dull drudgery. Transformation is an exercise in faith; and as Legrand put it, "faith in God cannot be lived in a vacuum". Rather, faith in God is amid "political events, social movements, and family situations, in an ongoing interaction of crisscrossing cultural and religious traditions and expressions."[65] Hence, though "our decisions in faith" remain partial and limited to our context, as Niebuhr reminds us, they are to be made in view of the fact that the resurrected Christ is both head of the Church and redeemer of our cultural world which "exists within the world of grace —God's Kingdom."[66]

59 Richard H. Niebuhr, *Christ and Culture* (New York: Harper & Brothers, 1951).
60 Niebuhr, *Christ and Culture*, 191.
61 Niebuhr, *Christ and Culture*, 192.
62 Niebuhr, *Christ and Culture*, 193.
63 Niebuhr, *Christ and Culture*, 194.
64 Niebuhr, *Christ and Culture*, 196.
65 Legrand, *The Bible on Culture*, 68.
66 Niebuhr, *Christ and Culture*, 256.

Conclusion

Jesus Christ came to bring abundant life to humanity. Every cultural tradition has attempted to give an answer to the fundamental questions behind the meaning and expression of life. It is not difficult to devalue the answers given by a cultural context in the light of one's own limited and culturally inherited answers. Life eternal remains a mystery and the testimony of the life that Jesus Christ brings; as witnessed in the New Testament documents; testify to that fact. The Apostle Paul calls the gospel of Jesus a mystery (Ephesians 3:4-6). It is the reality of Jesus Christ Himself that continues to give meaning to the *mystery* of Christ. The working out of the gospel, therefore, in any given cultural context is the realisation of life eternal; the life of God revealed in Jesus Christ. This requires more than one generation, because for Bediako, "gospel and culture engagement is about the process of coming together, the meeting of life with life … [thus] a process of conversion."[67]

We are most helped if we seek to find the *meanings* of the expression of life behind all the *forms* that cloud cultural activities. God's ultimate gift to humankind is life (John 10:10). Thus, the gospel proclamation should lead to life abundance for both hearer and speaker, where the past and present are reconciled for a common future. In this sense we can continue to appreciate, as Kwame Bediako proposes, that both the gospel and our cultures are "gifts of God"; and when we see them as such "a fruitful interaction between them is born."[68]

Allison M. Howell's journey of life has impacted many lives; hers has been a cross-cultural experiment for decades. She spent a considerable part of her chronological life among the Kasena for whom their religious itinerary has been a story of their coming to Christ and not to any denominational group.[69] Her commitment to the Lord Jesus Christ has enabled her to share a bit of that life which Jesus gives to all who have come her way. Friends, colleagues, and students would be remiss in failing to acknowledge their debt of gratitude for the impact of her wisdom and scholarship throughout the years regarding what Jesus Christ means to people in their cultural context.

67 Bediako, 'Scripture as Hermeneutic of Culture and Tradition': 6.
68 Bediako, 'Christian Faith and African Culture': 57.
69 Howell, *The Religious Itinerary of a Ghanaian People*, 313.

An Examination of the Significance of the Birifor Clan System and its Impact on the Church among the Birifor

Ini Dorcas Dah

Abstract

The Birifor have four main clans.[1] These clans are Palé/Palenfo, Dah, Kambou/Kambiré and Hien. The four main clans of the Birifor form two pairs of clan-allies. These two pairs of clan-allies constitute two pairs of clan playmates. The Da (Dah) are playmates with the Palé/Palenfo, and the Hien are playmates with the Kambou. The role of the allies bears an importance which is social, political, and ritualistic in nature. The clan system serves to promote peace in place of conflict. However, the Birifor clans are sometimes given so much importance in their communities, that people's lives, and even the acceptance of an individual, can be influenced by the clan to which s/he belongs. The clan system can also influence some churches among the Birifor either positively or negatively depending on the clan of the leader of the church. This paper first gives an overview of the myth of the Birifor clans. It then examines the relationship between people in their communities based on the clan to which they belong. Finally, it explores the influence of the clans on the Christian church among the Birifor and how Christian mission can bring about a real transformation so that Birifor Christians will be faithful and bear allegiance to Christ instead of their clans.

1 This has briefly been discussed in my book, *Women Do More Work Than Men; Birifor Women as Change Agents in Mission and Expansion of the Church in West Africa (Burkina Faso Cote d'Ivoire and Ghana)* (Eugen, Oregon: Wipf and Stock, 2018), 34-35.

Introduction

The Birifor have four main clans: the Da/Dah, Hien, Kambou and Pale. The origin of the four main clans has a story in connection with women's daily activities among the Birifor/Lobi. According to Andre Philippe Momo, "the Birifor did not have clan names. The current clan names are nicknames given to remarkable women in the society and they were finally adopted by their descendants as clan names".[2] Except for the Birifor living in Ghana, the clan names are also used as family names by the Birifor in Burkina Faso and Côte d'Ivoire. In this paper, I first give the myth of origin of the Birifor clans. Next, I examine the influence of the clans on social relationships. Furthermore, I look at the impact of the Birifor understanding of their clans on the churches among the Birifor. I finally engage the gospel with the Birifor understanding of their clan system in order to find points of entry for the introduction of the gospel and areas that need transformation. I proceeded by using published, as well as unpublished materials, written about the Birifor clan system. I also used interviews, observations, and informal conversations with people among the Birifor about their clans.

The Myth of Origin of the Birifor clans

The Da/Dah, according to Momo, is the largest clan. It is connected to the story of a woman who was skilled in the art of pottery. She taught her daughters this skill, and the Lobi started calling them "da me"; meaning, "the ones who do pottery". There are sub-clans within the Dah which are: Da Bir ("Black Da"); Da Siene ("Red Da"); Ban Youo Da ("Da whose ancestor wore cowries[3] around his head"); Layiere Da ("the Da of buffalo year"); Sikho Da ("Da, eater of fruit"); Djourbiel Da ("food beggar"); Djane Da ("Da living in the country of the Djan"); and the Tiole (from the village of Tiolo, Nako).

The clan name Hien is associated with the story of a woman who liked beans; called "*hɛ́*" in Lobiri. Therefore, her descendants were given the nickname, "he kho too" meaning, "the people of those who eat beans". Another version of the story has it that a woman was expert in the cooking of bean stew. She was finally named together with her relatives as "he

2 Andre Philippe Momo, 'Origine et signification des noms de famille Lobi—Birifor', in *Club de Promotion du Musee du Poni, (C.P.M.P), Connaissance des Peuples du Sud Ouest du Burkina Faso, Premier Atelier Regional sur l'Anthropologie Sociale et Culturelle des Peuples Lobi-Birifor, Recueil des Travaux* (Centre de Conférence Madeleine Père, les 05 et 06 mars 2010), 72-78 (73).

3 Cowries were used as currency before the introduction of the French currency in West Africa. Among the Lobi/Birifor it is still used for traditional practices.

kho", meaning, "eaters of beans". What is important in the two stories is that there is a connection between a woman; beans; and the clan name, "Hien". The sub-clans are: Timbarbi Hien (from Timbarbitionao; "they do not eat red monkey"); Gongouon Hien ("people from the hill country of the Lobi land"); Bolo o too ("descendants of Bolo"); Dagnouor Hien ("from a village called Dagnora"); Danbo o too ("descendants of Dambo"); Tokpo Hien (from Tokpora).

The Kambou/Kambiré are believed to be the descendants of two sisters who went to the bush for firewood. On their way back home, they reached a crossroad and were confused about which was the right road to their village. As they could not agree on one road, each one decided to go on the road she judged to be right. One eventually reached home as her choice was correct, but the other one got lost and the villagers had to go and look for her. The one who found her way home was named "*Kha Bir*", meaning, "break and return", from which the name Kambiré is derived. The other sister who got lost was named "*Kha Bou*", meaning, "break and get lost" in Lobiri, and that became the name "Kambou".

The sub-clans of Kambiré are the Bouogne/Bouo Yemi; Be Kambiré ("Dogs Kambiré"); Doli (from Doliro); Gongo (from Gongora); Kimpe (from Kimpeo); Lanta (from Lantao); Orko o too ("the descendants of Orko"); Tokala (from Tokalao); Belin (from Bele); Tioye (from Tioyo); and the Momo.

The Kambou sub-clans are Bambour (from Bambouro); Bobouor o Too ("they like celebrating the last funeral of their departed people"); Dankar ("go beyond your target"); Nadjin Kambou ("their village had a lot of acacia trees appreciated by cattle"); Ognona ("descendants of Ognona"), Sab Kambou (from Sabra), Wirdja Kambou (from Ouridiara).

The clan Palé is connected to the story of a woman who swept so well that people started calling her "Sonsouone Palamn Dar", meaning, "rubbish gatherer". Her descendants were called, "Palana" which was misspelt, "Palé". The sub-clans of Palé are: Diolompo (from Diolompo); Koumiena o Too; Youboulo o Too; Kakal Pale ("Pale dedicated to River Kakal"); "Youl or Wil" (from Youlao); "Sib, Som or Some" (Dagara Wile origin). However, as indicated in the introduction, the clans have an important role which goes beyond physical activities to have spiritual impact among the Birifor.

The Role of Birifor Clan System in Socio-Religious Activities

The origin of the clan-ally system is not known. However, Henry Labouret indicates that, according to the Dagari and the Oule living on the Black Volta River bank in Diébougou area, "Two head of families made a blood covenant that they would never fight each other. Therefore, their descendants decided to respect that covenant". [4] Hence the current existence of the clan allies among the Birifor/Lobi. Cecile De Rouville echoes the same idea but does not specify the place where those two ancestors lived.[5] Neither Labouret, nor De Rouville, give specific dates of the covenant between those clan ancestors.

The Birifor clan is very important in its socio-political organisation. The clan is the largest element in the Birifor social division. Like the Gikuyu clan described by Jomo Kenyatta in his book *Facing Mount Kenya*, the Birifor clan consists of several families "who have the same clan name and are believed to have been descended from the same family group in the remote past".[6] R. S. Rattray pointed out that the Birifor clans are "known by names which are, or are associated with, the clansmen's common remote ancestors".[7] Therefore, among the Birifor clans, whether the people are living in different villages or even different countries, those with the same names are believed to be descendants of the same ancestor.

The four main clans form two pairs of clan-allies. These two pairs of clan-allies constitute two pairs of clans' playmates. The Da (Dah) are playmates with the Pale/Palenfo, and the Hien are playmates with the Kambou. People can insult each other without any offence, so far as they are playmates. The clan structure is very influential on funeral and marriage practices. One thing that happens during the Birifor funeral is the *lɔfʋ*, which means joking of the clan-allies. For instance, when a Hien dies, the Kambou or Kambiré are the ones who come to joke. As soon as the *lʋlʋɔrba* (allies/jokers) hear that one of their clan-allies is dead, they go straight to that person's house and eat whatever food they find. They usually behave as if they were happy about the person's death. They are always at the funeral ceremonies joking, laughing at the family members who come to weep and mourn their relative. It often happens that a dying person also shows things to his family members which are to be given to the *lʋlʋɔrba* (allies) which may be a cow, or a big pot of cowries. For

4 Henri Labouret, *Les Tribus du Rameau Lobi* (Paris: Institut d'Ethnologie, 1931), 217.
5 Cécile de Rouville, *Organisation Sociale des Lobi, Une Société bilinéaire du Burkina Faso et de Côte d'Ivoire* (Paris: Harmattan, 1987), 165.
6 Jomo Kenyatta, *Facing Mount Kenya, The Traditional Life of the Gikuyu* (Nairobi: Kenway Publication, 1938), 1.
7 R., S., Rattray, *The Tribes of the Ashanti Hinterland* (Oxford: Oxford University Press, 1932), 426.

instance, when my grandfather was dying, he left a cow and a pot full of cowries for his *lʊlʊɔrba*. On the second morning of his funeral someone stood on the roof and let the pot down with the cowries and the allies looted them.[8] The cow which was with one of his nephews in another village refused to come to the funeral and they had to cut a part of it[9] and bring it to symbolise its presence for the *lʊlʊɔrba*. Later on, my aunt related that when her father was dying, he gave an order to give three cows: one for the *lʊlʊɔrba;* one for his children; and one to be killed and cooked for the people). His nephew refused to obey his uncle's order and gave only one. According to my aunt, the cow refused to go to the funeral because of the disobedience of her cousin. She further claimed that all those cows disappeared after that event, and nothing remains today because our grandfather has taken them with him.

The allies can also use the favourite clothes of the departed (such as his walking stick, his hat, etc.) and wear them while they are joking. Even at the burial time, if they are aware of it, one of them can go and lie on the grave and the departed's clan members must pay them something before they allow the burial to take place. This attitude of the allies should not offend the bereaved family according to the tradition. The *lʊlʊɔrba* are the ones who take the body in and out when needed. They also carry it to the grave for burial.

Allison M. Howell, in talking about researching gospel and cultural issues indicates that, "Looking only at the external visible forms can lead to wrong judgements about culture, for we fail to understand the meanings behind a ritual, an activity, or the history of a sacred place".[10] This is the case with the Birifor clan system; for besides laughing and eating, it has a religious impact. According to Philip Andrew Evans, the role of the allies goes beyond mere joking to bear "an importance which is social, political, and ritual in nature".[11] Spiritually, there are major sacrifices that require only the intervention of a clan ally in order to be accepted. For instance, Madeleine Père recorded the historical oath of the Birifor – that is, to have nothing to do with the white man – because of the fact that the French colonial government maltreated their ancestors to a point of hanging some of them in Malba (southwest of Burkina Faso). According to Père's

8 Observation by writer, Dikar, January 10th 1991.
9 Usually, they do not kill the animal when it refuses to go, but its tail can be cut and taken to the funeral to symbolise its presence.
10 Allison M. Howell, Researching Gospel and Culture Issues: Tools of Research', *Journal of African Christian Thought*, Vol. 2, No. 2 (December 1999), 22-28 (22).
11 Philip Andrew Evans, "The LoBirifor/Gonja Dispute in Northern Ghana, A Study of Inter-Ethnic Political Conflict in a Post-Colonial State" (Thesis Submitted in Part Fulfilment of the Requirements for the Degree of Doctor of Philosophy at the University of Cambridge, May 1983, Unpublished Document)', 30.

account, the Birifor believe that a person from the Hien clan has to go from Lawra (upper west Ghana) to Malba to perform the sacrifice because only a member of the Hien clan can intervene to pacify the divinities and resolve the problem of the Kambou in Malba.[12]

The clan system also serves to promote peace in case of a conflict among people. When a person is selected to settle disputes, this individual comes among the fighters shaking shea branches with a calabash full of ash in his or her hand. He or she draws a line with the ash on the ground between the fighters. When this is done; one has to forgive whatever the offence. Any person who continues to fight following the ally's actions can bring a curse upon themselves or their family.[13]

It also happens that an ancestor may be angry with a family member and cause misfortune in that person's life. If all required sacrifices fail, the person must look for a clan ally to bring the shea leaves and ash to plead with the angry ancestor in order to experience peace. For instance, a Birifor man died in 2000. His wife decided to build a house and to move out of the family house without discussing her plan with her husband's senior brother, who represented the father in the house. As she was about to move out, she fell seriously sick and could not recover despite all the care she received from hospitals. She was finally advised to send 25 francs[14] to her uncle in the village so that he could use that to consult a diviner about what wrong she had committed that had resulted in her suffering. The consultation revealed that her deceased husband was angry because she had not respected his senior brother who represented her husband's father after their father's death. The woman had to look for *lʊlʊɔrba,* who came with the shea leaves and ash to plead on her behalf before she could recover. After that incident, the woman gave up her project. She still lives in her husband's senior brother's house, even though he is also deceased now.[15] The Birifor, therefore, had their own way of reconciling prior to the introduction of Christianity to their culture. The clan is very important for the Birifor and for the other ethnic groups in Lobi land; to the extent that an individual's safety can depend upon which clan they belong to in differing locations.[16]

12 Madeleine Père, *Villages en Transition*, Tome II (Laval Cedex: Edition Siloë, 1988), 548.

13 Ini Dorcas Dah; 'A Theological Interpretation of the Birifor Practice of Funerals and Its Implications for the Christian Ministry to the Birifor of Burkina Faso' (A Dissertation presented to the Akrofi-Christaller Institute of Theology, Mission and Culture in partial fulfilment for the MTh degree in 2011, unpublished document), pp. 21-22.

14 Traditionally these 25 francs were supposed to be in cowries, but diviners accept it in CFAF now because of the scarcity of cowries.

15 Names of people involved in this story have been omitted to avoid disclosure of their identity.

16 In Burkina Faso, the joking system sometimes goes beyond clans to ethnic groups. For instance, the Birifor, the Lobi, the Dagara, the Pougouli, the Gan and Djan in Burkina Faso are playmates with the people from Cascades and Kenedougou Regions. These relationships also help in bringing peace when there is misunderstanding between communities in the same region. I am not going to dwell on this relationship in this paper because of the limitation of length.

The Influence of the Clans on the Christian Church among the Birifor

Some stories of Birifor conversion to the Christian faith show that the Birifor clan system played a major role in some areas. People not only considered the clan of the one sharing the gospel with them, but they converted in larger numbers when the first person to respond to an appeal for conversion was a clan head. This attitude was not only evidenced throughout Birifor Christian history, but especially during the Birifor itinerant preachers' phase. The Western missionary phase was the most difficult phase; to the point that some missionaries nearly gave up. The Birifor itinerant preachers' phase, however, was the period when large numbers of people converted to the Christian faith among the Birifor. Most of the time they considered the clan of the evangelists before deciding whether or not to convert.[17]

For instance, in 1973, Pastor John Danah of the Church of Pentecost (COP), travelled from Sawla, Ghana, to Marsountew to share the gospel with the Birifor in Côte d'Ivoire. Sakpa, the son of Marsoun, converted to Christianity the same day. His family and other people in the village also converted; forming the first COP among the Birifor of Côte d'Ivoire.[18] After Marsountew, Pastor Danah preached at *Mɩnɛtẽw, Dojɛnɩ̃* and *Kurbin-juu*, where other people converted to Christianity because of their relationship with the first converted Christian in Marsountew.

In 1978, Pastor Danah returned to Côte d'Ivoire to evangelise the Birifor and Lobi in Ansoum with two Birifor men; the late Pastor Samuel Zieme and his twin brother James Naaba. A man named Signarté Hien and all his relatives converted, and a church was opened there the same year.[19] Danah explained that the people of Ansoum were Hien. They accepted the gospel, because they realised that Danah and his companions were from the patriclan of the Hien. This attitude of the people of Ansoum demonstrates how the Birifor clan system is important to them in terms of their relationship with others; and even extends to issues related to their spiritual life. After evangelising the Lobi villages of Ansoum and Hondèfdʋɔ, Danah and his team went to share the gospel in Vargbor.

17 Ini Dorcas Dah, *Women do More Work Than Men; Birifor Women as Change Agents in the Mission and Expansion of the Church in West Africa (Burkina Faso, Cote d'Ivoire and Ghana)* (Eugene, Oregon: Wipf and Stock, 2018), pp. 88-130. In Chapter Four of this book, I gave details on the conversion stories among the Birifor in West Africa and also defined the different phases of Birifor Christian history.
18 John Danah, Interview, 28 May 2015, Sawla.
19 Danah, Interview, 28 May 2015.

Konouor Dah was the first person to convert in this village. Followed by his family, many other people joined him to form a church in 1978 in Vargbor. Like the people of Ansoum, Danah recounted that all those who belonged to the matriclan of Dah converted when Konouor Dah accepted Christ. On their mothers' side, Danah and his fellow companions are Dah. The Birifor being matrilineal, this connection opened the door for them among the Dah as well. According to Danah and the twin brothers' account of their work in Côte d'Ivoire; they always found favour among the Dah and the Hien clans.

A recent case in northern Ghana is the conversion of Tingan; a clan head and a traditional priest in Kpangri. Tingan's conversion led to the conversion of his children, some of his wives, and other people in the community in 2013.[20] When I visited Tingan on 4 February 2019, his brothers, who had been living in southern Ghana and had returned home, had also decided to convert to the Christian faith. According to Tingan, his brothers converted because he, Tingan, is the eldest in the family and since he had changed direction by giving up his divinities and embracing the Christian faith, they also decided to move in the same direction.

Tingan and his children have put up a church structure in the village where they worship on Sundays.[21] One of his sons has accepted the call to ministry and has been trained as a pastor and helps in teaching other people in the area.[22] This attitude of the Birifor can be explained by the fact that "ritual office and shrine custodianship is transmitted patrilineally, from brother to brother and father to son".[23] It is usually to the first male in the line that the office is transmitted if the father is no longer alive.

This Birifor attitude to the Christian faith bears similarities with John Garrett's discussion of the conversion of Pacific Islanders in the 19th century. According to Garrett, the conversion of chiefs—Tupou in 1830; Tafa'ahou in 1831; and Finau in 1833; —led to mass conversion in Tonga. Garrett argues that this occurred because Tupou held a crucial title in Tonga. He explains that because Tupou's "title had force of holy investiture, his decision carried weight with both Taufa'ahau and Finau". Tauf'ahau is reported to have said that "When I turn, they also turn";

20 Dah, *Women Do More Work than Men*, p. 196.
21 Observation, 4 February 2019, Kpangri
22 Informal interview with Tingan, Kpangri, 4 February 2019.
23 Evans, "The LoBirifor/Gonja Dispute in Northern Ghana," 27.

demonstrating how his conversion to the Christian faith following the conversion of Tupou led to his people following him into the church.[24] What does this imply about conversion both among the Birifor and among the people of Tonga? Does this mean that conversion to the Christian faith occurs merely because of clan fidelity, and without comprehension of the Christian faith? What does this imply about the depth of comprehension of the Christian message? The implication of this is addressed in the paragraph below.

While the clan can have a positive impact on the church by leading to mass conversion when the gospel is introduced by a clan member or when the first convert is a clan leader; it can also have negative impact. There have been instances where disputes between denominations turned out to be disputes between clans. One such case occurred in 1985 in southwest Burkina Faso between the Church of Pentecost (COP) and the Eglise Protestante Evangélique (EPE).[25] A dispute arose between Abraham Danyuo and one of the EPE leaders. The pastor of the EPE insisted to Danyuo that there was no need for the COP to be established in the area while the EPE was already there. The matter grew in such a way that it became a dispute between clans. Those bearing the clan name Som (Somé) disagreed with the EPE pastor's decision because Danyuo was from the clan of Som, while those with the clan name Palé agreed with the withdrawal of the COP, because the EPE pastor was from the Palé clan. Sometimes, people will also leave their church to join a different church if the leader is from their clan.

Another illustration is of a church division that occurred in the southwest of Burkina Faso. Around 2012, a pastor and one of the elders in a Birifor church disagreed over a matter. The pastor was from the Da clan. The elder left the church; and because he was a Palenfo (Palé clan), almost all the Palenfo in the church went with him. They put up a new structure and asked a different denomination to lead them. They are still under the leadership of that new denomination to the present day.

It is important to explore how the gospel can engage the Birifor understanding of their clans and how there can be transformation to help them better embrace the Christian faith instead of conducting church relationships based on clan dynamics.

24 John Garrett, *To Live among the Stars; Christian Origins in Oceania* (Geneva and Suva: World Council of Churches in Association with the Institute of Pacific Studies, University of the South Pacific, 1982), 70-87.
25 Dah, *Women Do More Work Than Men*, p. 102.

Engaging the Gospel with the Birifor Clans in Relation to their Conversion

Kwame Bediako, writing about gospel and culture issues, notes that, "there is within every tradition of culture, history, identity and continuity, elements which lead to Jesus and affirm Him as Lord: but equally, there are within every tradition elements that lead away from Jesus and deny Him".[26] This confirms that in people's traditions or cultures, not everything is evil. There are things that constitute a point of entry for the gospel as well as some that hinder the spread and in-depth growth of the church. As discussed earlier in this paper, it is obvious that the Birifor clan system has aspects in its practice that affirm Christ. For instance, the Birifor have a reconciliation method through their clans which can help in explaining the reconciliation of human beings to God. The Birifor traditionally know God as the supreme being who was close to the Birifor, but who went far away from them due to one person's failure to obey God's rule. Thus, the Birifor use various divinities as intermediaries to reach God.[27] Not only that, but the fact that the clans are major social structures used in the promotion of peace among the Birifor points towards affirming the identity of the Messiah as the prince of peace described by the prophet Isaiah (Isaiah 9:6). The fact that the Birifor give value to their clan heads is also an asset in evangelism that can be used to reach out to them by first investing in the clan heads in their communities.

However, Bediako further points out that,

> We are not converted unless our past is converted, unless we are brought to a place where we too can see how God has dealt with us, to the point of being now consciously able to say we believe in Jesus. It does not mean we have not responded in honesty to the Gospel, but conversion involves more than raising our hands at a meeting. Maybe that is why we do not feel, sense and experience the power of the Gospel, which has come into our lives and into our history and our tradition.[28]

In other words, the fact that people can easily put up their hands to show that they have accepted Christ is not enough if they cannot allow the gospel to transform some aspects of their lives, bearing complete allegiance to Christ in their own cultural context. As mentioned above, the Birifor tend to convert to Christianity through a clan member.

---

26 Kwame Bediako, "Gospel and Culture: Some insights for our time from the experience of the earliest Church", *Journal of African Christian Thought*, Vol. 2, No.2 (December 1999), 8-17 (12).
27 Dah, Women Do More Work Than Men, 46-50.
28 Bediako, 'Gospel and Culture', 15.

However, there is a problem if an individual is only attracted because another clan member is sharing the gospel with them; or if the first converted Christian in their community is part of their clan; but they do not understand the gospel and do not apply it to their life.

Andrew F. Walls, in his discussion of world view and Christian conversion, indicates that people do not automatically do away with their past realities when they convert to the Christian faith.[29] They add new things to their map of realities; increasing some aspects and decreasing others depending on their understanding of the elements that they had on their mind. Walls further notes that, "…while some elements on the map may change drastically, others change little or not all".[30] Kathryn Tanner also echoes this idea when talking about Christian culture and society and indicates that, "People do not simply discard their other identities when they take the Christian one".[31] One can understand from both Walls and Tanner that cultural transformation after conversion is a gradual—not sudden—event. It can be slow; or may not happen at all. This also helps us understand that when most people become Christians, they do not automatically think about Christ when faced with life circumstances; but rather refer back to their cultural background until there is a real transformation in their lives.

Walls, in discussing cross-cultural Christian expansion, indicates that there are tests for measuring Christian expansion. The first test, which he called, "the Church test", is the presence of a community of people bearing the name of Christ.[32] The second test is "the Kingdom test". For Walls, "The Kingdom of God is declared when demons are cast out by the finger of God. The kingdom of God has drawn near in the presence of Christ with his acts of mercy and power".[33] Another test Walls talks about is "the Gospel test" which is where the gospel impact is, not only felt on individuals, but in society.[34] He finally suggests a fourth possible test which is "the interaction of the Gospel with cultures and languages". This, according to Walls, is "the expansion of the Christian faith by its interaction with different cultures and even languages, so that by cross-cultural diffusion it becomes a progressively richer entity".[35] Looking at

29 Andrew F. Walls, *Crossing Cultural Frontiers; Studies in the History of World Christianity, Edited by Mark R. Cornik* (Maryknoll, New York: Orbis Books, 2017), 38.
30 Walls, *Crossing Cultural Frontiers,* 38.
31 Kathryn Tanner, *Theories of Culture; A New Agenda for Theology, Guide to Theological Inquiry* (Minneapolis: Fortress Press, 1997), 109.
32 Andrew F. Walls, *The Cross-Cultural Process in Christian History; Studies in the Transmission and Appropriation of Faith* (Maryknoll, New York: Orbis Books, 2002), 10.
33 Walls, *The Cross-Cultural Process in Christian History*, 14.
34 Walls, *The Cross-Cultural Process in Christian History*, 18.
35 Walls, *The Cross-Cultural Process in Christian History*, 9-10.

the examples of Birifor conversion to the Christian faith, one can say that through their understanding of their clan system, churches are physically in existence among the Birifor. Many activities are also done among the Birifor which show the impact of the gospel upon both individual and community life.

However, there is still a problem if the Birifor, after conversion, regard their allegiance to clan affiliation as superior to their allegiance to Christ. This illustrates that a cultural problem of intra-ethnic discrimination exists among the Birifor. If those within the same ethnic group are easily divided and churches split according to clan affiliation, then one is left to wonder how a Birifor congregation would react if a leader was not even from the same ethnic group.

Conclusion

According to Bediako, "In the gospel and culture engagement, our concern is to seek ways in which the gospel may be relevant to our cultures. In order to discover this, cultures must practically pass through Scripture for its light and shade to be discerned".[36] The Birifor clan is the largest division within their social organisation.[37] It is so important for them that it goes beyond mere family names, or activities to bear religious significance.

Even though the transition between the clan connection with women's daily activities to the religious importance is not clear, it is still important for Christian mission to pay attention to the Birifor clan system. It is also worth noting that the Birifor already had their own reconciliation system through the clan-ally system. As the conversion story of the Birifor shows, the clan of the one presenting the gospel to the Birifor is so significant for the conversion of both his matriclan and patriclan members, that the Birifor can convert to the Christian faith en masse following the conversion of their clan leaders, or the clan of the evangelists.

However, the danger with the clan system among the Birifor is that when a clan leader leaves the church, all his clan members are likely to follow, resulting in a negative impact on the church. It is therefore necessary to

36 Kwame Bediako, "Scripture as the Hermeneutic of Culture and Tradition," *Journal of African Christian Thought*, Vol. 4, No.1 (June 2001), pp.2-11 (2)
37 Dah, *Women Do More Work Than Men*, 34-35.

consider how best to teach the Birifor to bear allegiance to Christ, —because in Christ we are one body and there is no longer Jew or Gentile, gender, or clan (Galatians 3:18)—; rather than allowing clans to be of greater influence. As Andrew Walls indicates, "The great travail of the Christian Africa is over the conversion of the African past. Perhaps no conversion is complete without the conversion of the past".[38] Thus, the Birifor conversion will not be complete until all aspects of their culture —including their understanding of their clan system—have been converted to Christ.

38 Andrew F. Walls, *The Missionary Movement in Christian History: Studies in the Transmission of Faith* (Maryknoll, New York: T and Clark, Orbis Books, 1996), 53.

The Christian's Response to Burial and Funeral Performances of Elderly Women of the Kasena of Northern Ghana

Jonah Dise Kwotua and Judith A.K. Bawa

Abstract

This paper sought to investigate how Christians in the Kasena area of northern Ghana deal with the issues that surround the traditional funeral celebrations of elderly women. The work was mainly qualitative, and purposive sampling was used to identify respondents. Fourteen persons; made up of twelve males and two females between the ages of forty and eighty; and of Christian and Traditional belief systems were interviewed for primary data. Desk study from journal articles, books and other write-ups on the topic by others were also used for secondary data. It was found that while Christians had justifiable reasons in reacting against some of the rites that accompany such funerals because of the spiritual beliefs they entail; and the implications of these beliefs to their faith; other rites of Kasena funerals are social in nature and have the objective of cementing familial ties. Funeral occasions are part of the cultural practices that bring the paternal, maternal and marital families of both the deceased, and her husband together for social action, and therefore do not pose a danger to the faith of the believer. The paper ends by recommending that the church in the area attempt to fully understand the traditions of the people it seeks to evangelise by getting involved in their cultural lives so as not to antagonise them and miss out in sending Christ's message of salvation and deliverance to them.

Introduction

Sometimes when people observe rituals performed in a culture, or see artefacts used in certain ways, they assume immediately they understand them, and make judgments about what is happening. However, looking only at the external, visible forms, can lead to wrong judgments about culture; for we fail to understand the meanings behind a ritual, an activity or history of a sacred place.[1]

These words of Prof. Allison Howell, an Australian who lived for many years among the Kasena, motivated us to put this paper together. For, one socio-cultural event that has become a challenge for both some indigenous and foreign Christians in Kasena churches is the burial and funerary rites of deceased females which sometimes demand primal religious rituals that most Christians judged to be unchristian.

In many African societies death is not considered an end to life, but a transition into another life that requires a rite of passage.[2] A. K Abasi explains that in "traditional" societies, death introduces forces of physical, spiritual, and social rupture. To heal these ruptures and ensure the renewal and continuity of life, a transition must take place: the deceased must move from a state of impurity or contagion, to one of purity and harmony with the spirits.[3] This must be guided by the living through paying close attention to ritual preparations for, and internment of, the body. In this paper we investigate qualitatively how and why indigenous Christians in the local churches among the Kasena respond to bereavement; particularly the organisation of careful and elaborate funeral rites for demised adult female members. The aim is to articulate and document the understandings or meanings of the cultural symbols in the ceremonies, and their practical theological and pastoral implications for the appreciation of both the indigenous and non-indigenous (visiting) members of the local church. For the gospel to interpret culture it is necessary to learn the stories behind events and learn the meanings behind rites.[4] To this end the paper elicited data qualitatively by both critically reviewing literature and analysing responses from some interviewed church leaders. These leaders were

1 Allison M. Howell, "Researching Gospel and Culture: Tools of Research," *Journal of African Christian Thought*, Vol. 2, No. 2, (December 1999): 22-28 (22).
2 Ebenezer Yaw Blasu, *African Theocology: Studies in African Religious Creation Care* (Eugene, OR: Wipf and Stock Publishers, 2020) 210.
3 Abasi A.K., " 'Lua-Lia', The 'Fresh Funeral': Founding a House for the Deceased among the Kasena of North-East Ghana," *Africa: Journal of the International African Institute* Vol. 65, No. 3 (Cambridge University Press, 1995): 448-47.
4 Howell, "Researching Gospel and Culture: Tools of Research," 22.

purposively chosen from both the historical/mainline congregations and Pentecostal-charismatic assemblies from the three culturally adjoining towns of Paga, Navrongo and Chiana, which constitute some of the major traditional areas of the Kasena.

A total of fourteen persons were interviewed for data for this paper. This number is made up of twelve males and two females between the ages forty and eighty-two and was mainly comprised of pastors and church deacons and traditional African worshippers. This is to bring both a Christian and Traditionalist perspective to the subject under discussion.

The Kasena of Ghana

The Kasena are a minority tribe in the Upper east region of Ghana who, as a result of an early contact with the Catholic missionaries, had formal education before the rest of northern Ghana.[5] They are located around the borders of northern Ghana and southern Burkina Faso. Their language, Kasem, falls within the Gur group of languages. Kasem has many dialects including the Fera, spoken around Tumu, and in Burkina Faso. The people are located at the main towns of Navrongo, Chiana and Paga on the Ghana side. The traditional area is made up of the Kasena/ Nankana municipal and the Kasena/Nankana West district assemblies. The Nankana are another Gur speaking group. The belief systems and the cultural practices of both ethnic groups are similar, but with slight differences even within the Kasena speaking areas. Agriculture is their mainstay and livelihood. The 2010 population census puts the population of the Kasena/Nankana at 180,611. The Kasena/ Nankani Municipality has a population of 109,944; while that of the Kasena/Nankani West district has 70,667. The majority of the Kasena are Christian (55%); 26% believe in Traditional African religion; 13% are Muslim and 6% of the people did not align with any religion.[6] Although a patriarchal society, women occupy a very important socio-cultural space in the daily life of the Kasena; including in the performance of funerals but within their space.[7]

5 Roger T. Thomas, "Education in Northern Ghana 1906 –1940: A study in 3 Colonial Paradox," International Journal of African Historical Studies, Vol 7, No 5. (Boston University Press, 1974) 427 – 467.
6 Ghana Statistical Service (GSS), Population & Housing Census. District Analytical Report, 2010.
7 Abasi, "'Lua-Lia', The 'Fresh Funeral," 450.

Cultural Understanding and Responses to Death by the African

We have intimated earlier that many African societies do not consider death as an end to life, but a transition into another life that requires a rite of passage. All the same, in "traditional" societies, death introduces forces of physical, spiritual, and social rupture.[8] Consequently, these ruptures need to be healed to ensure the renewal and continuity of life. For this, the deceased must move from a state of impurity or contagion, to one of purity and harmony with the spirit.[9] Van Gennep argued that societal disintegration occasioned by a death has to be repaired through its own transitional process. As above, this assertion agrees with Zimon, and Ademiluka, who, who opine that death, to the African, is perceived as the beginning of the person's deeper relationship with all of creation; the completion of life on earth and the beginning of the communication between the visible and the invisible worlds.[10] S.O. Ademiluka argues that burial of the dead is an essential rite of passage as the deceased needs to be "detached" from the living in order to make a smooth a transition to the next life because the journey to the world of the dead has many interruptions.[11]

Agreeing with the views espoused above, Abasi describes the ceremonies that accompany the death of an elderly person as heralding the deceased into the realm of the honoured ancestors.[12] Among the *Sokpoe-Eve* of south *Tɔŋu* in the Volta region of Ghana, both primal and Christian religionists in some clans, such as the *Alɔlɔ,* perform *hlɔ̃tsilele* (clan ritual bath) for two reasons. The ritual bath symbolises socio-cultural disintegration of the deceased from the physical world and integration into the spiritual world; and it also signifies and informs ancestors in the spirit world of the moral worthiness of the deceased to be welcomed.[13]

Unlike the Sokpoe, for whom ancestors are not dominant components of their religious worldview, other African cultures respect and covet the ancestral cult. For such cultures, the goal of every aged male while

8 Lee R & Vaughan, "Death and Dying in the History of Africa since 1800," *The Journal of African History*, Vol. 49, Issue 3 (2008): 341-359.

9 Lee and Vaughan, "Death and Dying in the History of Africa since 1800," 341-359.

10 H. Zimon, "Burial rituals of elderly people among the Konkomba of Northern Ghana", *Hemispheres: Studies on Cultural and Societies*, Issue 20 (2005): 59 – 75.

11 S.O. Ademiluka, "The Sociological Functions of Funeral Mourning: Illustrations from the Old Testament and Africa" *OTE* 22/1/ (2009): 9 – 20.

12 Rita Kusi,'Ayie; 'The Akan Funeral Celebration Rituals' Online Siro 360.com/ayie-akan-funerals-celebration/accessed, 21 May 2018.

13 Blasu, *African Theocology*, 211.

alive is to attain the status of an ancestor after death; and so strives to live according to the moral dictates of the society. Attaining ancestral status occasions the performance of a "proper" funeral celebration with appropriate ceremonial rituals.[14] Some cultures believe that if these are not done, the dead person may become a wandering spirit, unable to "live" properly after death; thereby posing danger to the living. It is therefore in the interest of the living that "proper" funeral rites are performed. Expounding further on this, Peter Sarpong explains that the ancestors constantly check how funeral performances are done, and would deliver "justice" on the living for non-compliance in the proper performance of the rites.[15] He states, "The Ghanaian is constantly preoccupied with the thought that the ancestors are watching him,"[16] which thus serves to "regulate his daily life and behaviour", leading to a high moral lifestyle.[17] S. Van der Geest revealed that death is seen as either good or bad by the Kwahu of southern Ghana[18] but Abasi identified death as Normal, Abnormal, or Bad among the Kasena.[19] A person who dies at a very old age has died a normal death. Abnormal deaths constitute those who die young; or close to, or shortly after marriage. Bad death includes dying alone, in the bush, or as the result of lightning, drowning, dying away from home, and dying from an accident.[20] Such deaths do not receive a proper burial but are treated like an infant who is said to have "returned", as is done by the Sokpoe-Eʋe of the Volta region.[21] The death of an aged person, however, is considered good and honourable and so deserves celebration by the Kasena.[22] They believe that the elderly has achieved greatness by well lived lives, qualifying them for the status of an ancestor, and should be celebrated.

The society, status, and circumstances of death may determine if the deceased will be buried soon; and a formal funeral scheduled for a later time. For example, ancient Egyptians would hold elaborate funeral celebrations for their aged dead, spanning days or months. Consequently, important social and religious rituals are employed to complete the rite of passage. The rites differ in the richness and social significance and

14 Abasi, "'Lua-Lia', The 'Fresh Funeral'," 451.
15 Peter Sarpong, *Ghana in Retrospect: Some Aspects of Ghanaian Culture* (Accra, Ghana: Tema Publishing Corporation, 1974), 41.
16 Sarpong, *Ghana in Retrospect*, 41.
17 Sarpong, *Ghana in Retrospect*, 41.
18 S. Van der Geest, "Dying Peacefully: Considering good and bad death in Kwahu – Tafo", *Ghana" Journal of Social Science and Medicine*, Issue 38 (2004): 899 -911.
19 Abasi, "'Lua-Lia', The 'Fresh Funeral'," 451.
20 Abasi, "'Lua-Lia', The 'Fresh Funeral'," 451.
21 Blasu, *African Theocology*, 210.
22 Abasi, "'Lua-Lia', The 'Fresh Funeral'," 455.

vary in the burials of adults, children or infants.[23] The Konkomba of northern Ghana perform burial rituals of older people in a very solemn way whereas among the Kasena, mourning is interspersed with rejoicing with the aged as described by Van der Geest.[24]

Biblical Conceptions and Attitudes to Funerals

God's pronouncement of death on Adam (humankind) in Genesis 3:19 has since brought a great socio-cultural challenge to human life on earth. We experience loss of a beloved demised person, and so culturally organise befitting funerals involving levels of elaborate rituals in an attempt to ease the sense of social loss. Not much is recorded about elaborate funerals in the Bible. But in Genesis 49, the account shows Joseph and his brothers mourning their father Jacob in an elaborate ceremony after he died in Egypt; and the body was transported back to their homeland, Canaan, for burial.

Funeral celebrations of some biblical characters have been mentioned in the Bible, but few of them are described in detail for Christians to emulate; excepting that of Jacob in Genesis 50:1-14. It is, however, safe to assume that the living had activities outlined for the burials of their dead relatives. Christians could thus use Jacob's the narration on funeral as an example demonstrating aspects of mourning the dead performed by the ancient Israelites; to serve as signs of grief or mourning for any generation. Mourning, for the ancient Jews, depicted calamity to the people or nation. A man covered his beard and placed his hands over his head as sign of grief and self-abasement. Olyan explains that these self-abasing mourning rites were intended to serve as identifying with the dead for the duration of the mourning period.[25]

Other rites included cutting the body and fasting. For example, King David kept a day's fast for Saul and Jonathan, as well as for Abner.[26] After the burial of the remains of Saul and his sons, the inhabitants of Jabesh fasted for seven days, the usual period of strict mourning, as a lamentation for the dead.

---

23 Joshua J. Mark, "Ancient Egyptian Mortuary Rituals." *Ancient History Encyclopedia*. https://www.ancient.eu/article/1022/. Last modified March 01, 2017.
24 Van der Geest. "Dying Peacefully", 899 -911.
25 S. M. Olyan, "What Do Shaving Rites Accomplish and What Do They Signal in Biblical Ritual Contexts?" *Journal of Biblical Literature*, Issue 117/ 4, (1998): 611- 622.
26 Ademiluka, "The Sociological Functions of Funeral Mourning," 9 – 20.

The ancient biblical forms of mourning relate to Jewish or Israelite culture, and in some cases may be similar to the practice in some African primal cultures, but do not necessarily describe Christian understanding and praxis of mourning. Potocnik, in differentiating between African traditional and Christian perspectives on life and death, argued that traditional African societies try to maintain a cyclical view of time from their ancient world view, while Christianity and modern science maintain linear time.[27] He explains that African traditions employ the interconnected concepts of life, death, and rebirth unto the earth that are also well known in major Asian religions. This contradicts the Christian view of death as an end to life on earth, but opens a continuum of life in the spirit world in eternity with God.[28] The Kasena belief that ancestors visit living relations from time to time in dreams explains why they are articulate in the performance of the funeral of a deceased person; to ensure the dead are secured in *churu* (land of the dead).

Kasena Religious Understandings and Attitudes to Funerals

In Africa, various ceremonies or rituals are performed during the burial and funeral of a loved one, and the Kasena of Northern Ghana are no exception. How these ceremonies are performed may vary between cultures, but the principle reasons are in most cases the same. The African primal world views that are enacted in funerary ceremonies are many but can have a common structure.[29] Africans believe that funerary rites are meant to pave the way for the dead person to go to the land of the dead in a way that is acceptable to the traditions of the community; and that will guarantee him or her fitting welcome by, and a place with, the ancestors. Blasu observed this among the Zoyi (*Alɔlɔ*) clan of the Sokpoe-Eʋe in southern Ghana.[30] This shows the difference between humans and other creations of God since only humans are welcomed into, and exit the cosmos, with special cultural ceremonies.[31] Since God created humankind after His own likeness, humans are not just any living organism. They are unique among the creations of God, and thus require special ceremonies to herald their cosmic entry and departure. These ceremonies involve ritualistic symbols that are mysterious in nature, but enact world views

27 Mitya Potocnik, "A History of Death and Funeral Rites: A case study of the Ga in Jamestown (Ghana)" PhD diss., (University of Ghana, 2018).
28 Potocnik, "A History of Death and Funeral Rites"
29 Blasu, *African Theocology*, 43.
30 Blasu, *African Theocology*, 211.
31 Blasu, *African Theocology*, 210.

and convey meanings that identify the people with a cultural self-understanding.[32] We infer from Patrick Curry that the custodians of the meanings of cultural symbols are often the very old in the eco-community – "those who live longest", — who "pass them down generations mainly through oral traditions."[33] So, the elderly play very important roles during funeral ceremonies, ensuring culturally befitting burial and funerary rites to bid farewell and symbolically disintegrate a beloved departed from the physical living world.[34]

However, the need to ensure that cultural rituals are appropriate is an invitation to the African Christian to engage the gospel with their community's primal cultural values and praxis for the rites to be truly Christian, and yet truly African. This is necessary if we consider that the shift in the centre of gravity of Christianity to the Southern continents and to Africa especially. One significant implication of this demographic shift is the possibility of African Christians determining more of what world Christian thought and praxis should be in the twenty-first century and beyond.

Considering that the highest proportion of the world's Christians is now in Africa, Andrew Walls opines that, "Africa may be the theatre in which some of the determinative new directions in Christian thought and activity are being taken."[35] This expectation invites African Christians to wrestle with their Christian experiences vis-à-vis the realities of their primal imagination; to formulate globally appreciable theological basis for authentic African funerary ceremonies emanating from their gospel and culture encounter. For instance, Christianity has brought a new understanding of death and what happens when a Christian dies. In 1 Thessalonians 4:13-18, Paul implies that cultural rituals such as funerals are not wrong, but they do not necessarily pave the way for the dead to get to their ancestors, and definitely not to Christ.

When a person dies in Africa, it is not just the nuclear family that is affected. The entire community, and relatives linked by blood and marriage from other communities, come around to offer support; demonstrating social and spiritual implications as both the living and the living dead are involved. For the Kasena, a cousin clan (Kwoabia) takes over the funeral procedures and only ask for items needed for ritual performances from the

32 Blasu, *African Theocology*, 210.
33 Patrick Curry, *Ecological Ethics: An Introduction, 2nd edition* (Cambridge, UK: Polity Press, 2011), 176.
34 Blasu, *African Theocology*, 210.
35 Andrew F, Walls, *The Cross-Cultural Process in Christian History: Studies in the Transmission and Appropriation of Faith* (Maryknoll, NY: Orbit Books, 2002), 119.

bereaved family. A typical Kasena funeral is performed in three phases depending on the age of the deceased. The first phase is the burial (*too keim*); the second is the "whipping of the legs" (*nɛ ferem*) when the blackening of the grave stone is done; and the "charring" (*fulim*) which is the final rites. This last phase is completed after one or more years; depending on the financial strength of the family and is consistent with a typical African funeral.[36] For a younger person, the first two phases can be combined, but not so for an aged person. Each phase has specific rituals to be performed and the rituals differ according to the sex of the deceased.

Issues with Funerary Rites of Deceased Females in Kasena

As alluded to earlier, the Kasena perform burial and funerary ceremonies either simultaneously or separately depending on the age, status, and gender of the deceased. While the burial and funeral of an elderly male is a straightforward event involving only his family, that of females is not.

During the funeral of women, it is common to witness issuance of threats from the elders who are most of the time Traditionalists against the Christian immediate family members of the deceased on how to proceed with the burial due to a clash of belief. To broker a compromise, the deceased is allowed to be buried with a Christian ceremony and immediately after that, a second ceremonial burial is done according to the traditional values. Only then is it perceived that the person is properly buried according to tradition, and that her "soul" will be sent to the land of the dead appropriately.[37]

Moreover, it is not until the traditional burial has been completed that the final funeral rites of the person can be performed according to the culture of the Kassena. These rites can only be performed with the grave as the focal point. This has placed the Church in Kasena communities in a contentious situation, because even Christian children of the deceased have a significant role to play in each ceremony in respect to their beloved mother. Apparently then, the funerary rites done by traditional Kasena

36 Sarpong, *Ghana in Retrospect*, 41.

37 A Kasena woman belongs to two families, natal and marital; and both have equal say in determining her burial and funeral performance procedures. Culturally, each of the two families need to send the deceased off fittingly in accordance with their respective traditions and customs because she was a daughter and aunt to the natal family, and a wife and mother to the matrimonial family. While some of the rites are social in nature and aim to forge togetherness, others are ritualistic with blood sacrifices. Consequently, burial of the deceased female and her funeral performance has often generated conflicts between Christians and their extended family members who are not Christian, but traditionalists. The conflict is usually on whether to agree or not for a Christian to be buried in a way considered consistent with Christian belief and principles without the primal religious ritual attachments.

seem to assist the aged male to be assured of a place with ancestors without any controversy, while that of an aged female depends on the ability of the elders to broker a compromise between her husband and parents.[38]

It is in light of this situation that this paper sets out to do an in-depth analysis of the ceremonial rituals around the second burial and the handling of the soul during the burial or final funeral rites of an elderly woman among the Kasena in the hope of answering four research questions. Firstly, how do the Kasena perceive death, and what are the procedures that they follow to bury their dead; particularly in the case of an elderly woman? Second, what is the significance of the second burial and the procedures involving the handling of her "soul"; and how should the Church in the area respond to demands by family to partake in these ceremonial rituals? Thirdly, how can the Church in the traditional area deal with the conflicts that emanate from it for an amicable resolution? And, finally, what are the recommendations for the growth of the church? We sum up the findings in the following paragraphs.

Findings on Views Elicited on Rituals Associated with the Dead

In our discussions with all the respondents, we sought to understand the different rituals that go with the burial of the elderly woman; the reasons for the rituals; and to determine how best to engage the gospel with them, and then reconstruct what can be African Christian praxis for the churches in Kasena. Generally, we realized that for most part, the people do some of the things simply as inherited traditions passed down by oral communication without an understanding why they do them. Thus, even in some cases where the people had justifiable reasons to discard the traditional rituals, they would not for fear of the unknown. This suggests how rooted and influential the primal religious consciousness is within them. Consequently, although some of the practices are of more social significance than religious; those rites still remain prominent due to religious sacrifices that are added to instil fear and induce adherence from the people.

38 A Kasena woman belongs to two families, natal and marital; and both have equal say in determining her burial and funeral performance procedures. Culturally, each of the two families need to send the deceased off fittingly in accordance with their respective traditions and customs because she was a daughter and aunt to the natal family, and a wife and mother to the matrimonial family. While some of the rites are social in nature and aim to forge togetherness, others are ritualistic with blood sacrifices. Consequently, burial of the deceased female and her funeral performance has often generated conflicts between Christians and their extended family members who are not Christian, but traditionalists. The conflict is usually on whether to agree or not for a Christian to be buried in a way considered consistent with Christian belief and principles without the primal religious ritual attachments.

Funeral Procedures

Kasena tradition demands that when a person dies, male or female, three groups of people take care of the funerary rites from burial to the final funeral. These include: women from the *kwoabia sam* (agnates from the paternal line); elders from the *kwoabia sam*; and *Bayɛ* (undertakers). During the procedures, the children of the deceased (*too bia*), friends and other relatives are expected to *yïi* (appreciate) these people for the roles they play by intermittently giving cash or in kind. The children, and any person appreciating those in charge of the funerary rites, must drop the gift onto the ground signifying that they are giving the gifts to the deceased to take along to *churu* (land of the dead), and to bless them when they get there. Appreciating people with monetary gifts for work done is a good cultural practice, (Galatians 6:9), but where it is meant for the dead; and the practice of dropping gifts to signify donation to the dead; it constitutes spirit/ancestral worship (Deuteronomy 18:9-14).

Sacrifice to the Totem Deity

On the death of a woman, emissaries are sent to inform her paternal family, as according to tradition they will have to jointly perform the rites of her funeral with her marital family. Upon confirmation of her death by her husband's family, the first of these rites is for her sons to go to her paternal home to sacrifice to her *doŋa*; the personal deity unto which she was dedicated. This deity could be the totem of the family, or borrowed; —if it was consulted for her birth due to barrenness; and could be in the form of an animal, water creature, or tree. This rite announces to her *doŋa* and the ancestors that their daughter is returning to them; and usually involves blood sacrifices. Someone is sent to inquire from her father's family if there remain any outstanding bride price payments, as these must be cleared before she can be buried. In most cases, the payment of last of the animals (cows) is reserved for this time and brings to finality the marriage rites that began during the courtship for marriage.

The Kasena do not usually dedicate their children to deities when they are born. Some children, however, are dedicated to a deity. If a couple, due to barrenness, consulted a deity for a child, then that child will be dedicated to it. Also, if in her old age, a woman suffers from a prolonged illness and death is delayed, her children will be required to take a hen, millet, and tobacco to their maternal home in order to sacrifice her *doŋa* which might be withholding her from being released to die. This ritual has now become a requirement for all women as the formal announcement of her death. For the Christian, the creation story in Genesis shows that all things were created by God who exhorts His creation to offer itself as a sacrifice of worship unto Him. On this basis, any sacrifice man makes to anything other than God is not biblical, and goes against the Ten Commandments. To maintain the cultural significance, however, the practice could be revised to sending the fowl to the maternal clan solely to announce the death; since it is then usually reared, or sold, and not used for sacrifices.

Borem (Ritual of Inquiry into Cause of Death)

Not all Kasena communities practice the *Borem* ritual. This ritual is performed when a person dies outside the home and the body is brought back for burial. Before the body is taken inside the house, the head of the clan stands at the entrance of the household (*menchwoŋo ni*) with a calabash containing millet flour mixed with water— *mun na* (used for sacrifice)— and speaks to the "spirit" of the dead; to welcome her back home, and to reveal to all gathered whether or not the death is of natural causes. This is necromancy; a practise that was condemned in the Old Testament (e.g. Deuteronomy 18:10-13, Leviticus 19:31, Isaiah 8:19-20) and also in the New Testament of the Bible as the "sin of witchcraft" and banned in Israel. As such, it should be frowned upon by Christians unless the Holy Spirit gives a Scriptural application as an interpretative response to the cultural provision of the ritual for its modification. After all these rites are performed, the burial procedures may now proceed. The *borem* ritual has usually caused family splits of serious dimension, when some individuals or family members were accused of "killing by diabolical means" the deceased, and subsequently banned by some communities. This definitely should not be condoned by Christians. Scripture encourages believers to go through funerals of their dead in the hope of Christ's return, rather than participating in traditions of those without hope in Christ for the sake of cultural significance. (1 Thessalonians 4:13-17).

The Second Burial

When a Christian dies, a compromise is often brokered amongst the family for the body to be first buried with a Christian ceremony which is then followed by a second burial according to tradition. The process of the second burial involves a re-enactment of the burial process. Personal effects of the deceased such as: fingernails, hair, clothing, or soil from the grave of first burial, are then placed in the burial mat (traditional coffin) and the spirit of the deceased is invoked into it, and carried out for reburial. According Kan Sergei, personal belongings such as clothing are an extension of the body.[39] If the first burial took place outside the family cemetery, then the second burial will be completed in the family cemetery. If the first burial was in the family cemetery, then a small grave is dug by the original grave depending on the specification of the town.

This is done to satisfy cultural requirements; ensuring that the dead is recognised by her ancestors when she gets to the land of the ancestors. Otherwise, it is believed, she will be left wandering around without any welcome or rest in the ancestral world.[40] It is worthy of note that family heads, —and in some cases, their wives—are buried in the compound of the family house.

Seeking the views of both traditionalists and Christians on the second burial, all the traditionalist respondents defended the second burial as a good compromise with their Christians relatives; having allowed them to flout the tradition in the first burial. Some Christian respondents disagreed, arguing that the only acceptable compromise is one that will not force believers to partake in traditional rituals that corrupt their faith and cause them to revert to ancestral worship; which they had denounced in favour of their new faith in Christ.

The Rev. Roger Wegurih of the Presbyterian Church of Ghana, however, was of the view that the grave is a reminder and a proof that the person once lived and died, so the ritual should be permitted among Kasena believers.[41] Apostle Patrick Aseyoro of the Church of Pentecost disagreed with this assessment. He argued that a second burial is not necessary because when the believer accepted Jesus Christ as Lord and personal Saviour,

39 Sergei Kan, *Symbolic Immortality: The Tlingit Potlatch of the Nineteenth Century* (Washington, D.C.: Smithsonian Institution Press, 1989).
40 Sarpong, *Ghana in Retrospect*, 41.
41 Roger Wegurih, *Personal Interview*, 2007.

he was identified with Christ in His death and resurrection and became a new creation with the promised new hope in 1 Thessalonians 4:16-17. He, however, favoured a funeral service conducted in accordance with Christian practice held in the hometown of a deceased for identification; if the person died and was buried outside his hometown.[42] Both ministers cited Genesis 50:24-26 in reference to Joseph's instruction that his bones be returned to Canaan—his home town— when leaving Egypt in order to support his argument; but differed in the mode the liturgy was to be held. Kidner explains Joseph's charge concerning his bones as a gesture of faith in the promises of God. He argued that Joseph's silence on a funeral procession back to Canaan as was done for Jacob his father could be that he considered that the matter could wait for God's timing for a better Exodus Gen. 46 26 - 27.[43] Kidner re-iterated that, "the promise was signified as well as spoken, and would germinate one day in the mind of Moses to awaken him to his mission".[44]

Wegurih's argument on a second burial could be accepted if the dead person was buried outside the hometown, but not when the person died and was buried at home; a practice the Kasena engage in. If the reason for a second burial is to enable deceased to get to the land of the ancestors (*churu*), 1 Thessalonians 4 describes what becomes of the soul of a Christian who died in Christ.

The *Swogo zeŋem* (carrying the *Swogo*)

The *Swogo* is a basket with a small pot and calabash inside it which serves as a cabinet where a woman keeps important grains, soup ingredients and meat. Traditionally, every married woman keeps these valuable ingredients in the *dinia* (inner room) for use when an important visitor arrives very late at night and food has to be prepared for him. It is a basic requirement for a married woman. When the death of a woman is confirmed, her paternal family mobilizes the whole clan to go and mourn their daughter. This mourning involves drumming and wailing as they enter the house of the deceased with women carrying baskets with the same ingredients mentioned above. After the mourning ceremony, they are formally welcomed, refreshed and seen off to go back home. The Kasena believe that when the deceased paternal family is returning home after the mourning, the deceased woman's soul goes with them, and therefore,

42 Patrick Aseyoro, *Personal Interview*, 2007.
43 Derek Kidner, *Genesis* (Leicester, England: Inter-Varsity Press, 1967), 224
44 Kidner, *Genesis*, 224.

will be the need to be brought back to her husband's home with her *swogo*—which symbolizes her soul—and will be used for the performance of final funeral rites.

At her death, a woman's paternal household and her husband's household put the ingredients mentioned above in a basket along with with dry okro, salt, pepper, etc (denoting her role in the household - cooking). Amidst the singing of dirges (*lu-seim*), her eldest daughter and daughter in-law carry the basket to a crossroad towards her paternal house where they are burnt. The procession indicates guiding the woman to the land of the dead as they bid her farewell with everything she needs for the afterlife. Christians will be cautious about active participation in this ritual because of the spiritual connotations attached to it (Deuteronomy 18:9-14).

Some proposals were made based on insights from Mbiti,[45] and Bediako[46] on the Christian attitude to cultural issues. Christians have a powerful tool in the Bible which, with the right interpretative insight, could be used to deal with imported as well as traditional issues within the framework of any culture.[47] Using Galatians 3:26-29, Bediako argues that because of the Christian's adoptive past in Abraham, one has access to God irrespective of whichever culture one comes from, because of the universality of God.[48] He insists that the Christian's adoption to Abraham through Christ gives him or her access to Abrahamic inheritances, since his past is connected to Abraham, and not the individual's cultures.[49] Thus, the Kasena could be a descendent of Abraham through adoption in Christ, and still a Kasena by birth. And, through Christ, God's Word gives a better interpretation of the Kasena culture than any cultural authority.

It was revealed in an interview with one of the traditional respondents, that the people decided to discard the ritual of putting the *chira ŋona* (thread of the living dead) around the waist of a dead woman in preparation for her burial, because some wicked undertakers took advantage of the secrecy involved in the burial process; removed the thread from the deceased's waist in order to use it cause "spiritual harm" to their adversaries.[50] This shows therefore, the processes can be revised to meet modern demands, which calls for proposals to be made for the consideration of the church among the Kasena.

45 John S. Mbiti, *Bible and Theology in African Christianity* (Oxford University Press, 1986), 74.
46 Kwame Bediako, *Jesus in Africa* (Akropong-Akwapim, Ghana: Regnum Africa, 2000), 3-5.
47 Mbiti, *Bible and Theology in African Christianity*, 74.
48 Bediako, *Jesus in Africa*, 3-5.
49 Bediako, *Jesus in Africa*, 3-5.
50 Atigidebonga, *Personal interview*, Navro – Pungu, 2020.

Conclusion

The death of a woman within the Kasena cultural setting can be a challenging experience for her Christian family. Not only do they face the grief of mourning their dead relative, but also the challenge of how to deal with extended families who do not share their faith on how the funeral processes to proceed. This puts a lot of strain on such families as the process can lead to ugly disputes that leave social scars that, in some cases, result in separation. This has affected the growth of the church in the area since people equate Christianity with alienating adherents from one's roots.

This paper has tried to understand and appreciate what the challenges are, and to find an amicable solution. It was observed that most of the rituals associated with the burial of the dead have social and communal significance, but in order to put fear in the people, sacrifices are added to ensure strict adherence. It is only as the Church understands the significance of such practices, that she can shape observances into Christian standards and assure the people that Christianity is not anti-culture.

Recommendations

1. To demonstrate the above, the Church should increase its involvement in the cultural life of the people with the intention of gaining understanding. This will aid in differentiating between social and religious rites. Scripture says that Christians are salt and light of the world and need to make their presence felt in all circumstances (Matthew 5:13-14). If Christians isolate themselves from cultural practices, such as funerals, how will they reflect the light of Christ within the culture in which they work? Therefore, Christians should acquaint themselves with these cultural practices with the expectation that the Holy Spirit can guide them to take the right decisions when it matters.

2. Christians should not shy away from responsibilities when it falls on them to inherit the rights of headship upon the death of a clan head. For, in that position, they can influence decision-making on traditional matters. As the head, his wife equally earns the right to an equal place in the *kunkɔlɔ* (compound of the deceased) when women of the

clan gather for deliberations. They can then give godly counsel and Holy Spirit led decisions to the elders and the elderly women when the need arises. A great opportunity for influence will be lost if they decline to assume such responsibilities.

3. The Christian community can influence and transform the Kasena culture by their involvement and participation in cultural activities. For instance, the church could always make a representation, such as when women sit around the corpse as it is laid in state; or identify mature deacons and church elders recognized by tradition to sit with the clan elders to make contributions to family decisions.

4. Prior to the burial service, the church should be present at the funeral house to identify the possible challenges and fears of the bereaved family in order to offer moral support and guidance to the family to avoid possible entanglement. In so doing, the church would act as true salt and light to the community — not just to the bereaved family and clan; but as those who bring dynamic change to the culture. After all, culture is not static, but dynamic.

5. Giving gifts to people who come to help with funeral is a good practice, but Christians are against the dropping the gifts to the ground, as the practice symbolized giving to the dead. Instead, we propose giving gifts directly to the women sitting by the corpse as it is laid in state; to the elders at the *vɔŋɔ*; and to the gravediggers through their leaders.

An Exploration of the Interplay between Faith and Life in the Practises of Ethiopians

Seblewengel Daniel

Abstract

This article explores how average believers work out their faith in their day to day lives and where they are finding the spiritual resources to survive and flourish in difficult and challenging times. Their responses to practical questions that were gathered through interviews, questionnaire and observation uncover their spirituality. The findings are also discussed with the lenses of secondary data.

Key words: spirituality, Evangelical, Orthodox, minister, priest, church, prayer, traditional

Introduction

It is not uncommon to hear people say that "African Christianity is a mile wide and an inch deep". Neither is it uncommon to witness efforts aimed at "deepening" our "shallow" faith.[1] It seems that depth is measured in terms of intellectual articulation of the creeds and reformed theology.[2]

Spirituality can be defined in different ways. Daniel Louw defines it as "the human soul in action".[3] As for its role in Africa, Kofi Asare Opoku writes African spirituality "provides answers to the stirring questions of the human spirit and to the ultimate questions posed by men and women in Africa. Answers deriving from our own unique experiences in Africa were given to their myriad questions."[4]

1 Ben Byerly, "Why African Christianity is 'a mile wide and an inch deep'", 11 December 2008, https://benbyerly.wordpress.com/2008/12/11/Why-African-Christianity-Is-A-Mile-Wide-And-An-Inch-Deep/.
2 Ben Byerly, "Why African Christianity is 'a mile wide and an inch deep'."
3 Daniel Johannes Louw, *Mechanics of the Human Soul: About Maturity and Life-skills* (Cape Town: Sun Press, 2005), 133.
4 K. Asare Opoku, "Cooking on Two Stones of the Hearth? African Spirituality and the Socio-Cultural Transformation of Africa," *Journal of African Christian Thought* 13, No.1 (June 2010), 3.

What is presented below is part of a larger research project carried out in five African countries (Ethiopia, Burkina Faso, Zimbabwe, Ghana, and Cameroon) in which the writer of this article had the privilege of serving as the investigator for Ethiopia and Anthony O. Balcomb with Allison M. Howell served as principal investigators.[5] The premise of this research is that spirituality could not be separated from the everyday experience of ordinary people and that people should be given an opportunity to express their experiences and beliefs without outside interference.

The following working definition of spirituality, which was adopted by the team of researchers, further elaborates it: "Spirituality has to do with the beliefs, attitudes, and actions that people have, arising out of their religious faith as it is shaped by the circumstances of their lives and influencing the way they live in the world and shape the societies around them."[6]

This research took place between March 2016 and February 2017. In the first phase sixteen church leaders were asked to record over a period of one month the forces, factors, issues, problems, and questions impinging on the lives of people over which they had spiritual oversight, as well as any dreams, visions, and prophecies that they might have had. At the end of the four months most of them gave an oral report based on their notes. An Imam and former practitioner of primal religion were also interviewed. The researcher also observed healing services on two prominent churches in Addis Ababa.

The data emerging from this first phase of the project were categorized, and the issues which surfaced more frequently were brought together in the second phase of the research and principal investigators thematized the issues and then formulated thirty-one questions around these themes which were answered by fifty people. Most participants filled it out in Amharic. Few used English and the non-literate ones and some who were not comfortable writing down their answers were interviewed orally. The distribution of the actual research is as follows, with figures in parentheses showing percentages:

- Religious affiliation: Christian (76%) Muslim (24%)
- Age group: 25–34 (40%) 35–44 (24%) 15–24 (18%) 45–54 (12%) 55+ (6%)

5 Balcomb, Anthony et al., "Spirituality and Hope in Africa: A Study in Five Countries", *International Bulletin for Missionary Research,* Vol. 41(4), 2017, 336-346.
6 Balcomb et al., "Spirituality and Hope in Africa", 337.

- Churches: Ethiopian Orthodox Church (46%), Evangelical (30%).
- Marital Status: Single (48%) Married (42%) Separated (8%) Widow/er (2%)
- Gender: Male (56%) Female (44%)
- Education: University/Tertiary (56%) Secondary (30%) Primary (10%) None (4%).

The fourth phase was analysis of the data collected concerning a wide range of issues that informants raised as being important including marriage, customary tradition, relationship with spiritual beings, witchcraft, dreams, spirit possession, gender, the sacred environment, divination, sacrifice, ritual, success and failure (in business, politics, and sport), doubt, fear and uncertainty, poverty and prosperity, exclusion and/or embrace of others, corruption, political engagement, spiritual authority, handling of disputes, and substance abuse.

The data emerging from the questionnaire interviews were divided into a number of themes and in the final process of writing up, the researcher decided to reflect on five of the themes: Marriage, Spiritual Issues, Authority/Power, and Human Flourishing/Prosperity. In what follows the findings from the sixteen participants of the first phase is described, a brief analysis of the above four issues conducted and reflections follow.

Marriage

Premarital Issues

One of the premarital issues that appeared repeatedly was conflict between engaged couples. The pastors noted that couples were quick to interpret the conflict as an indication of God's disapproval of the relationship. The expectation is that if one has God on his/her side, things are to be smooth. Disagreement and difficulty are taken as indicators of a lack of God's blessing on the relationship. Such spirituality, which was part of their belief system, seems to have been immensely strengthened by the teachings of the prosperity gospel and word of faith movement. It was observed that believers were reluctant to work out differences but expected a trial-free life. On the other hand, all of the pastors reported that finding a husband was an issue for women in the church.

The passage which many evangelical pastors used to discourage single people from marrying unbelievers (including people from other Christian traditions), and caution Christians in their business partnerships with unbelievers for that matter, is 2 Corinthians 6:14 which reads, "Do not be yoked together with unbelievers . . . What does a believer have in common with an unbeliever?" Maintaining deeper relationships with non-believers is feared to cause believers backslide. Relationships with unbelievers usually aim at leading people to Christ. One of the pastors rhetorically asked, "Would it be easier to pull down a person from a higher ground or pull him up from a lower ground? The answer is obvious; marrying an unbeliever with a hope that s/he would come to faith is like committing to pull them up."[7]

The levels of intimacy single people have with the opposite sex is used by pastors as one of the litmus papers to test the quality of their relationship with God. Spirituality in this case is tied with sexual purity as we shall see further below. Similar conviction was expressed by an Imam who noted that they teach young people how to keep themselves pure and parents to strictly discipline their kids. He remarked, "All of the problems Christians have, especially Protestants, come from not teaching their kids properly. Your women dress like prostitutes even when they go to church. We teach our people the Quran and that is why we do not have as many moral problems as you do."[8]

Marital Issues

All participants of the second phase regarded marriage as sacred. Most of them were of the opinion that neither unfaithfulness nor childlessness should lead to automatic divorce. In case of unfaithfulness: 57% said divorce should not be entertained, 19% said it is a valid ground for divorce, and 24% indicated that it depends on the circumstances surrounding the unfaithful spouse so they may or may not seek divorce. Some felt that unfaithfulness shakes the very foundation of marriage, which is trust. A female Evangelical replied, "In the case of unfaithfulness the marriage covenant is nullified, and it is acceptable for a Christian to divorce his/her spouse."[9]

7 Informant 1, April 20, 2016.
8 Informant 17, March 15, 2016
9 Informant 8, August 8, 2016.

In the case of childlessness, prayer and endurance were mentioned as prime ways of dealing with it. 70% of the respondents acknowledged that children are gifts of God and 40% said they will pray. Only 2% said childlessness would not bother them much. People's spirituality plays a big role in these responses because nearly all of them focused on the sacredness of marriage and the fact that it is God who gives children. Educational status was not significant in the responses given.

On the other hand, the data gathered in the first phase showed that childlessness is one of the main things which shakes marriages and leads to separation and even divorce. Religious leaders indicated that childless couples find it difficult to accept their status but seek God's intervention as much as they possibly can.10 The desperation of infertile women is so great that some are driven into pleading with their pastors to bless the husband to have a child from another woman. Such desperate measures aim at saving the marriage.

Infertility is particularly difficult for women. "As in many traditional societies around the world, the worth of an Ethiopian woman is measured by her role as a mother and wife and not so much by her contribution outside of the home."11 However, pastors testify that women persist in prayer. The stories of the patriarchs in the Old Testament, who encountered barrenness in one form or another but were visited by the Lord later in life give them hope. In primal religions, infertility is associated with God's disfavour. It is even considered as a punishment by God for wrong doing. The general expectation is that with the right approach, appeasing the gods, the situation can be averted.12 Among Christian couples there seems to be a somewhat similar expectation of God.

Muslim participants, on the other hand, seem to have less difficulty handling infertility. 66% of them said that they would pray and acknowledged that it is Allah who gives children, but if this prayer is not answered some of them were open to marrying another woman or having their husbands marry another woman. The rest (33%) said the solution is taking another wife.

10 One of the pastors shared with me the testimony of a woman who came with a medical certificate that she will not have a baby because her uterus was removed when she was fourteen. She later got married and came for prayer. The pastor gifted with healing prayed for her and she went back to her seat. She then claimed to see a vision in which the doctor who removed her uterus was putting it back. The pastor sent her back to see a doctor and it was confirmed that she now has a uterus. Informant 3, April 25, 2016.

11 Seblewengel Daniel, "The Role of African Women in Bible Translation: The Case of Ethiopia", *Journal Of African Christian Thought*, Vol. 19, No., 2, December 2016, 47-51.

12 Vishanthie Sewpaul, "Culture Religion and Infertility: A South African Perspective," in *The British Journal of Social Work*, Volume 29, Issue 5, 1 October 1999, 741-754.

The second most frequently mentioned challenges in marriage, as indicated by fifteen of the sixteen church ministers, are unfaithfulness and abuse. Nearly all of the complainants were women. In almost all cases, the men seemed to deny any wrong-doing and accused their wives of mistrusting them. Women asked pastors if this can be treated under "the small window" Jesus allowed for divorce (Matt 19:3–12).

In the responses given by participants of the second phase of the research towards abuse, gender is not significant. Out of the 22 females only 5 said they would divorce and out of 28 males, only 5 talked about separation or divorce. The rest talked about endurance, examining oneself if they are causing it, and involving elders as mediators. Similarly, all ministers indicated that they counsel the wronged to forgive based on the teaching of the New Testament. Most of the pastors said that they encourage wives to endure the abuse and try their best to be good witnesses of Christ according to 1Cor. 7:16 and 1Pet. 3:16. None of the ministers save one recommended separation, not even in the face of physical abuse, but insisted on reconciliation and implored women to change the way they approach their husband.

Ministers also reported that they deal with conflict which arises as a result of one of the spouse's conversion; some from Islam but many from an Orthodox to Evangelical Christian tradition. One Imam noted that many people want to convert to Islam these days. He explained, "When people want to convert to Islam, we do not accept them right away. We want to make sure that they are not converting for money or because they are in love with a Muslim girl. We explain to them that no one should change his religion for the sake of material gain, but only out of love for Allah."[13]

One of the Orthodox priests also noted that women who wish to establish their marital vows through holy sacrament complain that their husbands are unwilling to do so because it is believed that being unfaithful after such a vow would trigger the wrath of God. Moreover, marriage established through holy sacrament is indissoluble. Such wives, who try their best to subdue their flesh, regularly celebrate the Eucharist and try to attain righteous life, fear that sleeping with the "non-consecrated" husband would defile them.[14]

13 Informant 17, March 15, 2016.
14 Informant 3, April 25, 2016.

Here we can see that spirituality is strongly tied with adherence to the law of God as mediated through the Eucharist. God's wrath seems to be specially associated with participating in the Eucharist while being unfaithful in marriage. Traditionally, sex and the life in the world is resented as leading one to sin. Putting the flesh in check by denying it earthly pleasures is a higher state to be attained by few. Ascetic lifestyle is sought as a mark of spirituality. Ever since the introduction of monasticism in the 5th century by a group of monks referred to as the *Tsadikan*, the rule of St. Pachomius is said to be widespread in monasteries in Ethiopia with extreme forms of ascetism practised by members of some monastic communities.[15] Monastic life is highly praised and ordinary Orthodox Christians at times look at themselves as weak and the monks and nuns as the ones who have attained righteous standing with God. One cannot help but notice a striking similarity between the practises of Orthodox Christians and the medieval Cathar (Albigensian) movement in the church of France. Cathars rejected the material world and classified celibate people who lived rigorous moral lives as *perfecti* and the rest as just believers. Needless to say, the believers aspired to attain the status of *perfecti* before death.[16]

Spiritual Issues

Relationships with spiritual beings

The findings indicated that there are believers who claim to have been visited by departed family members. A woman asked her pastor whether she should receive practical advice from her late husband, who would visit her in her dreams. Some of the congregants recalled the story of Samuel appearing to Saul in order to validate their experiences. The pastors said that they take time to educate people who have had such experiences that dead people cannot communicate with the living ones. They explain the visitation as being caused by evil spirits and say that they should rebuke the spirit to depart in Jesus' name when it appears to them. One pastor said that he helps the grieving person to come to terms with the loss of a family member because he feels that denial of his/her death may result with such experiences.[17] Some pastors also indicated that they ask people to go to mental health centres when the complaint about hearing voices does not go away upon prayer.

15 Taddesse Tamrat, *Church and State in Ethiopia 1270 – 1527* (Oxford: Clarendon Press, 1972), 108; Krzysztof Piotr Błaśewicz, Institute of Oriental Studies Warsaw University, Ethiopian Monasticism, *Warszawskie Studia Teologiczne* Xii/2/1999, 31-46, 41.
16 Irvin, Dale T. And Scott W. Sunquist, *History of the World Christian Movement. Volume I: Earliest Christianity to 1453* (Orbis Books, 2001).
17 Informant 2, April 21, 2016.

A young man shared with an Orthodox priest that he always feels that he has a bad body odour and that people hate him. He also said that he was too shy to socialize with people. The priest noted that he discussed God's love, faith and prayer with the young man. The priest noted, "When I prayed for him spirits of sorcery and *ayne-tella* (spirits which make people too shy and cause others to avoid them) were confronted by the power of God and forced to leave him. I advised him to read the bible, pray and fellowship with Christians and also encouraged him work on socializing with other people."[18]

One of the pastors indicated that people possessed by evil spirits usually have a strange body odour which can easily be identified by ministers who formerly were part of *yeba'ed amleko* (pagan worship). The pastor noted that he immediately prays for deliverance and nearly all the time spirits manifest themselves. Psychiatrists, too, pay attention to various sensations reported by patients which include the sensation of being infested with insects, and the perception that they emit a foul odour.[19]

Among Orthodox and Muslim participants of the second phase of the study, only one person in each looked at relationships with spiritual beings as satanic. The rest understood it as something undesirable but not necessarily demonic in nature. Among the evangelicals, however, 46% directly associated it with demons. Gender and educational status did not result with a significant difference in the responses. When asked if they believed that people can be possessed by a spirit, some wanted to know what kind of spirit. 94% of all of the respondents believe in possession by spirits. As techniques for dealing with spirit possession, Orthodox believers subscribed to the use of holy water (*Tsebel*),[20] Muslims to reciting the Quran, and Evangelicals to prayers of deliverance. In relation to healing power of *Tsebel* (holy water) Aymro notes, "… demons are exorcised with holy water. If a man is sick, sometimes Holy Water is supplied for drinking, pouring over his hands, and sprinkling his face and body. Holy water sanctifies whoever is touched by it, frees him from uncleanness and attacks of the power of darkness, and ensures that wherever it is sprinkled there is freedom from pestilence and the snare of Satan."[21]

18 Informant 3, April 25, 2016.

19 Seblewengel Daniel "Exploration of the Approaches of Evangelicals to Mental Disturbance: The Case of Addis Ababa", (MA Thesis in Counselling Psychology, Addis Ababa University, Ethiopia, 2016), 59.

20 *Tsebel* can be drunk in the morning prior to any meal for some consecutive days. On some occasions believers travel afar to receive treatment in a particular church and stay in the church's guest house or stay with the nuns and monks. Any fresh water within or near the church can be considered holy or *tsebel*. Otherwise for water to be considered as *tsebel* it needs to be blessed by the priest using the cross.

21 Aymro Wondmagegnehu And Joachim Motova (eds.), *The Ethiopian Orthodox Church* (Addis Ababa: The Ethiopian Orthodox Mission, 1970), 72.

Unlike Christians in the rest of Africa who freely talk about their ancestors (the living dead), Orthodox Christians do not necessarily seem to associate claims of having relationship with or encountering spirits with departed family members (ancestors), but the appearance of spirit beings. Any claim of encountering spirit beings and having a relationship with them is rated as demonic by Ethiopian Evangelicals who seemed to have little room for the ancestors. Those who torment and demand "sacrifices were believed to be evil spirits and they were to come out in the name of Jesus . . . They are not to be prayed to or appeased through sacrifice to have mercy on the people they possess."[22]

Therefore, the belief about one having a wholesome relationship with the ancestors, which is common in the rest of Africa, does not seem to be shared by Ethiopian Christians, at least not openly. Perhaps the long-lived (more than sixteen centuries) interaction of Christianity with the culture has to do with it. At any rate, the reasons behind such perception are beyond the scope of this research.

Authority/power

Often the issue of authority tended to be gender specific, as the findings of the second phase indicates. In the responses to the question about consulting a female spiritual leader, both religious affiliation and gender are significant. Orthodox and Muslims said they have no female spiritual leaders whereas all Evangelicals said they would be comfortable with female leaders; perhaps thinking of the priesthood of all believers. 62% of female Orthodox and 57% of female Muslims were against seeking spiritual counsel from a female even if there was one. The rest of the Muslim and Orthodox female respondents indicated that they would have been more comfortable with a woman spiritual leader if there was one. Again, it is interesting to note that having a female counsellor in the secular arena may not have been unacceptable but religious circles are mostly reserved for men.

The findings showed that seeking counsel from prophets and prophetesses was common in the Evangelical circle, with no evidence of gender preference. Nearly all of the pastors shared that they talk to many disappointed people who are frustrated that what God has said to them through prophets/prophetesses has not come to pass. With the usage of the popular Old Testament phrase, 'Thus says the Lord,' divine

22 Seblewengel Daniel, *Perception and Identity: A Study of the Relationship between the Ethiopian Orthodox Church and Evangelical Churches in Ethiopia*, (Carlisle, UK: Langham Publishers, 2019), 42.

authority is attached to messages and recipients are not always keen about examining them. One pastor noted that many people do not specify what they think God promised them but tend to claim any prophecy or word of knowledge they come across anywhere. He said he takes time to counsel them not to hold on to a message that might not have come for them. He chastises them, "If you continue to go this path, you might lose your mind. Lead your life based on God's promise in the Bible."[23] As for the immense authority ministers exercise over believers, Cyril Okorocha maintains that the essential features of African spirituality have to do with power:

> To the African, power is the essence of true religion…a lethargic Church of perfunctory liturgy is inimical to spiritual growth and therefore unacceptable to the African. The people shift again and again from a "powerless" religious system to a "more powerful" one in search of salvation. This is the meaning of religious conversion in Africa. The implication is that African or primal peoples do not come to a new religion passively. They come to get something for themselves and for their group or community. The pragmatist approach to religion accounts for the rise of new religious movements and new forms of older religions in Africa. [24]

However, the primal consciousness about wholesome mediation with the spirit world (for example by *Awaki*, or wise persons, in Ethiopia) was suppressed, left unengaged, or worse still, categorically rejected as being of the devil. The following true story which is part of the Ethiopian Kale Heywet Church's history provides us with a vivid illustration to my point. Abuye, who lived in Kembatta area in the 1920s, claimed to have received a revelation from '*Magano*', the High God of Kembatta. He was a known '*qalicha*'[25] in his area:

> While Abuye preached he would hold up the palm of his hand and appear to be reading from it and say, 'This is what God says' and went on to urge his hearers to stop worshipping Satan and worship only Christ."[26] His teaching was said to be similar to the teachings of the missionaries, so Aba Gole, one of the 'Jesus Men' (as the believers were referred to then), went to hear for himself. Upon hearing the preaching of Abuye, Aba Gole was astonished and said, 'What you taught previously was Satan's work.[27] Now teach the

23 Informant 2, April 21, 2016.

24 Cyril Okorocha, "African Spirituality in the Context of Mission," Unpublished Paper Presented at West African Consultation, ACI, March 23-29, 2009, 3.

25 This is the rightful person to do the rituals and communicate with spirits in the context of Traditional Religions.

26 Seblewengel, *Perception and Identity*, 101.

27 "Such a conclusion appears to have come from the conviction that anything that has to do with traditional religion was demonic even with the clear teaching of Abuye against Satan's worship, Aba Gole still called his teaching 'Satan's Work'." Seblewengel,

> truth. Pull down your old house. Build a new one. Have your hair cut off. Drink water and eat your food with gladness.'[28]

It is striking to note that despite his astonishment, Aba Gole categorized Abuye's service as "Satan's work". In the footsteps of the missionaries, Aba Gole could not imagine continuity between primal religions and biblical Christianity. Even though the missionaries did not necessarily engage in power encounters, the Ethiopian converts did. They confronted witchdoctors and destroyed objects of traditional worship fearlessly. The fact that nothing happened to them led many to follow Christ, who is more powerful than the traditionally feared forces.[29] When Pentecostalism came, it succeeded because "it presents an immediate experience of the power and presence of God."[30] The search for more powerful shrines or diviners, which was part of the primal worldview, seems to have endured in that African Christians continue to go from church to church in search for the person with the manifestation of more of God's power.

Baye notes that in the Ethiopian Orthodox Church, all sickness is attributed to evil spirits. Healing, therefore, is believed to come through exorcism, which involves prayer, the use of holy water, *emnet*/holy ash, and anointment of oil. He adds that exorcisms in the EOTC have two forms: the one that involves a human medium, either a monk or a priest, and an exorcism without a human medium (between a victim and just the holy water or/and saintly pictures and the victim). Baye notes that it is common to see people screaming in front of pictures of the saints in the monasteries. Their experience is attributed to St. Mary's acts of confronting the demoniacs.[31]

In the Evangelical circles, it is common to hear people claim to have received a prophetic word that God would give them a breakthrough in their marriage, business, education, ministry, etc. The problem, according to the pastors' experience, is that most of the time the breakthrough has no human responsibility but is perceived as God's doing. Some of the pastors also indicated that people come to them for prayer but expect

---

Perception and Identity, 101, footnote 50.

28 Cotterell, Peter, *Born at Midnight* (Chicago: Moody Press, 1973), 114.

29 Wondiye Ali, በመከራ ውስጥ ያበበች ቤተ ክርስቲያን *(Church Out of Tribulation)* (Addis Ababa: Ethiopian Kale Heywet Church Literature Department, 1998).

30 Anthony O. Balcomb, "Lost and Found in Translation – Two Case Studies at The Interphase of Inter-Cultural Communication in The Christian Mission," *Journal of Theology for Southern Africa* 140 (July 2011) 20-33, 23.

31 Baye Berihun Asfaw, Demonic Possession and Healing of Mental illness in the Ethiopian Orthodox Tewahdo Church: the Case of Entoto Kidane-Mihret Monastery, *American Journal of Applied Psychology*, Vol. 3, No. 4, 2015, 80-93. doi: 10.12691/ajap-3-4-2.

the ministers to know what is in the congregants' minds and hearts. One of the pastors fears that they are being treated like diviners. [32] The pastor went on to share that people do not tell their ministers the truth but when the Lord reveals to the ministers what the congregants have hidden, some repent with tears, some would be overjoyed. "But still, I do not wish to be regarded as all knowing, someone who reads their thoughts all the time, because I am not!"[33]

At times there is some similarity between the way the Spirit of God is approached by Evangelical prophets/prophetesses to that of spirits in primal religions. Some people who claim to have gifts of prophecy and healing try to manipulate the Spirit. Like primal religions, much singing and dancing is done while anticipating the coming of the Spirit. There is great interest in having a blueprint of one's future. There is little room for human responsibility. What is propagated and believed is that if God says it, he will do it no matter what.

Divination

This is a tricky subject in Ethiopia because of the long-lived Orthodox Christianity, as shall be explained at the end of this section. The Orthodox priests who participated in this research shared stories of people who came to see them and confessed that they went to consult diviners. None of them appeared to be surprised at this. In their answers to the question relating to consulting a diviner, 44% of the participants indicated that they either have been to a diviner or knew someone who goes there. Some of the reasons listed for people's visits to diviners included seeking success, prosperity, or healing; when a family member disappears; when a business goes bankrupt, or to increase earnings; success over others, seeking revenge, etc. One interesting reply was that people consult diviners when their religion seems to offer no solution to their existential problems.

Neither educational status, gender, nor religion were significant for the question on whether people would consider the opportunity to increase their earnings by performing rituals. Religious affiliation, however, seemed to have significance: 80% Orthodox, 59% Muslims and 20% Evangelicals responded in the affirmative. The Orthodox respondents associated it with preparing pilgrimages, almsgiving, etc. The Evangelicals who said yes added the following qualifications: if it

32 Informant 2, April 21, 2016.
33 Informant 2, April 21, 2016.

is prayer; I will do anything for God as long as it is legal; I will support God's work financially.

Some Evangelicals associated their struggle in business to their neighbours using witchcraft against them. In addition to prayer and instruction from the Bible, some of the pastors asked believers to come with water or oil for them to pray over. One pastor shared a personal example of the experience of a young businessman who said to him, "My restaurant was closed because of lack of customers. I came for prayer. You asked us to lift up oil, but I had a half full bottle of water and I lifted it up by faith. You prayed against demonic oppression and the power of witchcraft. I took the water home and sprinkled it all over my restaurant and now my business is flourishing."[34]

The same pastor shared another story of a young lady who came for prayer. She told him. "I am trained and have applied for jobs but could not find any. Please pray for me." The pastor said, "I prayed over her credentials and prophesied that she will receive a phone call right at that moment. And she did and was employed by Ethiopian Airlines."[35] There are more stories which are not easy to fit into an Evangelical worldview. In fact, conservative Evangelicals discard them as following on the footstep of traditional diviners. At any rate, they are quite common in Ethiopia nowadays. It seems that people are more prone to the power of God mediated through objects or fluids (water or oil). Proponents of such approaches cite the story of Paul (Acts 19:12) where people took his handkerchief and were healed. Needless to say, the Old Testament is cited as much as the New Testament while validating similar experiences.

Power encounter and casting out demons were part of Evangelical Christianity in Ethiopia long before the coming of Pentecostalism, which mainstreamed them.[36] Balcomb notes that Pentecostalism is "so popular in Africa because it takes seriously the spiritual universe of African people."[37] He adds, "The success of Pentecostalism is due to the fact that it presents an immediate experience of the power and presence of God. Holiness, discipleship, prayer and commitment in terms of classical pietism are presented as hallmarks of true spirituality."[38] Pentecostalism in its old form, however, did not go as far as focusing on objects and

34 Informant 2, April 21, 2016.
35 Informant 2, April 21, 2016.
36 Cf: Wondiye Ali, Awakening at Midnight, Vol. 2 (1942 – 1973), (Amharic) (Addis Ababa: the Ethiopian Kale Heywet Church Publishing Department, 2000); Eshete, Tibebe, The Evangelical Movement in Ethiopia, (Texas: Baylor University Press, 2009).
37 Balcomb, "Lost and Found in Translation", 15.
38 Balcomb, "Lost and Found in Translaton", 23.

people as mediators of God's power as much as the faith movements are doing now.

Pastors noted that the kinds of prayer requests that people came with seem to have a hint of desire for manipulation, similar to some primal religious practices. The function of divination, magic, and charms appears to be strong among some members of the Ethiopian Orthodox Church.[39] They tend to seek help from traditional medicine men and diviners in times of deep trouble. Some clergy take part in providing traditional cures and charms as a means of protection. The "domain of the sacred" and "domain of the profane" is evident in the Orthodox Church that magic is practised covertly.[40] There are people who look at Zar spirit as demonic, but there are others who believe that it has its origins in God; ordained to protect and guide humanity.[41]

Meron Zeleke differentiates *zar* from *wuqabi* and writes that *bale zar* is a mere subject and even a victim of the spirit *zar*, and the possession is likened with sickness. He or she is expected to appease the spirit regularly by taking care of its particular cravings." On the other hand, she writes that *bale wuqabi* is not considered to be a victim: "In fact, he or she is a spirit expert who has domesticated and harnessed the power of *zar* with the capacity to heal, settle disputes, and to control fortune and misfortune. The source of knowledge for both the Muslim and Christian *bale wuqabi* is said to be God, drawing from each respective tradition."[42]

Similarly, Baye's findings indicate that the Zar spirit possesses when invited; during dancing and celebration; whomever it chooses to; or when a child is dedicated to it. At times it is credited with providing protection depending on how it is treated.[43] There is tremendous apprehension about harm brought by spirits who at times are referred to as handed

39 Seblewengel Daniel, *Perception and Identity*, 39-47.
40 De Ménonville, Siena. "In Search of The *Debtera*: An Intimate Narrative On Good And Evil In Ethiopia Today," *Journal Of Religion In Africa* 48 (2018) 105-144, 109-135.
41 Timkehet, Tefera, "ያገሩን ሠርዶ በገሩ በሬ *[Yagärun Särdo Bagäru Bäre]:* Zar Spirit Possession Among The Amhara And The Role Of Music", In Hadžić, Fatima (Ed.), Music In Society, The 9th International Symposium, October, 23–26, 2014, Sarajevo, The Embassy of Austria In Bosnia And Herzegovina, Viewed 4 January 2010, https://www.academia.edu/11694243/Timkehet_Teffera_2016_._%E1%8B%AB%E1%8C%88%E1%88%A9%E1%8A%95_%E1%88%A0%E1%88%AD%E1%8B%B6_%E1%89%A3%E1%8C%88%E1%88%A9_%E1%89%A0%E1%88%AC_Yag%C3%A4run_S%C3%A4rdo_Bag%C3%A4ru_B%C3%A4re_Zar_Spirit_Possession_among_the_Amhara_and_the_Role_of_Music._Music_in_Society_The_Collection_of_Papers._Fatima_Had%C5%BEi%C4%87_ed._._pp._441-469.
42 Meron Zeleke, "The Gendering Discourse in the Debates of Religious Orthodoxy", In *Muslim Ethiopia, The Christian Legacy, Identity Politics, And Islamic Reformism* (Patrick Desplat and Terje Ostebo, Eds) (New York: Palgrave Macmillan, 2013), 119, 120.
43 Baye Berihun Asfaw, "Demonic Possession And Healing Of Mental Illness In The Ethiopian Orthodox Tewahdo Church: The Case Of Entoto Kidane-Mihret Monastery", *American Journal Of Applied Psychology*, Vol. 3, No. 4, 2015, 80-93, Doi:10.12691/Ajap-3-4-2.

down from the ancestors.[44] Unlike the rest of Sub-Saharan Africa, therefore, reverence for the ancestors (the living dead) seems to be more limited in Ethiopia.

In addition, there is a long-time experience of using charms as protection from evil spirits. In the 1830's, missionaries with the Church Missionary Society (CMS, the first mission agency to Ethiopia) wrote about how people asked them for a piece of paper in order to write charms and were even asked to wear them for protection. Christians did not see much incongruence between their faith and traditional practices. In fact, they were astonished when the CMS missionaries told them that such practices lead people to hell.[45] Having visible objects for protection, therefore, was a strong temptation that even the Bible or its portions were used as tools of protection.[46]

The endurance of such practices implies that traditional world views are powerfully at work. Power encounter, however, was part of the ministry of monks of the Orthodox Church who spread Christianity. In the footsteps of the legendary Nine Saints[47], who attempted to eradicate paganism from Ethiopia, indigenous monks such as Tekle Haymanot confronted witchcraft head-on. Endorsed by Zer'a Ya'iqob[48], the fifteenth century evangelists such as *Aba* Merha Kristos and *Aba* Tekle Hawaryat publicly challenged witchdoctors, burnt their books of magic and flogged them. They even expelled people from highland districts on the basis of their involvement in pagan worship. The aim of such violent measures was to demonstrate 'the powerlessness of the pagan gods and their human agents.'[49]

Violence/Rape

With regard to the question "If you are experiencing abuse in your marriage, what would you do?" most male respondents assumed that it referred to women. Two even wrote, "this question is for women." Prayer and endurance are mentioned as prime ways of dealing with

44 Baye Berihun Asfaw, "Demonic Possession And Healing Of Mental Illness In The Ethiopian Orthodox Tewahdo Church: The Case Of Entoto Kidane-Mihret Monastery", *American Journal Of Applied Psychology*, Vol. 3, No. 4, 2015, Pp 80-93, Doi:10.12691/Ajap-3-4-2.

45 Seblewengel, *Perception and Identity*, 160-162.

46 Seblewengel, *Perception and Identity*.

47 They are a group of monks who came to Ethiopia from the Roman Empire in the year 480 A.D. It is believed that the Nine Saints rejected Chalcedon and faced persecution at the hands of Byzantine emperors and eventually fled to Ethiopia. Traditionally, the monastic order these saints followed was connected to the order of St. Pacomius of Alexandria. Sergew Hable Sellassie, *Ancient and Medieval Ethiopian History*, 120, 121; Taddesse Tamrat, *Church and State*, 108.

48 Emperor Zer'a ya'iqob is depicted as a ruthless person, who did not spare his critics. Even Aba Tekle Hawaryat died from torture for confronting the king about the massive shedding of blood. Zer'a ya'iqob also remained polygamous and ruthless in his judgements 'which convey very little of the sense of justice of a deeply religious man.' Taddesse Tamrat, *Church and State*, 243.

49 Taddesse Tamrat, *Church and State*, 239, 40.

abuse. 18% of the women said they would endure abuse, whereas 6% said they would see if they were to blame in one way or another. 32% said they would involve other people (close friends, family members, spiritual mentors, etc).

Out of the 22 females, only 5 said they would seek divorce if abused and out of 28 males, only 5 talked about separation or divorce. The rest talked about endurance, examining oneself if they are causing it, and involving elders as mediators. Similarly, all ministers indicated that they counsel the wronged to forgive based on the teaching of the New Testament. None of the ministers apart from one recommended separation, not even in the face of physical abuse, but insisted on reconciliation and imploring women to change the way they approach their husbands.

The passage which pastors quote is Malachi 2:16 in which God says, "I hate divorce". There is a strong conviction that women can work out their relationship with their husbands if only they put in more effort. Women also complained about sexual assault by prophets. The Orthodox priests recounted the story of several women, who as young girls or teenagers were raped by a close family member. Their feelings of intense resentment extended not only to the ones who assaulted them but also other family members who forced the girls not to tell anyone. Some of the men were bread winners and women feared that their economic support would be discontinued if they told their story to anyone.[50]

Evangelicals who participated in the second phase of the study highlighted the honour of God being at stake when answering the question "what would you do if you or a member of your family was sexually abused by a spiritual leader/man of God?" Most Christian women said they would first tell the church/religious leader. It is interesting to note that gender is not significant in these replies. With regards to pressing charges in case of sexual abuse, educational status is significant among Protestants and Orthodox respondents (more people with tertiary education said that they would press charges). For Muslims, neither gender, nor educational status were significant; apart from one participant, all said they would seek justice in a civil or Sharia court.

Women who are wronged, on the other hand, fear being accused of flirting with the man who sexually abused them. Some blame themselves

50 Informant 3, April 25, 2016.

for having been raped or sexually abused. Such a false guilt is inflicted on them by the society, which goes to great lengths to justify the man's actions and condemn the woman. Moreover, women fear that they would be subjected to enduring shame and stigma if they expose the man who abused them. Even in Evangelical churches, men are let off the hook with little difficulty but for women the stigma sticks to them for the rest of their lives, and they may never be restored to ministry. So, they choose to suffer quietly.

But there is hope for women. A growing number of Evangelical churches are willing to involve women in leadership. More women are undertaking higher education and assuming key positions in government and private organizations. With the Prime Minister Abiy Ahmed openly acknowledging the important role women play (including home makers) and appointing women as half of his cabinet members, the future looks brighter.

Human Flourishing/Prosperity/Health

The ministers indicated that the next most pressing issue for which people came to seek their counselling was economic struggle. One pastor said that people queued for hours to see him and ask him for prayer. "Most of the time, what they seek prayer for is not beyond my reach so when such people ask me to look up in prayer on their behalf I at the same time reach down into my wallet to share with them what I have."[51]

Minsters also observed that people expect quick solutions to their problems and that they expect miracles all the time and seem to be wary of long-term solutions. One of the pastors lamented, "At times I feel as though people approach us as magicians who can quickly fix their problems."[52] One of the pastors said, "I challenge them to work hard and teach them that God blesses hard workers and not lazy ones. I warn them with the words of Prov. 6:11: "If you do not work, just like the Bible says, poverty will come upon you like a thief and scarcity like an armed man."

Writing about the effect of the prosperity gospel in Southern Africa, Paul Gifford contends that the doctrines conveyed in prosperity gospel preaching divert attention away from

51 Informant 11, April 14, 2016.
52 Informant 2, April 21, 2016.

> the socio-structural causes of the region's ill: By advocating the gospel of prosperity, it [born-again Christianity] dissuades adherents from evaluating the present economic order, merely persuading them to try to be amongst those who benefit from it. With its emphasis on personal healing, it diverts attention from social ills that are crying out for remedy...By emphasising personal morality so exclusively, it all but eliminates any interest in systemic or institutionalised injustice. By making everything so simple, it distracts attention from the very real contradictions in the lives of so many in Southern Africa.[53]

Ojo Matthews argues that based on their traditional worldviews, Africans constantly select and deselect what constitutes their identity as Christians. Some of the values to which they subscribe, which Matthews presents as this-worldly, are success, power, and health. On the other hand, biblical values such as "self-discipline, sacrifice, self-denial, obedience, holiness, which are Christ-centred and other-worldly" are deselected. "This conscious selection and de-selection, which resembles the traditional African propensity to worship a variety of gods at different times and for situation-restricted benefits, invariably produces Christians who behave ambivalently depending on time and situation. . . Therefore, it is often possible to find a Christian serving as a public official who takes bribes but who will defend the faith against any Islamic onslaught."[54]

Jesse Mugambi contrasts the religiosity of Africans to their desolate condition and rhetorically asks, "how [can we] explain the apparent contradiction that contemporary Africa continues to be perhaps the most religious continent in the world and yet its peoples remain the most abused of all in history. How could it be that people who continue to call on God most reverently are the ones whom God seems to neglect most vehemently? Could it be that irreligion is the key to success and that religion is the key to backwardness?"[55] According to Mathew, the vast corruption and other woes partly have their root in a "disconnection between spirituality and morality".[56] Believers, therefore, continue to pray to break the chains of poverty. There are many gospel songs which celebrate breakthrough; cursing Satan and telling him what a loser he is.

53 Paul Gifford, "Prosperity: A New and Foreign Element in African Christianity, *Religion*, 1990 Vol.20, 4, 65-66 quoted by David Maxwell, "'Delivered from the Spirit of Poverty?': Pentecostalism, Prosperity and Modernity in Zimbabwe", *Journal of Religion in Africa*, Vol. 28, Fasc. 3 (Aug., 1998), 351.

54 Ojo Matthews, "African Spirituality, Socio-Political Experience and Mission", in Wonsuk Ma And Kenneth R. Ross (eds), *Mission Spirituality and Authentic Discipleship*, Regnum Edinburgh Centenary Series, Volume 14 (Oxford: Regnum, 2013), 50, 51.

55 J. Mugambi, "Christianity in Africa, 1910-2010" in *Atlas of Global Christianity*, eds. Todd Johnson and Kenneth Ross, (Edinburgh: Edinburgh University Press, 2009), 111.

56 Matthews, "African Spirituality, Socio-Political Experience and Mission ", 49.

The words in one popular song say, 'God will move me to a higher ground while the devil watches.' Fantini observes that there is a connection between Pentecostalism and a strong desire for upward mobility and success.[57] Such expectation from God, however, is associated with the prosperity Gospel, which according to Gifford, persuades people to be among the beneficiaries of the present economic order and nullifies human responsibility for societal evil. It blames every ill on the devil and prescribes prayer as the remedy. [58] A primal world view, too, seems to be weak in helping people take responsibility for their actions. Balcomb observes that many traditional cultures in Africa blame sin and evil on malevolent forces.[59]

The data collected in the second phase has interesting replies for the question whether one's faith would guarantee good health and prosperity. Most Muslims deferred everything for divine providence and predestination that they diminished human responsibility. It is as though human beings have no role to play but passively accept what is predestined for them by Allah. Some are predestined to live a good life and enjoy good health, others are not.

A single Muslim man with a tertiary education responded, "It depends. Allah tests people; some are tested through wealth and Allah would ask them how they used it; some are tested with poverty and Allah would ask them how patient they lived as poor people. It is a destiny as decided by Allah. If he so decided that I should be poor, I will pray that he would compensate me in Jennet."[60] However, 36% of Muslims said that people can work hard and turn their lives around. Religion, therefore, played a significant role in the responses of Muslims. Educational status and gender, however, were not significant.

Evangelicals and Orthodox, on the other hand, separated faith from prosperity and good health. Some Orthodox noted, "If I enjoy good health, I consider myself a rich person because accumulating material wealth does not matter as much as having physical health."[61] Most ofthem did not see any relationship between prosperity and faith. Prosperity depended on working hard. Health on the other hand comes from God. Some talked about the responsibility of human beings in minding what they eat and how much they exercise. As for what they

57 Emanuele Fantini, Crafting Ethiopia's Glorious Destiny Pentecostalism and Economic Transformation Under a Developmental State, *Archives De Sciences Sociales Des Religions* 175 (Juillet-Septembre 2016), 67-86, 82.

58 Paul Gifford Joseph, "Prosperity: A New and Foreign Element in African Christianity, *Religion*, 20, no. 4, October 1990, 373-388.

59 Balcomb, "Lost and Found in Translation".

60 Informant 18 (Interview No. 34), July 25, 2016.

61 Informant 19 (Interview No. 23), July 21, 2016.

do in order to succeed in their work or business, the following came up repeatedly: integrity, good time and resource management, creativity, prayer, hard work. Religion, education, and gender were not significant in the responses above.

The role of faith for healing and deliverance is emphasized in some of the mainline churches too. A prominent deliverance minister of the largest Pentecostal church in Ethiopia mentioned how Jesus asked the two blind people, 'do you believe that I can heal you? And when they responded in the affirmative, he said, let it be according to your faith.' He said, if people believe, they will be healed, but if they do not, we send them to physicians.[62]

Nodding to such lines of thinking, another pastor from the largest Evangelical denomination in Ethiopia said, "The only ingredient needed for healing is faith." [63] When asked what he would say to people who are not healed by his prayer, he replied, "That is between the individual and God. I am called to pray by faith, and it is God who heals. These people are desperate, tormented physically and psychologically by poverty and so many things. Most of them have God and him alone! We give them hope, hope in the intervention of the living God and He comes for their rescue accordingly."[64]

The authority which is laid behind the words of such ministers is enormous. People beg them for prayer. I witnessed family members of sick people begging healers to touch the sick, coming very close to revering them as the ones in whom God's power resides. The difference people made between such healers and other ministers was quite visible. In worship services which lasted from seven to nine hours[65], there was time for testimony by people who received their miracle in the previous services. Women went up with their infants whom they had borne after receiving prayer. At the end of each of the services, the minister asked people to lift up whatever they had brought with them for prayer, such as oil or water, and people lifted the liquids up and he prayed and asked them to apply them. The growing attention given to objects as mediators of God's grace and the ministers who pray for the sick is troubling.

62 Informant 4, 15 March, 2016.
63 Informant 2, April 21, 2016.
64 Informant 2, April 21, 2016.
65 The researcher observed healing services in Qetena Hulet Muluwongel Church and Kolfe Kale Heywet Church on April 9 and 16, 2016 consecutively.

When asked about the kind of needs people come to him with, one Imam said, "Most Muslims want to know what Allah requires of them. They ask me, 'what does Allah expect me to do?' He said that he tells them from the Quran that Allah wants them to be loyal to their faith and their country.'[66]

Conclusion

The findings indicated that the kind of spirituality that has emerged has more room for traditional religious practises than people may care to admit. It is also a spirituality that yearns for divine intervention to such a degree that it may have little interest in propositional truths which lack concrete experiences. These different forms of spiritualities are expressed in congregants' reverence for 'anointed' people and greater openness to their utterances, at times more than to the Bible itself. This is exemplified by a growing weariness towards carrying one's cross and following Christ. There seems to be 'this world too is my home' kind of spirituality which measures the depth of one's spirituality by his/her material gains and physical wellbeing. In other words, it seems that deliverance from trouble and not the traditionally upheld perseverance within it is praised as a mark of true spirituality. Followers of folk Islam and traditional adherents of the Ethiopian Orthodox Church incorporate various practises which are not strictly upheld by the Quran and the Bible respectively. Similarly, among Evangelical Christians, there is a growing tendency of indulging in practises which are not easily justified by the Scriptures.

It is widely recognized that the centre of gravity of Christianity has shifted to Africa and Latin America. Andrew Walls notes that the implications of this are enormous: "Whatever might happen in the economic and political and military spheres" he says, "the future of Christian operations will be determined by the Christians in Africa, Asia, and Latin America."[67] Therefore, as shapers of the face of Christianity, churches in these continents have immense responsibility for safeguarding and showing the relevance of biblical Christianity. As Balcomb rightly observes: "[The shifting] is now. It is not something that will necessarily remain with us forever. Indeed, the centre of gravity has shifted, but there is no telling when and where it will shift next."[68]

66 Informant 17, March 15, 2016.

67 Andrew F. Walls "Christianity Across Twenty Centuries" In *Atlas of Global Christianity 1910-2010*, (Edinburgh: Edinburgh University Press, 2010), 48-49, 48.

68 A.O. Balcomb, "A Hundred Miles Wide, But Only a Few Inches Deep!"? - Sounding the Depth of Christian Faith in Africa, *Journal of Theology for Southern Africa* 140 (July 2011), 20-33, 33.

This chapter has discussed the ways in which spirituality in Ethiopia is being shaped by many factors other than biblical Christianity despite the country having one of the most ancient forms of Christianity in the world. Therefore, blaming Western missionaries for the kind of gospel they preached in Ethiopia is not necessarily legitimate. Rather, there is a need to sift through ancient Christian tradition and examine how and where it is failing to address questions which arise from the context. The burden of asking whether its theology resonates with the average Ethiopian Christian is on the shoulders of the church.

This calls for making an intentional effort to listen to the questions and issues and to critically engage with the solutions offered by average Christians. There is a need for engagement through participatory theologizing in mother-tongues. As opposed to offering a ready-made theology in a language which people do not fully understand, communities are to be engaged in the language they use for deeply spiritual activities, namely, prayer and pronouncing blessings. Examining everyday lived experiences of average Christians in our pluralistic contexts and journeying in the process of formulating answers from the Scripture, Christian traditions and primal world views is vital to address contextual hurdles and maintain the relevance of the gospel to communities of faith.

Allison Howell and Relational Pedagogy: Meeting the Pastor and Counsellor in the Theological Educator

Victor Zizer

Abstract

This paper examines relational pedagogy as an effective teaching approach for theological training. It reflects on the author's teacher-student relationship with his doctoral supervisor and advocates for teachers and theological institutions to consider ways in which relational pedagogy may become a key element and approach in theological education. Examining this case study reveals how the Christian teacher cultivated a trusted shepherd-counsellor relationship with one of her students by adopting this positive educational approach, and how this contributed to the student achieving the expected outcomes successfully. The study proposes that promoting shepherding and counselling roles in teaching is a supportive way to foster such trusting relationships for effective theological training. It creates an enhanced environment to achieve educational goals and encourages positive change in students. The chapter considers the place of dialogue as a vital component of relational pedagogy. It sees the need for teaching personnel in theological training institutions to assume shepherding-counselling roles in order to provide students with the right support to become effectively trained and impactful leaders.

Key terms: Relational pedagogy, Theological education, Counselling, Shepherding, Christian Leadership

Introduction

Relational pedagogy enhances teacher-student relationship to achieve educational goal(s). Researchers Crownover and Jones; Boyd MacNeill and Sullivan; and Aspelin, see relational pedagogy as a model/approach where educators, administrators, and those involved in the teaching-learning process cultivate "positive relationships with students"[1] through meaningful social interactions and well-considered instructional approaches.

As Christian educators pursue the transmission of information, impartation of knowledge, and promote skills training for impactful service, it is significant that they go about this not just as conveyors of thoughts and views. Teaching that is done with a sense of empathy in dealing with people, whose needs and lives extend beyond the physical environment of the learning hall, is rewarding. The author, reflecting on the transforming teacher-student relationship with his supervisor, sees the need for teaching personnel in theological training institutions to foreground relational pedagogy and to assume shepherding-counselling roles in order to provide students with the right support to achieve the goals of theological training.

The study begins with the author's narration of a specific experience in his theological training and uses relational pedagogy as a framework. It discusses the place of dialogue as a vital component of relational pedagogy. It then attempts to reveal how counselling and shepherding intersect in the teacher through relational pedagogy to facilitate effective theological training for impactful Christian leadership. The paper uses the terms education and training interchangeably.

A Particular Journey

My journey to study at the Akrofi-Christaller Institute of Theology, Mission and Culture (ACI) started in 2006 with an invitation from the Presbyterian Church of Ghana to attend their General Assembly and convey fraternal greetings from our Church, the Presbyterian Church of Sierra Leone. Following that meeting, we travelled to Akropong-Akuapem, the cradle of Presbyterianism in Ghana, where I was

1 Adam Crownover and Joseph R. Jones, "A Relational Pedagogy: A Call for Teacher Educators to Rethink How Teacher Candidates are Trained to combat Bullying", *Journal of Thought*, Vol. 52, No. 1-2 (Spring/Summer 2018), 17-28 (p. 18). https://www.jstor.org/stable/10.2307/90022688 03-03-2020. See also: R. Boyd N. MacNeill and G. Sullivan, "Relational pedagogy: Putting balance back into students learning", *Curriculum and Leadership Journal*, 4, 13, (2006); J.M. Aspelin, "Beyond individualised teaching: A relational construction of a pedagogical attitude", (2014), http://www.tandfonline.com/doifull/10.3402/edui.v5.23926. 03-03-2020.

introduced to the late Reverend Professor Kwame Bediako. He was founder and first Rector of the erstwhile Akrofi-Christaller Memorial Centre (ACMC), now ACI. It took no time for me to discern and appreciate the Professor's heartbeat for sound theological education and training of African Christian leaders. He personally took me on a tour of the Zimmerman Library at ACI and observed from our brief conversation that I had an interest in furthering my theological training, although I had not expressly stated a plan. I left Akropong and returned home to Sierra Leone.

A few months later, I was delighted to receive a letter from Professor Bediako with the offer of a scholarship to pursue a PhD degree programme. However, family and ministry concerns prevented me from immediately seizing that opportunity. I requested that I defer my enrolment, though at the cost of losing the scholarship.

In 2008, I made another brief visit to Ghana and again had the privilege of meeting with Professor Bediako to discuss concrete plans for my enrolment in a postgraduate degree programme at ACI in August that year. We had fruitful discussions during which he mentioned something about his health condition but remained optimistic that we would meet again at my enrolment later that year. We prayed for each other, and I left. It was our last meeting; he took his eternal rest before I registered for the Master of Theology (MTh) programme on my way to pursuing a PhD. The ensuing years of study at ACI were full of varied experiences—some pleasant moments as well as challenging times. This chapter is my reflection on episodes in the latter that enabled me to discover how a teacher's use of relational pedagogy significantly contributed to alter what I refer to as a disengaged teacher-student relationship. It interweaves these reflections in foregrounding relational pedagogy as an effective teaching approach for achieving the goal(s) of theological education.

Progress with my PhD research work had stalled for some time due to health issues with my primary supervisor, Professor Andrew Walls. The Academic Board later appointed Professor Howell to that role. Previously, I had mainly interacted with her in lecture-room situations and on official matters. This next period of engagement with her enabled me to see a kind, empathetic, and self-sacrificing person veiled behind the image of a stern, disciplined, and officious lecturer. This transformed my interactions with her beyond lecture-room related issues to other personal concerns that directly and indirectly affected my studies. I recall a number of selfless endeavours she undertook on my behalf, including spending a good part of a night to digitise a document I badly needed for my research and also purchasing a set of relevant books I had requested and allowing me to use them until I had completed my studies.

My PhD defence delayed for some time, but the viva voce finally took place very close to the graduation date. ACI gave me three months to complete my corrections and I was required to work with Prof. Howell to do my revisions before I could graduate. This meant that I missed graduating that year. After that meeting, Prof. Howell invited me to her office to go through the examiners' reports and recommendations. Two of the reports were very good but the third required major changes in the thesis. After reading the report, I remember asking her this question: "Prof, do you believe in dreams?" And she answered, "Yes, I do!" I then narrated a dream I had had a few days before my defence and how it predicted the outcome of my examination. She shed tears as I recounted my dream. Whatever caused her tears, whether they were related to the reality of the dream or to what we would discuss about completing the corrections prior to graduation, I never asked. But another crucial event overtook us. Prof. Howell was critically ill and required emergency surgery. She was mostly unavailable for the next three months. Although I missed graduating that year, I was able to complete corrections in good time and graduate the following year.

The period that followed her recuperation and partial resumption of duties gave me an additional opportunity to draw from her empathetic heart as we worked through my revisions. I felt much more at ease in relating to her as a friend. We shared prayer concerns, testimonies, and sometimes prayed for each other at the end of the revision meetings. Encouraging emails and telephone calls were also not unusual during this period, and these continued for some time even after graduation. The shepherd-counsellor role she cultivated through a dialogical approach had transformed the disconnected student-teacher relationship into a liberating one of trust and care that greatly contributed to me achieving my goal. In a way, this chapter also endorses Nodding's view on the need to reposition theory and foreground the need for a caring and a relational attitude with the learner in educational systems.[2]

2 Nel Noddings, *The Challenge to Care in School: An Alternative Approach to Education*, (New York: Teachers College Press, 2005).

Theological Training and Relational Pedagogy

Christian theological education is relational in nature. It comprises the activities of teaching and studying about God as they relate to the experiences of humankind, and the interpretation thereof. This process of teaching and the principles that guide it constitute what is referred to as pedagogy. Bishop and Starkey see pedagogy as "the profession, art, and science of teaching".[3] This means, seeing teaching as a vocation (calling) and a discipline that requires learning to acquire right skills to demonstrate the needed ability. Although the root word "pedagogue" has acquired less professional and distasteful nuances such as pedantry and dogmatism, its origin from the Greek, *paidagogus*, refers to a boy's tutor; and it carries the idea of an agent of learning, one who looks after, attends to, escorts, or leads a child to school.[4]

Pedagogy has the potential to greatly influence teacher-student relationships in ways that articulate the meaning of theological education for the student. Larry J. McKinney outlines the duty of theological education in four areas of commitment: commitment to biblical training; commitment to the Great Commission; commitment to holy living, and commitment to ministry formation. How these translate in the context of a changing world is crucial, and keeping the balance between academic excellence and spiritual formation should remain a key engagement of theological educators.[5] This is clearly captured in Budeslić's summary that the chief goal in theological education is "shaping lives and practices of believers and the church".[6]

Theological education uses the Bible (as a sacred text) as its foundation, and it is grounded in God's self-disclosed desire to establish a relationship with humanity and creation. This construct is evident in the fact that humans are social creatures that grow and acquire knowledge through interaction with their social contexts. Knowledge acquisition as a social construct is represented by various paradigms including mentor-mentee and personality compatibility (Mintz); bonding and pairing (Lev Vygotsky); modelling (Bandura); mutuality and dialogue (Thayer-Bacon), who asserts that "we become knowers and are able to contribute to the constructing of knowledge due to the relationships we have with others".[7]

---

3 Wendy Bishop and David Starkey, *Keywords in Creative Writing Book*, (University Press of Colorado/Utah State University Press, 2006), 119. Stable URL: https://www.jstor.org/stable/j.ctt4cgr61.28.

4 See: Bishop and Starkey, *Keywords in Creative Writing*, 120. See also: www.Collinsdictionary.com.

5 Larry J. McKinney, "Evangelical Theological Education: Implementing Our Own Agenda." Paper presented 20 Aug 2003 at the ICETE International Consultation for Theological Educators High Wycombe, UK (2003), 1-16.

6 Ervin Budeslić, "An Apology of Theological Education: The Nature, The Role, The purpose, the Past and the Future of Theological Education", *KAIROS - Evangelical Journal of Theology* / Vol. VII. No. 2 (2013), 131-154 (132).

7 See: A. Mintz, "The midwife as matchmaker: Socrates and relational pedagogy", *Philosophy of Education Archive*, (2007), 91-99; L.S. Vygotsky, *Mind in Society: The development of higher psychological processes* (M. Cole, V. John-Steiner, S. Scribner & E. Souberman, Eds.). (Cambridge: Harvard University Press, 1978); A. Bandura, *Social Learning Theory* (NJ, Eaglewood Cliffs: Prentice Hall, 1977); B. Thayer-Bacon, *Relational "(e)pistimeologies"*. (New York: Peter Lang Publishers, 2003), 2.

Aspelin describes teachers' work as involving both a knowledge aspect and a social dimension.[8] The former addresses the content and presentation of information and the latter, embraces areas of moral education/ discipline—that which promotes social cohesion and care: responsible living, consideration directed towards self and others, especially showing interest in students and attention to those who are suffering. Relational pedagogy therefore focuses on the importance of relationships that are created in the learning environment (classroom, lecture hall or in any other learning sites). Relationships in education refers to the positive connections and inter-connections between students, teachers, other staff and members in the learning community that "foster positive social interaction and establish a nurturing environment of trust and support".[9] Two basic forms of relationships, including student-student and teacher-student, exist in this context. Our concentration here is on the latter as pivotal in the education endeavour.

A growing number of research in pedagogy speak in support of a genuine, trusting teacher-student relationship as a fundamental element in the education processing.[10] They observe that a trusting relationship explains a number of positive outcomes in students, including their empowerment, adjustment to education, academic performance, individual initiative and engagement with studies, empathy, and cooperation in the teaching-learning environment and process. The converse may result in "increased levels of anxiety and depression"[11] and demotivation in students. They also maintain that this inter-human phenomenon connects and influences other levels of relations in the social web in which the student participates—from the individual up to the larger societal stage. Teachers' expected outcomes have also been observed to increase with positive teacher-student relationships.

This is why Crownover, and Jones describe relational pedagogy as "the systematic construction of appropriate relationships embedded within the schooling [training] process."[12] This involves a deliberate effort to not only build, but also, to maintain relationships in ways that aid the teaching-learning process in order to realise the transformative goal of theological

8 Aspelin, 'Beyond individualised teaching'.

9 American Institutes for Research (AIR, 2020). 'Safe Supportive Learning Environment', www.safesupportivelearning.ed.gov 16-08-2020.

10 See, for example, Paulo Freire, *Pedagogy of the Oppressed*, M.B. Ramos, Trans., 30th ann. Ed, (New York: Continuum, 1970/2000) p. 85. C. Murray and M.T. Greenberg, "Children's relationships with teachers and bonds with schools: An investigation of patterns and correlates in middle childhood", *Psychology in the Schools, 38*, (2000) 425-446. N. Noddings, *The challenge to care in schools: An alternative approach to education* (New York, NY: Teachers College Press, 1992). Aspelin, "Beyond Individualised Teaching", Crownover and Jones, 'A Relational Pedagogy'.

11 Crownover and Jones, "A Relational Pedagogy", 21.

12 Crownover and Jones, "A Relational Pedagogy ",18.

training. Since relational pedagogy promotes a shared "relational commitment" among all those involved in the learning community, such an endeavour goes beyond the four walls into amorphous social interrelations. It does not place value on students based on a form of gradation. Worth and respect are premised on the basis of a common humanity[13] and perhaps, we may add, a common cause. Reflecting on my MTh studies at ACI, I see Prof. Howell's attempt at outlining the steps for each of us on how to overcome our first major hurdle in the programme, the Integrated Presentation, as a commitment to a common humanity and a common cause.

The Integrated Presentation was an examination, essentially a practice viva voce in itself, that MTh students had to pass in order to progress to the next level of their studies. For this examination, each student was randomly assigned a comprehensive question/problem to address, based upon the programme content. They then undertook research on the chosen question and prepared a paper within twenty-four hours for presentation before a panel of select faculty. This, in addition to semester papers on each course, as well as a dissertation, constitute the major assessments for ACI's MTh degree. On the panel, there was one faculty member who was responsible for graduate studies, academic, and all issues relating to quality assurance in addition to teaching specific courses. This lecturer pontificated about the expectation for each student, from research to writing, preparedness, punctuality, presentation, etc. The examination created a very tense atmosphere, coupled with a sleepless night and loss of appetite for a few of us! Although some unfortunate things happened on the appointed day, including illness and computers crashing, we all managed to sail through the presentation. One thing that became more evident to all students during that period was Professor Howell's unbiased position on quality assurance issues: "you are here for business and business we would do!"

It is important to bear in mind that there is a huge difference between firm and fair, such as Professor Howell demonstrated, and abusive. Teachers, as instructors, wield a lot of power and inappropriate exercise of this influence may result in abuse of learners. This has led scholars such as Williams and Freire to believe that the classroom becomes a place that promotes oppression when teachers fail to understand the need to create a healthy environment for their learners.[14] One way to prevent this and foster conditions for growth is for teachers to initiate dialogue with students.

13 Crownover and Jones, "A Relational Pedagogy ", 25.

14 Candace L. Williams, "My Intimacy with Pedagogy of the Oppressed' Public Stories of Mathematics Educators", *Journal of Urban Mathematics Education*, Vol. 2, No. 2, (December 2009) 6-11, 6-7. See Chapter Two of Freire, *Pedagogy of the Oppressed*.

Dialogue in Relational Pedagogy and Theological Education

Theological education is dialogical in its accommodation of reasoning and encouragement of students to consider alternative viewpoints and interpretations. In basic terms, dialogue is a conversation between parties. It is a situation in which one person seeks to understand another through communication by expressing his/her opinion while trying also to fit the other person's view into his/her own. This encourages what Richard Paul describes as cooperative learning: a situation where individuals learn by reasoning together with others, drawing from each other's thinking, suggestions or proposals and analyses, and finding insights to problems and issues, and implications that may arise. In this way they experience support in learning.[15] Freire accentuates the significance of dialogue in education when he states, "Without dialogue there is no communication, and without communication there can be no true education."[16]

Dialogue becomes dialectical when it involves an "extended exchange between different points of view or frames of reference" and analyses of the strengths and weaknesses of the various perspectives/arguments to arrive at a conclusion.[17] As Paul argues, dialogue translates into dialectics when viewpoints vary in the conversation and require assessment of positions.[18] The underpinning assumption here is that knowledge acquisition and its application to situations as a goal of true education is not passive. It requires the learner's active participation, investigation, and analysis of issues, and formation of positions/conclusions and application of the knowledge gained.

In other words, theological education does not entertain "uncritical absolutism" or acceptance of absolute judgments without subjecting them to the scrutiny of reason. It is Howell's commitment to develop in students this quality of thought processing and engagement and the cultivation in them of the capacity to question and critically judge or justify positions that sets her apart and distinguishes her from some other theological educators, particularly those who equate education with "gathering content and a body of information" and who treat students "as boxes to be filled gradually with logically arranged packets of information."[19]

During my MTh studies, I took a course entitled *Aspects of Christian History of Africa* under Professor Howell; and as required, I wrote a final essay on an approved topic. I tried my best to submit a draft I thought would be

15 Richard Paul, Critical Thinking: What Every Person Needs to Survive in a Rapidly Changing World (California: Foundation for Critical Thinking, 2012), 316-17.
16 Freire, Pedagogy of the Oppressed, 92-93.
17 Paul, *Critical Thinking*, 309-310.
18 Paul, *Critical Thinking*, 312.
19 Budeslić, 'An Apology of Theological Education', 138.

commendable. When she returned my paper, it appeared as if I had written the original in red ink! As another colleague remarked upon receiving his own paper from Professor Howell, "she has literally painted my own paper red." This was to show us the extent of the revision required on our papers. In my case, I submitted a second and a third draft with revisions before she finally accepted that paper. Upon reflection, I realised that this rigorous exercise was part of her process of introducing students to sound theological scholarship; one that engages in dialogue and subjects others' views to scrutiny.

In George Hillock's assessment, teachers' effectiveness correlated with their belief that their students' work will improve. He argues that "Teachers… who are not optimistic about their students will have no reason to change. Because [these teachers] so seldom engage in reflective practice, they will have little evidence of any need to change. And because they have low expectations of their students, they will not be surprised when their students fail to learn."[20]

One significant way in which Professor Howell facilitated my improvement in learning was through her role as shepherd and counsellor. Impactful theological pedagogy creates a dialogical connection between the roles of shepherd, counsellor, and theological educator.

Shepherding and Counselling Roles of the Teacher

An effective and efficient Christian educator combines the roles of pastor and counsellor to facilitate the achievement of their own objectives and the goals of their students. As a teacher, the theological educator initiates dialogue with the students to support them to identify their individual goals and intentionally guide them to achieve the desired changes in their lives. By doing this, the teacher helps the students "discover for themselves what stops them from making progress, so they can move forward."[21] This care and support from the teacher to guide the student on what to do to achieve the desired learning outcomes is rooted in the nature of true shepherds and counsellors. Elizabeth Ebizie Nkechi et al. have observed that "counsellors…proffer guidance to the [student] in a quest of moulding the [student] in the right path to take in their life pursuit."[22] In doing this, the teacher assumes some shepherding and counselling functions in fulfilling the varied roles of a teacher.

20 George Hillock as cited in Bishop and Starkey, *Keywords in Creative Writing*, 121.
21 Peter C. Kratcoski 2017. *Correctional Counselling and Treatment*, Sixth edition (Springer International Publishing, 2017),199.
22 Ebizie Elizabeth Nkechi, Enajedu Esther Ewomaoghene and Nkechi Egenti, "The Role of Guidance and Counselling in Effective Teaching and Learning in Schools", *RAY: International Journal of Interdisciplinary Studies, E-ISSN: 2456-3064*, Vol. 1, No. 2, October, 2016, 6-48, 37.

I recall how this became apparent to me in one of my meetings with Howell after my viva/defence. We were revisiting and addressing comments of one of my two external examiners, who had requested a revision of the term 'Native' to 'Indigenous.' I had employed the former irrespective of the argument of derogation against it. In my view, the term communicates a stronger power or greater strength of something's connection with its origin, than its alternative. In my opinion, 'Indigenous' is a softer term. Noticing my insistence and reluctance to revise the expression, I remember Professor Howell firmly restating what my examiner had required. Then she asked me, do you want to complete this revision and move on with life? Of course! I desired to open a new chapter in my life, so I accepted the requirement to revise 'Native' to 'Indigenous' and proceeded with the rest of the revision and concluded that journey.

Soundararajan sees the counsellor's objective precisely in this regard: "to provide support to clients' goals by assisting in decreasing their stress, aiding the effort to provide a healthy environment, helping them focus on personal and career goals, thereby contributing to their clients' motivation, performance, and satisfaction with their life."[23] Successful counsellors do not only put themselves in clients' shoes, but, after listening and understanding, they also facilitate clients' development of a better understanding of themselves and their respective situation in order to arrive at "a realistic, practical solution."[24] This responsibility interconnects with shepherding.

Shepherding is a key pastoral responsibility but not the sole function. Anthony Yeo sees it as "a shared ministry" and as such, this task also falls to other members of the school community. In this sense it is not done in a formalised system but "a contextual, informal and interactive approach…facilitated through constructive relationships and experienced via conversations" or dialogue with students.[25]

A healthy shepherd-counsellor relationship rests upon trust. The true shepherd and counsellor has a strong relational capacity. In true shepherding and counselling within academia, the instructor relates to the student as a person not as an object that is acted upon or given a set of instructions to follow. Truly, "Teachers with a strong relational capacity can relate to a student's actual person and potential existence."[26]

---

23 Radhika Soundararajan, *Counselling, Skills and Practice:* (India: New Delhi: Tata McGraw-Hill Education Private Limited, 2012), 111.

24 Soundararajan, *Counselling, Skill and Practice.*

25 Anthony M.A. Yeo "Counselling in the Twenty-First Century – A Personal Perspective", in Isaac Lim (ed), *The Christian Church in the 21st Century Singapore* (Singapore: National Council of Churches, 2000).

26 Buber Martin cited in Crownover and Jones, "A Relational Pedagogy", 21.

Through teacher-student counselling, the teacher is better placed to understand some of the key issues students face that may adversely affect their performance. However, in this counselling role, there is need for the teacher to guard against the assumption of having complete knowledge of the student's challenges.

Jones and Augustine have specifically observed that, "knowledge about one's own students raises awareness of the [education-related problems]" that they go through. Awareness then becomes a significant first step in addressing students' challenges and is "best attained by developing quality teacher-student relationships" in which the teacher seeks to relate to the students as distinctive individuals with their personal needs, circumstances, experiences, and thinking.[27]

These dual roles of a teacher are perfectly represented in the person of the Holy Spirit and exemplified by Christ in his relationship with his students/disciples, as the Master Teacher. Good teachers fulfil changing roles in their relationship with their students; and Harden and Crosby define a good teacher as one "who helps the student to learn."[28]

The Need for Training

A teacher's intervention in a number of education related cases, school or classroom, is crucial in promoting and achieving the goal of theological education. Studies carried out in secular educational institutions by scholars suggest that teacher intervention helps to create a facilitating environment for students to learn.[29] The teacher's work as a counsellor involves a variety of individuals with varying problems in various settings. Stress, anxiety, finances, family, general planning, and time management are examples of common student problems in higher education, and those in theological training are no exception. To effectively address some of these issues and fulfil the counselling responsibilities, the teacher should possess certain skills.

Soundararajan outlines a list of competencies required of counsellors, including knowledge of the learning process; knowledge of educational programmes and their requirements; ability to teach effectively; ability to diagnose student problems; ability to help students form and clarify

27 Joseph R. Jones and Sharon Murphy Augustine, "Creating an Anti-Bullying Culture in Secondary Schools: Characteristics to Consider When Constructing Appropriate Anti-Bullying Programs", *American Secondary Education*, (Summer 2015), v43 n3 (Summer 2015) 73-84, 80.

28 R.M. Harden and Joy Crosby (2000). 'AMEE Guide No. 2: The good teacher is more than a lecturer—the twelve roles of the teacher' in *Medical Teacher*, Vol. 22, No. 4 (2000) 334-346, 335.

29 See: D. Olweus, *Bullying at School: What We Know and What We Can Do.* Oxford: Blackwells, 1993; P. O'Connell, D. Pepler and W. Craig, 'Peer involvement in bullying: insights and challenges for intervention', *Journal of Adolescence*, 1999, 22, 4, 437-452. doi:10.1006/jado.1999.0238; Jones and Augustine, 'Creating an Anti-Bullying Culture'.

their educational values and goals; ability to provide crisis intervention and support; ability to understand the world of the individual from both subjective and objective perspectives; ability to provide effective consultation to students and community members. Additionally, they should demonstrate experience-based capacity in their counselling roles.[30] In many respects, these are shared qualities in the teacher's role as shepherd. Consequently, to acquire some of these skills may require some form of training for teachers in basic counselling procedures and skills, a rethinking of theological pedagogy.

Conclusion

Relational pedagogy is favourable to theological education. Its benefits to the theological educator, the student, the educational process, and the community are far-reaching. Professor Howell's adoption of this approach in the teacher-student, supervisor-supervisee relationship with me, and its positive effective on my educational outcomes, highlights the need for agents of theological education to factor the place of dialogue, shepherding and counselling into the relational pedagogy equation. The connection between relational pedagogy and shepherding and counselling could impact how students facing academic challenges are supported within the context of theological training. The emphases should be on human qualities and individual potentials.

As learning facilitators, planners, role models, information providers, resource developers, standard accessors, etc., teachers play key roles in student learning. In these engagements, as they transition from teacher-centred strategies to student-centred approaches through relational pedagogy, they fulfil some of the shepherd-counsellor functions to their students. This becomes evident as they pay attention to each student's needs and guide the student to meet those needs in positive ways. My recommendation, therefore, is that teacher preparatory and refresher programmes should feature relational pedagogy when training theological instructors and deliberate workshops should also be part of institutional faculty development plans.

PART THREE

THEOLOGY, HUMAN NEED AND ENVIRONMENT

Politics, Economics and The Great Commission

Andrew F Walls[1]

Abstract:

Does the "Great Commission" to make disciples of all nations have any relevance in the fields of politics and economics? Noting that the Commission is premised on the assertion in Matt. 28:17, the chapter explores the "powers and authorities" behind structural evil in society, the Pauline view of frustration in the natural world since the fall, the presentation of the risen Jesus as Messianic King and the ongoing challenges to his rule. It concludes that structural evil is within the scope of Christ's atonement, and that disciples are called to maintain Messiah's authority over all human life—including the political, economic and environmental spheres—until his Kingdom is completed before the End.

The Great Commission

The name "'The Great Commission'" has long been given to the words which brings Matthew's Gospel to a close, where the risen Christ tells his followers to "make disciples of all nations" (literally "to disciple all nations"), baptizing them in the name of the Father, the Son and the Holy Spirit, and teaching them all that Jesus himself had taught. The Commission has long been a charter for proclamation of the Christian message, and the process of proclamation has been accompanied by countless works of mercy and by endeavours for human betterment beyond calculation. Even so, the implications of the Great Commission are perhaps wider than has often been recognized, so that closer inspection of even such a well-known passage may be justified.

1 In the composition of this paper the author is much indebted to Dr Ingrid Reneau Walls.

While the tendency (at least in recent times) has been to concentrate on verse 18 and 19, the Commission actually begins with the claim in verse 17 that "All authority in heaven and on earth is given to me," and the word "therefore" links these words to the command to go and disciple the nations. The whole mission of the Church to the nations in teaching and baptizing rests on the universal authority that the risen Christ has been given. The passage ends with the assurance that the one who has this authority will be with his disciples "to the end of the age." When reading the Great Commission as a whole, from verse 17 to the end of the Gospel, we may find a helpful commentary in Paul's great exposition of the significance of the Resurrection in I Corinthians 15.

The Messianic Kingdom and the End

Having established that Christ's resurrection is the first fruit of a great harvest in which those who have died "in Christ" will also rise, Paul points to a further stage—the End, when Christ will hand the Kingdom back to the Father, that "God may be all in all" (vs 24). This will take place after Christ has destroyed "all dominion, authority and power; for he must reign until he has put all things under his feet" (vs 24f.). This contains a clear reference to Psalm 8, in which the psalmist, in awe at God's creation and the dignity given to humanity within it, cries out, "you have put all things under his feet." Paul sees Christ, the Messianic King who represents the perfection of humanity, ruling until everything is subject to him. During his reign, however, there are still "dominions, authorities and powers"—entities that are at enmity with God and resist Messiah's rule—to be brought into subjection. The last of these entities to be destroyed will be death, the recognized enemy of humanity (vs 26), which entered the world with humanity's fall.

Paul thus sees the risen Christ, possessing power and authority, at present ruling as Messiah. That rule is currently challenged by alien dominions and authorities, but the defeat of these powers is certain.

The Frustration in the Natural World

We will return later to what Paul says elsewhere about the activities of these alien powers; but first we may reflect on what he says in Romans 8:18ff. about the present state of the created world. He represents this as being subject to frustration, suffering pains comparable to those of human childbirth, and condemned to decay. The natural world, the human environment, is affected—perhaps one should say, infected—by the outcome of human sinfulness. We may recall that in the Creation stories Adam finds after the Fall that the ground is cursed because of him; he has now to labour to get sustenance from it, and to contend with thorns and thistles, unknown in the garden (Gen. 3: 17ff). In line with this, Paul expects the liberation of the natural world of creation to come about when the work of human redemption is complete ("the redemption of our bodies" Rom 8:23). Decay is written into nature as we know it, and we share in that decay. We are part of the natural world, subject to death, which will be the last enemy to come under the feet of the Messianic King (I Cor. 15: 26). Both the natural world and humanity await the completion of the Messiah's rule.

At the time of writing this, the coronavirus, believed to have spread to humans from animals, is shattering lives and damaging economies across the continents. This is a reminder of the interconnectedness of the wellbeing of humanity and that of the environment; it is also an example of the dislocations and disasters that afflict the created world during what Paul describes as its frustration. The apostle looks for the regeneration of nature, the end of the frustration and groaning of the natural world, to come with the completion of the process of human redemption, of which Christ's resurrection is the first major landmark (Rom 8:23f).

Prophecies of the Messianic Age

In the Messianic prophecies of the Old Testament the transformation of the natural world is associated with Messianic rule. For instance, when Isaiah, who sometimes had difficult encounters with the monarch of the day, looks forward to the reign of a just ruler from the Davidic dynasty who will protect the poor instead of oppressing them. He also sees wolves and lambs then living peaceably together and children playing unharmed around snakes' nests (Isa. 11:1ff): "They will neither harm nor destroy in all my holy mountain." Both human society and the world of nature are healed of their destructive aspects under the messianic king.

The Gospel of the Kingdom

The Messianic prophecies of the Old Testament culminate in the message of the last of the prophets, John the Baptist. His message about the imminence of the Kingdom of God brings about repentance and moral renewal. Soldiers and petty officials respond to it by giving up abusive and exploitative practices, and modestly well-off people share the necessities of life with the poor and deprived (Luke 3:7–14). Then Jesus arrives, proclaiming the same message (Matt. 4:17). But with Jesus, the Kingdom begins to assume concrete and visible form. The sick, even the desperately sick, are healed; blind people see, disabled people walk, the most distressing forms of physical and mental affliction and the most dangerous behavioural disorders are relieved; evil forces are expelled and flee his presence. It dawns on followers of Jesus that the messianic king has arrived, and some of the implications gradually sink in (they were slow to grasp the idea that the Messiah must suffer). They realize that the righteous ruler with Davidic ancestry has arrived; the Messianic age was at hand.

Human Society and "Powers and Authorities"

To consider the messianic age in relation to human affairs, we may again begin with a Pauline commentary. In the Epistle to the Colossians (Col 2: 15ff), the apostle points to "powers and authorities" seeking to mislead the Colossian believers, at the same time making clear that in the resurrection of Christ these entities have already suffered a decisive defeat. He speaks of the risen Christ disarming powers and making a public spectacle of them, triumphing over them by his cross. The image is of a Roman general returned from the wars, riding in a public triumph with prisoners of war trudging behind him. The victory chariot in this case is the cross; the resurrection marks the victory; the captives trailing behind are powers and authorities defeated in the conflict.

Paul has already reminded the Colossian Christians that they had themselves been raised from spiritual death, their sins cancelled, the bill of their debts nailed to the cross. But the work of Christ in the atonement made by his death reaches deeper than this, to the evil embedded in the operations of society, the ways in which the world works. And here Paul introduces us to the role of the powers and authorities that operate in the intellectual and social realms.

In their pre-Christian life the Colossian Christians had been subject to what Paul calls "the elements" or "basic principles" (*stoicheia)* of this world which kept them in the ignorance, idolatry, and immoral and licentious behaviour, from which they were now delivered. Even so, Paul sees a danger that through "deceptive philosophy" dependent on human traditions, they might fall back under the sway of these "elements" belonging to the social and intellectual influences of a mode of life they have left behind (Col. 2:8). For Paul, the *stoicheia* are more than obsolete opinions or mistaken mental attitudes: they belong to an alien sphere, the realm of the powers that have been defeated by the cross and are now captives trailing behind the chariot of the risen Christ. Those who share by faith in Christ's risen life should not submit to the *stoicheia* by resuming the attitudes and habits belonging to the past life.

Evil exists not only in the sinful thoughts and words and deeds of individuals but also in the corporate processes by which human societies operate. It penetrates human activities: social, political, economic, intellectual, and religious. Paul describes these structural manifestations of evil in terms of "powers, dominions and authorities" opposed to God's rule. The well-known passage in Ephesians 6:10ff. is eloquent: Christians must stand against the devil's schemes, since "our struggle is not against flesh and blood but against the rulers, the authorities, against the powers of this dark world, and against the spiritual forces of evil in the heavenly realms."

Task for African Theologians

Modern Western theology has found difficulties with this aspect of New Testament language, since there is no space for such "powers" in the worldviews characteristic of the West that are generally called "modern." A generation or so ago the influential New Testament scholar Rudolf Bultmann argued for "demythologizing" the New Testament of such elements[2]; and there have been various attempts since to reckon with how the New Testament presents structural evil in the political and economic spheres, without reference to spiritual entities. The time may be ripe for African Christian theologians, free from the inhibitions imposed by the small-scale views of the universe now characteristic of the West, to give this aspect of New Testament language fuller consideration. Modern western theologies, both formal and popular, sometimes find difficulty in understanding the Gospel as addressing both individuals and the evils in social, political and economic structures. World Christianity needs a truly ecumenical theology of evil that recognizes both the personal and the structural dimensions of evil and reflects the saving activity of Christ in relation to both.

2 Rudolf Bultmann's *Neues Testament und Mythologie* first appeared in 1941. A convenient English version is available in Rudolf Bultmann, *The New Testament and Mythology, and other basic writings*, edited by SM Ogden, (Minneapolis MN: Fortress Press, 1984).

There is only one atonement. The atoning work of Christ is presented in the New Testament as a cosmic act reaching across time and space, dealing with all evil in the universe, personal and structural. As Paul writes, again to the Colossians, "God was pleased to have all his fullness dwell in Christ, and through him to reconcile to himself all things, whether things on earth or things in heaven (Col 1: 19f). The atoning work of Christ goes deeper than the forgiveness of the sins of individual sinners; it reaches to the evil embedded in societies.

Structural Evil and the Gospel Narratives

Structural evil appears early in the Gospel narratives, in the reaction of Herod the Great to the question about the whereabouts of the king of the Jews innocently asked by the Magi. The suspicion and fear of Herod at the thought of another king, even a baby; his anxious consultation with scriptural specialists; his disingenuous response to the Magi; and his drastically cruel measures to destroy a possible future claimant to his throne (Matt. 2:1-18) all reflect the ways that absolute rulers calculate. (We may note in passing that the portrayal of Herod and his actions in the Gospel narrative is in keeping with what we know from other sources about that consummate but ruthless political operator).

But the prime biblical example of how evil operates in ordinary political processes can be seen in the Gospel narratives leading up to the arrest of Jesus, the trials before Jewish and Roman authorities and his execution. We can identify the various interest groups: different branches of the leadership of the Jewish community, Roman imperial power, a Jewish crowd of probably varying composition. Behind the events arising from the interplay of these forces Paul sees the activity of the "powers of this age who are coming to nothing." He contrasts their ways of thinking with the hidden wisdom of God working for human salvation; had they known this divine wisdom, "they would not have crucified the Lord of Glory." (I Cor. 2:6ff.).

Such language envisages the "powers and authorities" as at work in the political field, using human agents such as Caiaphas and Pilate. The political reasoning of each of these is indicated in the Gospels. Caiaphas belongs to the upper ranks of the priesthood, seeking to accommodate to Roman rule, and fearing messianic enthusiasm as likely to provoke Roman repression, he concludes that "it is better that one man die for the people than that the whole nation perish" (John 11:50). The Gospel writer notes that these words had a deeper meaning than Caiaphas was aware of.

Pilate's thinking is equally intelligible. Jesus is brought before him on a political charge by the leaders of the province that he is appointed to govern. He knows that the charge is bogus, but does not want to offend them, and is sensitive to the potential threat to his career of appearing not to be Caesar's friend (John 19:12). He tries to evade responsibility by passing the case to the Tetrarch of Galilee (Luke 23:13) or by the device of a Passover amnesty (Matthew 27:15ff). Frustrated, and forced to a decision, he reluctantly authorizes the unjust execution, but still refuses to accept responsibility for it (Matt 27: 24ff).

The reasoning behind the essentially political decisions of Caiaphas and Pilate reflects the way that things often happen in human affairs.

Paul views this "way that things happen" as due to the "rulers of this age." In this case the "hidden wisdom of God" turned the crucifixion of the Lord of Glory from a triumph of evil into the instrument for the redemption of the world (I Cor. 2:6ff). Behind the thinking and the actions of such ordinary political figures, lay the workings of those unseen "rulers" at work in the structures of this present age—powers who are "coming to nothing." The resurrection of Jesus gives assurance that these unseen rulers of the age are indeed coming to nothing.

"The World" in the Johannine Writings

Johannine language differs from Pauline language but expresses similar truths. In itself the word *kosmos* means "world," but in the fourth Gospel its usual connotation is "the world as it is now"—that is, estranged from God and his ways. When Jesus says to Pilate, "My kingdom is not of this world" (John 18:36), he is not saying that his kingdom is purely spiritual with no reference to politics, as the words that follow the statement make clear: had his kingdom been "of this world" his followers would have fought to prevent his arrest by the Jewish authorities. The Gospel narrative indicates that some, at least, had in fact attempted to fight, and that Jesus had restrained them (John 18:11).

The prayer of Jesus for his followers is not that they may be taken out of the world but that while in the world they might be protected from the evil one, that is, the "Prince of this world" (John 17:15f). The Kingdom of Christ does not dispense with politics; it requires a different kind of politics from that of the world as it is; a picture quite consistent with Paul's account of what took place in the seen and unseen worlds in the crucifixion of the Lord of Glory. That Lord of Glory embodies the messianic kingdom, and his rule is to continue until all opposition has ceased. The healing of the world of its bondage to decay can then take place.

Modern Disciples and the Great Commission

We may now return to the Great Commission. We have seen that in interpreting it we need to stress the significance of its opening words, which present Jesus, the crucified Messiah, now risen from the dead and invested with "all authority" in heaven and earth (that is, both in the world we see and in the world outside our experience). His reign as the Messianic King has thus begun; an idea which we have seen that Paul expounds in 1 Corinthians 15. From the latter, we learn that Christ's authority is still challenged by dominions *(arche)*, authorities *(exousiai)* and powers *(dunameis)* which are to be "put under his feet" during his reign as Messiah.

We—like the first disciples and those who received Paul's letter—are living in the messianic age. During this contested part of his reign, the created world of nature remains subject to the frustration that has characterized it since the Fall; it will be subject to decay until the resurrection of the dead completes human redemption and ends the messianic age.

Matthew's Gospel closes before the Ascension; the Great Commission is given on a mountain in Galilee, not on the Mount of Olives. Luke tells us of Jesus being taken up, and of the angelic voice speaking of his eventual return. The currency of the Great Commission is the interval between Pentecost and the Return; in fact, the period of Messiah's reign, during which his rule will still be challenged. Paul tells us that after all opposition has ceased, nature will be healed of its bondage to decay, and death itself abolished. Then, indeed, God will be all in all.

During the interim, the task of disciples of Jesus is to "make disciples of all nations": disciples who have absorbed all Jesus is and did and taught. It is a task requiring interaction with all the cultures and institutions by which the nations operate.

We have noted how the New Testament speaks both of decay and dislocation in the natural world and of the evil embedded in social structures. This "structural sin" lies in intellectual climates, in the arts and literary and musical culture, in the values operating in commercial and economic life, "the way things work" in the political and legal realms. Structural sin represents what Paul calls "dominions, authorities and powers" not yet subjected to Messiah's rule. Disciples of Jesus must seek to reclaim these territories for their Messiah, bearing in mind that the decisive victory has already been won; not only has the Messiah's atoning work been completed; he is riding in the victory chariot of the cross with a trail of captive powers behind him.

The gospel is the good news of the Kingdom of God; our Messiah is reigning now. The gospel is not a formula, a form of words through which some people may be saved from a perishing world; it is a word from God that gives hope for the world itself; even the groaning natural world as it awaits its redemption. (Nowhere has the opposition to Messiah's rule been more intense than in the field of care for the earth and our environment, where Professor Howell has been such a staunch campaigner). We may be certain that when the Return heralds the approach of the End, it will not arise from some sudden act of divine despair about the world. At the centre of the gospel is the Kingdom of God, the high and holy one who inhabits eternity, who has known all from the beginning. The task of disciples is to continue to witness to the Messiah, giving evidence about him until his rule is no longer challenged, while God is creating a new heaven and a new earth (Isa.65:17ff; Rev.21:1).

The disciples of Jesus are a worldwide community, substantially represented on every continent, and will be called to witness to Christ and his kingship in many social settings. We may recall that when the Protestant missionary movement from the West reached its critical stage in the late eighteenth and early nineteenth centuries, it came into collision with structural sin in a particularly loathsome form. The Atlantic slave trade was devastating Africa as millions of Africans were forcibly transported to the Americas to be made human property to serve the economies of Europe and North America. The missionary movement and the anti-slavery movement grew up together, with shared interests and with many people active in both causes. Christians involved in these matters realized that the powers resisting Messiah's Kingdom in the commercial and economic and political fields could not be subdued simply by preaching at them. The slave trade was an economic institution and its abolition required economic arguments, and the devising of economic models. Bringing about abolition required immense research and documentation, and an unprecedented degree of organization, networking, and publicity. (It is arguable that the abolition of the slave trade was the first act of public policy brought about by mobilizing public opinion through the media).

As disciples of Jesus the Messiah across the world fulfil the Great Commission to make disciples of all nations, they can expect opposition from dominions, authorities and powers that resist Christ's rule. To respond will take them into active witness in every conceivable area of human thought and activity, from agronomy to art history and accountancy, from polymer science to political science, from medicine to music. No field is outside the scope of the Kingdom of God and Messiah's righteous rule.

Urbanisation and Religious Ecology: Muslims' Commitment to Islamic Environmentalism in Sokpoe-Sogakope Ecological Area

Ebenezer Yaw Blasu

Abstract

Sogakɔfe, is the capital of South Tɔŋu District in the Volta Region of Ghana. Its progressive growth into a semi-urban area has varied impacts on the religious space in the post-modern secular society. In particular are the challenges to Islamic commitment to environmentalism in zongos, which are eco-communities where Islamic religious beliefs remain widespread and central to the life of the dominant Muslim population. Theoretically, Islamic theocentric worldviews, the concept of *mizan* (cosmic balance) and the theomorphic understanding of humanity as *khalifa* (vicegerent of God) enjoin Muslims to rely on *fitra* (natural instinct) to care for creation. But for the Islamic eco-communities in Sogakɔfe, urbanisation tends to make Muslims compromise their ecological *fitra*. The basic reasons for this compromise analysed in this study include the demands of busy life-styles for survival, leaving no time for proactive environmental consciousness. But more significant reasons include cultural heterogeneity and the community's self-understanding as 'zongo' dwellers, both resulting in non-cohesion and cooperation around environmental issues. As a way forward, the paper proposes an African theocology curriculum for ecological education at all levels to awaken Islamic environmental *fitra*.

Key Words: Urbanisation, Religious ecology, Islamic environmentalism, African Theocology

Introduction

Faith communities and religious institutions have been pivotal in the growth of cities and urban communities in the world, usually as cradles around which large cities emerge. The growth of urban communities has varied impacts on religious life in the post-modern secular society, including both opportunities and challenges to religious life and commitment to the sacred. Muslim communities in the southern parts of Ghana develop as Zongos, where, often, Islamic religious beliefs remain widespread and central to the population. The capital of South Tɔŋu District in the Volta Region of Ghana is a fast-growing semi-urban town called Sogakɔfe. Its growth factors include the continuing influx of people, due to, among other reasons, rural-urban migration, river tourism, and the establishment of the West African Football Academy (WAFA) for hosting Ghana Premier league games. Sogakɔfe as a growing city is thus not without the impacts of urbanisation on the religious space, and particularly, Islamic religious motivation for creation care among Muslims.

Allison Howell is a passionate practitioner and strong advocate of religious environmentalism. She bemoans why 'there seems to be decreasing concern for the preservation of trees' as developers put up new housing estates in city areas; and the fact that 'in some new housing estates,' such as is often the case in zongos, 'the units are built so closely together that scarcely a tree can grow anywhere and drainage is neglected.'1 For Howell, a significant and fundamental explanation to environmental problems in African communities is due to the fact that 'the spiritual engagement with land and water, once part of the fabric of African spirituality, seems to have become unravelled in our time.'2 In addition, Howell believes, like Patrick Curry, that a concerted effort in responding to complex environmental challenges in a hetero-cultural community 'requires input from multiple sources to help interpret, and gain insight as to the best course we need to take.'3 Under the supervision of Allison Howell, I, a Christian, carried out research for my PhD in 2017, to determine the religious impulsion for creation care among Muslims in the Sokpoe-Sogakɔ*f*e ecological area. The aim was to find the best course to promote Christian-Muslim joint religious care for creation in the eco-area. This paper reviews literature and qualitatively

1 Allison M. Howell, "African Spirituality and Christian Ministry: 'Discerning the Signs of the times' in our environment and community", *Journal of African Christina Thought*, Vol. 20, No. 1 (June 2017): 12-23, 12.
2 Howell, "African Spirituality and Christian Ministry", 12.
3 Howell, "African Spirituality and Christian Ministry",13.

analyses the responses of participants regarding Islamic moral impulsions for creation care and some challenges of urbanisation to their commitment to Islamic moral care for creation.

Islamic Theoretical Impulsions for Creation Care in Literature

At least three theoretical or reconstructed factors are identifiable from Islamic literature as impulsions or motivators for Islamic participation in current global concerns about the environment. First, is the theocentric worldview, second, the concept of cosmic balance and, third, the theomorphic status of humanity as *khalifat* (vicegerent of God).

The first source of impulsion for a Muslim to be concerned about the environment and hence participate in creation care relationships and actions is the *taqwa*. It is reverence of and gratitude to the Creator for his creation, of which humanity is part. Muslims maintain their entire way of life with one major belief, which inspires their conduct, the belief in God (*Allah*). As John Azumah writes,

> Belief in God (*Allah*) is the first and central belief in Islam. He is depicted as sovereign, king, ruler, and master who is utterly other than his creation. His transcendent status is encapsulated in the familiar Muslim expression, *Allahu akbar* (God is great).[4]

Theocologically, the import of 'belief in God' in the Islamic worldview is the metaphysical affirmation of the Muslim that the cosmos belongs to God. God, according to the Qur'an is the real creator, owner, and sustainer of all reality (Qur'an 2:29). It suggests that all reality should be seen and read with the point of view in mind that nature originates from God and has an inherent purpose to impel creation's (both human and other-than-human) submission to God. The strength of a Muslim's claim of Qur'anic cosmology lies in the Islamic understanding that 'both the author of Qur'an and creator of nature are the same, God.'[5] Thus what the Qur'an ultimately reveals and what nature is ordered to manifest—divine glory in these two Books of God—are the same and obliges Muslims to submit to God.[6] Implicit in this affirmation is that the Qur'an enjoins Muslims to 'love creation for the sake of its Creator'.[7]

---

4 John Azumah, *My Neighbour's Faith: Islam Explained for Christians*, (Nairobi, Kenya: Hippo Books Ltd., 2008), 28.

5 Ibrahim Özdemir, 'Toward an Understanding of Environmental Ethics from Qur'anic Perspective' in Foltz, Richard C., Denny, Frederick M., and Baharuddin, Azizan, eds., *Islam and Ecology*, (Cambridge, Massachusetts, USA: Harvard University Press, 2003), 3-37 (9).

6 Özdemir, 'Toward an Understanding of Environmental Ethics from Qur'anic Perspective', 7- 9.

7 Özdemir, 'Toward an Understanding of Environmental Ethics from Qur'anic Perspective', 29.

Commenting ecologically on Qur'an 49:13 (*Most noble of you in the sight of God is he who is most reverent*), Llewellyn thinks Muslims need to revere God in everything, because he is Lord and will try humanity concerning his creatures.[8]

Taqwa as impulsion for eco-praxis receives further strength from *tawhīd*, the affirmation that Islamic worldviews are 'comprehensive, integrated, and holistic' and portray 'unity of reality'.[9] Özdemir explains that *tawhīd* in Qur'anic cosmology refers to the belief and affirmation that God is the very meaning of reality; implying that God is the dimension that makes other dimensions possible.[10] Known as the 'cosmological evidence of God's existence' in Islamic theological philosophy (*kalām*), *tawhīd* obliges humanity to morally respond by grateful submission[11] as well as being reverent to God and compassionate to all creatures.[12]

A significant theoretical inference is that when Muslims understand the ecological import of *taqwa* and *tawhīd* as a Qur'anic teaching, it can impel them to submit (be Muslims) by taking ecological actions that care for creation and sustain the unity of God (or integrity of creation) whether in a rural or urban setting. Patrick Curry believes that in religious ecology 'people will "naturally" do the right thing(s) when they apprehend the natural world correctly,' identifying oneself with that world and its fellow inhabitants.[13] The practical challenge, however, is with the right interpretation of Qur'anic texts. The Qur'an, according to S. Nomanul Haq, as the source of these teachings, is not a systematic treatise meant to convey ethical doctrines or principles. If this text is to yield a concrete system, it requires an imaginative reconstruction on the part of the reader.[14] Since large numbers of Muslims, particularly in Africa, even in cities are not literate in Arabic, the official language of the Holy Script, imaginative reconstruction that stimulates ecological action in caring for creation may be a non-starter. Even if Arabic literacy is not a challenge, classical Islam recognises epistemological difficulties in the finality of the reconstruction, unless there is 'overwhelming community consensus.'[15]

8 Othman Abd-Ar-Rahman Llewellyn, 'The Basis for a Discipline of Islamic Environmental Law' in Foltz, Richard C., Denny, Frederick M., and Baharuddin, Azizan, eds., *Islam and Ecology*, (Cambridge, Massachusetts, USA: Harvard University Press, 2003), 185-247 (189).
9 Özdemir, 'Toward an Understanding of Environmental Ethics from Qur'anic Perspective', 4.
10 Özdemir, 'Toward an Understanding of Environmental Ethics from Qur'anic Perspective', 9.
11 Özdemir, 'Toward an Understanding of Environmental Ethics from Qur'anic Perspective', 9.
12 Llewellyn, 'The Basis for a Discipline of Islamic Environmental Law', 189.
13 Patrick Curry, *Ecological Ethics-An Introduction*, 2nd ed., (Cambridge, UK: Polity Press, 2011), 106.
14 S. Nomanul Haq, 'Islam and Ecology: Toward Retrieval and Reconstruction,' in Foltz, Richard C., Frederick M. Denny, Azizan Baharuddin, eds., *Islam and Ecology*, (Cambridge, Massachusetts, USA: Harvard University Press, 2003), 121-154 (125).
15 Haq, 'Islam and Ecology: Toward Retrieval and Reconstruction, 125.

Notwithstanding these problems, the Qur'an remains a valuably rich and subtle stimulus to religious *imagination*,[16] particularly for Muslims who see themselves as *khalifas*.[17]

The concept of *khalifa* (theomorphic vicegerent) as impulsion for eco-praxis

The second source of impulsion for Islamic earthkeeping is from their belief that God has made humans his *khalifas* (vicegerents) in the world.[18] The Qur'an confirms this special functional position in the cosmos, by virtue of being theomorphic and a covenant or 'trust they have taken upon themselves in pre-eternity.'[19] In this position, human beings qualify to become 'stewards' of God on Earth as implied from these Qur'anic verses:

> He it is Who made you stewards on the earth, and raised some of you by degrees above others, so that He might try you by means of what He has bestowed upon you. (Qur'an 6:165).
>
> Thus, we have made you to succeed one another's stewards on the earth, that We might behold how you acquit yourselves (Qur'ran 10:14)[20]

The concept of *khalīfa* suggests a privilege and honour, yet it is more of a trust, a responsibility and a trial. Among all creatures, only humankind agreed to bear a trust or moral responsibility (Qur'an 33:72) for the Earth. According to Islamic theology it is a responsibility to 'be a shepherd over all the lives on Earth that he may touch for good or ill,' for which he shall be accountable to God on the day of resurrection[21]—the day 'when the earth throws out its burdens' (Qur'an 99:2). As Llewellyn explains a *khalīfa* acts not for himself/herself, but for his/her Lord and according to his/her Lord's purpose. He shall 'be asked about his flock' since all human beings 'shall be asked regarding every atom's weight of good that he or she has caused, and every atom's weight of harm' (Qur'an 99:7-8).[22]

As a concept, *khalīfacy* also suggests a trial of the integrity of humanity in managing the things Allah 'has bestowed upon you.' According to

---

16 Haq, 'Islam and Ecology: Toward Retrieval and Reconstruction', (Italic in original).
17 Mawil Izzi Dien, 'Islam and the Environment: Theory and Practice', in Foltz, Denny, and Baharuddin, eds., *Islam and Ecology*, 108-120 (110).
18 Llewellyn, 'The Basis for a Discipline of Islamic Environmental Law', 191.
19 Haq, 'Islam and Ecology: Toward Retrieval and Reconstruction', 127.
20 Llewellyn, 'The Basis for a Discipline of Islamic Environmental Law', 190.
21 Llewellyn, 'The Basis for a Discipline of Islamic Environmental Law', 190.
22 Llewellyn, 'The Basis for a Discipline of Islamic Environmental Law', 190.

Llewellyn, in a rigorously authenticated *hadith* of Abu Sa'id al-Khudri, Prophet Muhammad explained that God has made humans his 'stewards' in the world and 'He sees how you acquit [prove] yourselves.' All the same, it appears God had already foreknown humankind's inability to keep the trust since the Qur'an (33:72) indicates that humanity 'was unjust and foolish' and for which reason the Prophet strongly admonished 'whatever we do, we will not leave this world unchanged. We must take heed, then, that we leave it for the better.'[23]

The implication, as I see it, is that the *khalīfa* position in Islamic thought is gracious and rewarding, but it is also a fearful one, likely to determine the eternal fate and abode of humanity. It is a wilful choice of humanity on whom it behoves to do as Allah requires in being faithful 'stewards' of creation or else justly faces His wrath in the end for disobedience. It is my view that a good understanding and affirmation of this religious concept could (or rather should) be a strong moral impulsion for keeping integrity of creation even in urban settings. Yet, in practice, contrary to the Islamic belief in *khalifacy*, but true to the Qur'an's prediction (Qur'an 33:72) concerning humans' managing the Earth, Llewellyn observes that 'we have proven ourselves thoroughly unjust and foolish.'[24]

The observed failure of humanity, as Muslims see it, to be faithful *khalifas* of the earth is partly because of misrepresentation of the concept by overemphasizing the privilege and honour implied in the term as a mandate to exploit nature.[25] This excuse, however, seems to beg the question about the practical reality. It stands out more as an intellectual defence by Islamic writers regarding Islam's valuing of human beings. Llewellyn observes that the position of each human being as a *khalifa* on the earth has received considerable attention by Muslim writers in the twentieth century; and its misrepresentation (and misapplication) is because,

> Under the influence of European Humanism, and in response to allegations that Islam gives too little value to human being, Muslim writers have felt the need to prove that man (sic) has exalted status. As enthusiasm for "progress" and "development" swept the poorer countries of the world, some reformist thinkers even interpreted the concept of *khilafa* as a mandate to exploit and develop the earth on behalf of God.[26]

23 Llewellyn, 'The Basis for a Discipline of Islamic Environmental Law', 191.
24 Llewellyn, 'The Basis for a Discipline of Islamic Environmental Law', 191.
25 Llewellyn, 'The Basis for a Discipline of Islamic Environmental Law', 190.
26 Llewellyn, 'The Basis for a Discipline of Islamic Environmental Law', 190.

I argue, then, from a practical ecological point of view that most practising Islamists, particularly at grassroot levels, do not have a thorough and persuasive understanding of the *khalifat* concept in relation to Earth keeping.

Ibrahim Özdemir blames the loss of many animal species on 'our unawareness of Qur'anic values, which regulate...humankind's relations with other living species.'[27] Or the concept as a religious belief lacks the pervasive influence of a religious ecology that Mathew Clarke describes.[28] I agreeably infer from Patrick Curry that *khalifacy* or 'stewardship' as managerial ideology is religiously laudable; however its success requires the discipline of adhering to the concept of *qādr* or 'limits' both of the ecosystem and the human managers.[29] Moreover, since they serve not themselves but their Lord and his purpose as trustees,[30] *khalifats* necessarily need to be in tune with the eco-ethical and religious caring instructions of their Lord (God) from his Books, the Qur'an and/or the natural world. Significantly known and promoted concepts of such eco-information in Islam are *fitra* and '*mīzān*, balance in nature.'[31]

The concepts of *fitra* (instinct) and *mīzān* (cosmic balance) as impulsion for eco-praxis

For Muslims, humans have instinctual consciousness of their manifold but balanced relations with God and the rest of creation. This for me is a reason creation care can be (if not ought to be) a matter of course to the Muslim. In Islamic ecological reconstruction, ecological crisis is merely a symptom of the broader calamity that human societies are not living in accordance with God's will,[32] which is diligently and purposefully demonstrated in the ordered and just world that he created. Muslim scholars argue that a careful search into and comprehension of the Book of Nature, like the Qur'an, will awaken human instinctual consciousness of our manifold relations with God and the rest of creation. The reason is that Islam is *'din al-fitra'*; a religion which reminds that instinctual knowledge is true and primordial endowment by which we live in accordance with the environment. Therefore, environmental consciousness is something that needs not be taught, but merely awakened from observational knowledge of nature and/or reflecting on the

27 Özdemir, 'Toward an Understanding of Environmental Ethics from Qur'anic Perspective', 22.
28 Mathew Clark, *Development and Religion - Theology and Practice*, (UK: Edward Elgar Publishing Ltd., 2011), 1.
29 Curry, *Ecological Ethics – Introduction*, 35.
30 Llewellyn, 'The Basis for a Discipline of Islamic Environmental Law',190.
31 Adnan Z. Amin, 'Preface to Islam and Ecology', in Foltz, Denny, and Baharuddin, eds., *Islam and Ecology*, xxxiii-xxxv (xxxiii).
32 Richard C. Foltz, Introduction" to Foltz, Denny, and Baharuddin, eds., *Islam and Ecology*, xxxvii-xliii (xxxix).

Qur'an.[33] This sounds like the Akan maxim *obi nkyere abofra Onyame* (no-one points God out to a child), implying the Akan (and hence the African child) knows God instinctively from historical intimate experiences with and in the indigenous environment. In addition, it connotes the idea that the indigenous urbanised African child is culturally endowed with the potential for right and wrong about the environment in his/her consciousness.[34]

Patrick Curry suggests that any ecological ethic reconstruction today is only a 'reawakening of something very old' that we have forgotten from our intuitive experience of indigenous culture.[35] This affirms the Islamic assertion that eco-praxis arises from instinctual consciousness of our manifold but balanced relations with God and the rest of creation.[36] Muslims thus believe that carefully examining the heavens, the Earth, all creaturely things and natural phenomena in the environment, one cannot but marvel and praise God as the Creator. The learner would necessarily conclude: 'Our Lord! Not for nothing have You created (all) this! Glory to You (Qur'an 3:191).'[37] This is natural theology—affirming faith in God from his creation through doxological contemplation. Arthur Holmes refers to learning by doxological contemplation in the early centuries of Christianity and observes that it moulds a religious moral consciousness.[38] I infer from Allison Howell that a religious morality resulting from examining the cosmos or 'discerning the signs of the times in which we stand today'—times evidenced by environmental degradation—'enables one to engage in specific wise actions that lead to restorative transformation, renewal and well-being, both of humanity and for non-human creation.'[39] Similarly, Muslims believe such an experience changes the searcher's worldview, self-image, attitude, feelings and the patterns of relationships with reality.[40] For the Muslim, the aim of nature is then to point to humanity not only God's ownership of creation, but also his established moral laws of nature that ensure *mīzān* (cosmic and ecological harmony or balance).

Talking about balance in the ecosystem Fazlur Rahman, in his *Major Themes of the Qur'an*, explains that 'when God creates anything, He places within it its powers or laws of behaviour called in the Qur'an "guidance",

33 Saadia Khawar Khan Chishti, '*Fitra*: An Islamic Model for Humans and the Environment' in Foltz, Denny and Baharuddin, eds., *Islam and Ecology*, 67-82 (67).
34 Kofi Asare Opoku, *West African Traditional Religion*, (Accra: FEP International Private Ltd., 1978), 3-9 (5).
35 Curry, *Ecological Ethics*, 12.
36 Chishti, '*Fitra*: An Islamic Model for humans and the Environment', 67.
37 Özdemir, 'Toward an Understanding of Environmental Ethics from Qur'anic Perspective', 7-8.
38 Arthur F. Holmes, *Building the Christian Academy*, (Grand Rapids, Michigan: Wm. B. Eerdmans Publishing Co., 2001), 2.
39 Howell, "African Spirituality and Christian Ministry", 12-13.
40 Özdemir, 'Toward an Understanding of Environmental Ethics from Qur'anic Perspective', 6.

"command", or "measure" whereby it fits into the rest of the universe.'[41] He implies that God potentiates creation to fulfil its purpose without fail as *ayā* (sign) by submitting to the functional laws to ensure ecological balance (material sustenance) and justice (ethical relations) in the universe. The importance of ecological balance in Qur'anic discourse is further emphasised by Qur'an 55:5-9. It reads:

> The sun and the moon follow courses (exactly) computed; And the herbs and the trees - both (alike) bow in adoration. And the firmament has He raised high, and He has set up the balance (of Justice), In order that you may not transgress (due) balance. So establish weight with justice and fall not short in the balance. (Quran 55:5-9).[42]

This text portrays how that the firmament keeps its given height and the heavenly bodies, like sun and moon, also stick to their given orbits to sustain balance (rightful relativity) in the cosmos without fail.

That these cosmic bodies keep rightful relations is a warning-sign for humans everywhere 'not to transgress balance' (ethical relations) in all aspects of life. This includes 'how [people] *ought* to live and act'[43] ecologically, be it in the rural or urban areas. The phenomenon of cosmic and/or material balance or self-conservation in Islamic worldview corresponds with observations in cosmological and ecological sciences, except with the difference that observable self-conservation in nature is a doing of God. Arguing with evolutionary philosophy regarding the origin of the Earth, Swimme and Tucker refer to 'self-organisation dynamics' in nature as a process to maintain the delicate conditions of life on Earth. They see Earth as a creative community of beings that reorganises itself age after age so that it can perpetuate and even deepen its vibrant existence.[44] Ecologically the Qur'anic worldview suggests that the nonhuman creation, adhering to the *ạwamir* or natural laws, cannot cause perturbations of ecosystems if not interrupted by human beings. Rather, due to the divine *ạwamir* ordained by God, eco-balancing processes such as 'biogeochemical cycles'[45] exist in ecosystems. Nomanul

41 Fazlur Rahman, *Major Themes of the Qur'an*, (Minneapolis: Bibliotheca Islamica, 1980), 67, quoted in Özdemir, 'Toward an Understanding of Environmental Ethics from Qur'anic Perspective', 13.

42 Özdemir, 'Toward an Understanding of Environmental Ethics from Qur'anic Perspective', 13.

43 Curry, *Ecological Ethics: Introduction*, 28.

44 Brian Thomas Swimme and Mary Evelyn Tucker, *Journey of the Universe*, (New Haven and London: Yale University Press, 2011), 56.

45 William P. Cunningham and Barbara Woodworth Saigo, *Environmental Science - A Global Concern*, 6th ed. (New York: McGraw-Hill Inc., 2001), 595 define 'biogeochemical cycles' as 'movement of matter between or within ecosystems; caused by living organisms, geological forces, or chemical reactions. The cycling of nitrogen, carbon, sulfur, oxygen, phosphorus, and water are examples.'

Haq asserts that there is a due measure (*qādr*) to things, and a balance (*mīzān*) in the cosmos which humanity must not disturb but fulfil[46] looking unto the *amr* as the self-sustaining law of nature.[47]

In other words, since the 'natural law *is* never violated as things run their customary course, moral law *ought not* to be violated'[48] irrespective of habitation—in countryside or city.

Thus, it is arguable that these Qur'anic texts alone could be enough for developing an environmental ethic of respecting and preserving just and balanced ecological relations by all humanity.[49] The Muslim, even in urban cities, is thus expected to live in 'better harmony with his surroundings than any other type of man (sic)',[50] because of the strong theocological inferences in Islam. Yet, as Özdemir laments, Muslim jurists have lagged in contributing solutions to the intensifying environmental problems afflicting Islamic lands. It is because they lack (or are yet rediscovering and formulating) well-articulated Islamic environmental ethics and laws.[51] At the same time they reject those borrowed from the industrial West, seen as having been derived from alien beliefs.[52]

In Ghana, I noticed a similar attitude from my research into the motivation for and praxis of ecological ethics among Muslims in Sokpoe-Sogakɔ*f*e riverine ecological area in South Tɔŋu, Volta Region. Muslims participating in this study show no distinctively Islamic eco-ethics. Yet they vehemently oppose the primal religious eco-regulations and rituals, even though they share the same riverine ecosystem with the traditionalists and Christians. In their mind and explanations observing the eco-regulations of the indigenes would mean compromising the purity of their Islamic faith and fate. Allison Howell would have disagreed with this position of these Muslims. For her, as intimated earlier, responding to complex environmental challenges 'requires input from multiple sources to help interpret, and gain insight as to the best course we need to take.'[53]

The lack of practical Islamic ecological values, ethics and norms is not unique to Muslims in the urban zongo at Sogakɔ*f*e. Although the

46 Haq, 'Islam and Ecology: Toward Retrieval and Reconstruction,' 127.
47 Haq, 'Islam and Ecology: Toward Retrieval and Reconstruction, 137.
48 Haq, 'Islam and Ecology: Toward Retrieval and Reconstruction,' 132. (Italics in the original text).
49 Özdemir, 'Toward an Understanding of Environmental Ethics from Qur'anic Perspective', 13-14.
50 Özdemir, 'Toward an Understanding of Environmental Ethics from Qur'anic Perspective', 16.
51 Özdemir, 'Toward an Understanding of Environmental Ethics from Qur'anic Perspective', 28.
52 Llewellyn, 'The Basis for a Discipline of Islamic Environmental Law', 186.
53 Howell, 'African Spirituality and Christian Ministry':13.

Sogakɔ*f*e Moslems' life and living is highly determined by the teachings of Qur'an, yet they, like 'the majority of Muslims in the Islamic world', are unaware of the 'powerful and persuasive spiritual teachings of Islam about the natural world and the relations of human beings to it.'[54] Idrisu Ibrahim, son of the Zamarama *sarachi* of Sogakɔ*f*e urban zongo, laments how that the imams do not teach 'these things; they have only one message instead of addressing pertinent issues in our lives.'[55] Idrisu was virtually echoing the same feelings of Seyyed Hossein Nasr, writing on 'Islam and the Environmental Crisis,' who decried that even the '*ulamā*' (traditional guardians of Islamic knowledge in its various dimensions), do not teach or preach the Islamic views on the environment.'[56] He is emphatic that apart from governments being opposed to Islamic environmentalism, Islamic revivalists in urban cities do not emphasise environmental concerns.

Thus, there is lack of ecological awareness and preparation of the *ulamā* or traditional scholars who are custodians and preachers of Islam to the masses.[57] But it is also the case that the imams do not address environmental issues, because generally the exceedingly rich contributions that Islamic law and ethics have to offer in addressing environmental concerns in the Islamic world as a whole remain largely unarticulated, (not promoted) and unrealised.[58] Chief Imam Mahmud Abu Bakr of Sogakɔ*f*e urban zongo admitted with humility that it is not everything that 'I know because of the level of my education'.[59] Despite not being well informed ecologically, he and other Muslims in the study detest any ecological regulations not specifically attributable to Qur'an, and for that matter, Allah. All these notwithstanding, it is encouraging to know that Islamic eco-ethic is being reconstructed and practised 'today, at the dawn of the twenty-first century and in a time of worldwide environmental crisis.'[60] As Nasr assesses, efforts to raise serious Islamic ecological concerns among Muslims have been generally advanced in the Muslim world particularly since the last three decades (1980s).[61]

54 Seeyed Hossein Nasr, 'Islam, The Contemporary Islamic World, and the Environmental Crisis,' in Foltz, Denny, and Baharuddin, eds., *Islam and Ecology*, 85-105 (85).
55 Idrisu Ibrahim, interview at Sogakɔ*f*e, 23 April 2016.
56 Nasr, 'Islam, the Contemporary Islamic World, and the Environmental Crisis', 87.
57 Nasr, 'Islam, the Contemporary Islamic World, and the Environmental Crisis', 86.
58 Llewellyn, 'The Basis for a Discipline of Islamic Environmental Law', 186.
59 Imam Mahmud Abu Bakar, interview at Sogakɔ*f*e, 5 April 2016.
60 Özdemir, 'Toward an Understanding of Environmental Ethics from Qur'anic Perspective', 29.
61 Nasr, Islam, the Contemporary Islamic World, and the Environmental Crisis', 86.

Islamic Eco-Valuing, Ethical Principles and Praxis

In Islam, ecological values and ethics are together reconstructed from the Qur'an and Hadith as part of the legal and moral principles in the fiqh-law. Islam in its essence is a religion of law—the sharī'a, which literally means the guided Way to Life.[62] According to Nomanul Haq, 'Fiqh, or the Islamic science of jurisprudence, is a systematic and fully structured theoretical search for God's sharia, or Way [of life], that had to be gleaned from and constructed out of the myriad of adilla (here, legal indicators) provided for reflection throughout God's āyāt.'[63] Practically, fiqh includes axiological and ethical principles for understanding or determining the legal status of an act, 'a determination arrived at through the application of correct, though not epistemologically certain procedural rules.'[64]

The ultimate ethical and legal objective of fiqh is the welfare of God's creation on Earth and beyond, known as 'Masālih al-khalq: the universal common good'.[65] Other guiding principles derived from this include 'Masālih' and 'mafāsid', the law of benefits and detriments. This law operates through emphasis on maximising ecological benefits and minimising detriments; universal versus individual welfare, which encourages preserving eco-community interest over the individual interest; or the greater preferred to lesser ecological needs. The rest of the ethical principles include choosing the lesser of two ecological evils; the interest of the powerless over the powerful in eco-justice; and averting detriments by taking precaution to prevent ecological harm rather than insist on benefit.[66]

Islam tends to articulate practical environmental ethics more from the Hadith than the other āyāt of God. As Haq notes, in the Hadith there are several concerns expressed with a degree of urgency pertaining to the natural environment, its status, its relation to human life and, hence, what we may term environmental ethics.[67] Among many others, two pertinent creation care or practical ecological models in the Hadith include the institutions of himā and harām. They had a long history of pre-Islamic abuse of land exploitation and dispossession. But Muslims claim the

62 Llewellyn, 'The Basis for a Discipline of Islamic Environmental Law', 186.

63Haq, 'Islam and Ecology: Toward Retrieval and Reconstruction', 142.

64 Haq, 'Islam and Ecology: Toward Retrieval and Reconstruction', 142. (Italics in original). According to Llewellyn, 'The Basis for a Discipline of Islamic Environmental Law', 187, acts are evaluated with a five-tiered scale: an act may be obligatory, recommended, permitted, reprehended or prohibited. Thus, it provides prohibitive, injunctive and prescriptive ethics enforceable by individual and social conscience in addition to imperatives enforced by the courts.

65 Llewellyn, 'The Basis for a Discipline of Islamic Environmental Law', 193. (Italics in original text).

66 Llewellyn, 'The Basis for a Discipline of Islamic Environmental Law', 194-197.

67 Haq, 'Islam and Ecology: Toward Retrieval and Reconstruction', 141.

Prophet transformed them to become environmental and ethical policies. Himā literally means protected or forbidden place for natural life[68] and may be considered the Islamic equivalent of contemporary reserved forested land, natural parks and nature conservancy.[69] Four conditions determine declaring himā: need and fairness ensured by the community, ecological proportionality relative to total land area of community, resisting commercialised development and envisaged economic gains to be in interest of societal welfare.[70] Similarly, harām as sacred territory is often associated with wells, natural springs, rivers, and forests on waste land (mawāt).[71]

Undoubtedly it is not difficult to conclude that Islam as a religion has much, at least, theoretically, to provide great impulsion for Muslims in both rural and urban settings to care for creation. However, the situation in practice seems confronted with many challenges, especially due to urbanisation, which tend to close praxis of the faith regarding religious environmentalism.

The Pressure of Urbanisation on Practising Islamic Religious Ecology in Sogakɔ*f*e

Seyyed Hossein Nasr discusses many obstacles to practising Islamic environmental ethics globally, which I see as not only due to modernity, but also to urbanisation, particularly at Sogakɔ*f*e. For it is in urban spaces that modernity and its developmental impacts on socio-cultural and, hence, religious faith and life become more obvious. Nasr takes note of the strong influences on the Islamic world of science and technology. A characteristic of modern and city life in most non-Western cultures is Western value setting in socio-economic agenda with its associated consumer lifestyles that affect the environment. Nasr bemoans how that both modern and fundamental Muslims prefer to and promote Western science against Islamic science[72] and, hence, Islamic religious approaches to ecological praxis. Inferably, the effects of modernity on Islamic eco-praxis are greatly experiential through migration and urbanisation.[73]

For, city immigrants tend to lose their pre-migration rural ecological instincts, and while this may be due to many factors, the urgency of urban survival seems a highly significant factor.[74]

68 Haq, 'Islam and Ecology: Toward Retrieval and Reconstruction', 144.
69 Nasr, 'Islam, the Contemporary Islamic World, and the Environmental Crisis', 98.
70 Haq, 'Islam and Ecology: Toward Retrieval and Reconstruction', 144.
Haq, 'Islam and Ecology: Toward Retrieval and Reconstruction', 144.
72 Nasr, 'Islam, the Contemporary Islamic World, and the Environmental Crisis', 87-93.
73 Nasr, 'Islam, the Contemporary Islamic World, and the Environmental Crisis', 87-93.
74 Nasr, 'Islam, the Contemporary Islamic World, and the Environmental Crisis', 87-93.

That city-immigrant tends to lose eco-instincts in the struggle for survival is an opinion shared by Muslim respondents in the research in Sokpoe-Sogakɔ*f*e eco-area. The aim of the study was to determine impulsions and commitment of Muslims to Islamic environmentalism. Most of the respondents admitted that rural zongos are often environmentally friendlier than city or urban zongos. They explain that rural folks are more committed to eco-praxis. Hajia Fatti Sanni, objected to unfounded, generalised and blatant allegations of zongos being environmentally unhygienic, but did not deny the fact that some Muslims, particularly in metropolises, are, without doubt, truly guilty of the allegation. Comparing environmental cleanliness in village and city zongos she surmised,

> Rural zongo is better, because in truth some city zongos are really unclean. If the city Muslim community is said to be ecologically unhygienic, I shall not deny, because it is true.[75]

To emphasise her view, she describes inmates of a city zongo as *'gota huɖehuɖe, xɔme nyãnga'* (having an outwardly clean house, but which is messy within). She meant that while some city Muslims dress up neatly to depict being socially sophisticated, yet ecologically they live within unhygienic or messy surroundings. On her part, in a separate interview, Hajia Hawusatu Eleas based her agreement to the allegation on what she had personally witnessed in Nima, a suburb of Accra.

Other informants, such as the chief Imam Muhammad Abu Bakar, Zongo sarachi Abdullah Muhammad and Madame Adiza Garba, comparing their experiences in rural and urban zongos, are unequivocally not different from Hajia Fatti Sanni and Hawusatu Eleas. For the former not only are ecological unsanitary conditions relatively more pronounced in urban than rural zongos, but surprisingly, without doubt, most of these 'messy' city zongo dwellers were once from 'neat' village zongos. Asked why rural Muslims tend to drop their environmental ethos when immigrated to city *zongos* (urban Islamic eco-communities), respondents had almost the same perceptions in separate interviews. They see city immigrants having become environmentally passive and irresponsible due to modernity and busy-city-influenced lifestyles. The major contributing factors in their views include the site of the zongo, population size and heterogeneity, eco-character of inmates and what I call 'the zongo-effect' - a psycho-social self-understanding and attitude related to the meaning of the word 'zongo'.

75 Hajia Sanni Fatti, interview at Sogakɔ*f*e, 14 April 2016.

Sogakɔfe urban zongo, like others, was initially located at the outskirts of and entrance to the town. Answering the question why it appears that zongos are located at the outskirts of towns and villages the zongo sarachi of Sogakɔfe Abdullah Muhammad explains that usually the hosting traditional leaders release sites that are ecologically very challenging for habitation. Recalling his father, Muhammad Sokoto's experience in starting what has now become the current urban zongo at Sogakɔfe, sarachi Abdullah Muhammad decried that 'the indigenes or landlords released only the place they knew was not habitable, to the Hausa [Muslim].'[76] In a separate interview Abdulla's sister, 75 years-old Zinabu Muhammad, expressed the same view when she lamented that 'the Eʋe hesitate to coexist with the Hausa; so the Eʋe landlords usually provide land for zongo at outskirts of their towns to keep the Hausa at a distance.'[77] Thus to begin with, the Muslim sojourner may have location-related ecological problems, which discourage being grounded, and hence, de-motivate moral responsibility to care for the locality. Grounding or being rooted in a land of habitation is essential in motivating moral care for the area.[78] Sarachi Abdullah Muhammad did not identify the specific types of ecological challenges. However, he was certain the locations have often not been the place indigenes would naturally want to reside; yet the indigenes turn to describe zongos as ecologically non-sustaining.[79]

The challenges with environmental sustenance increase with population as more immigrants arrive and settle in the zongo, gradually turning Sogakɔfe into a semi-urban town. The contribution of increasing human population to ecological challenges lies in the dwindling inability of the Earth to produce food and absorb wastes - that is, drastic weakening of the nurturing and disposal functions of the ecosystem.[80] But at Sogakɔfe, the most significant influence of population increase on the religious environmental sustenance in the views of these Muslim participants lies in its cultural heterogeneity. In separate interviews the *sarachi* (zongo chief) of Sogakɔfe, Abdullah Muhammad and Imam Alhaji Ali answered questions on the social ecology, particularly, why zongos in villages appear relatively neater and more peaceful than those in urban places. They observed that an urban zongo is a conglomeration of people from different ethnic extractions. The immigrants converge only around the Islamic religious faith and worship, but not on ecological concerns. Each group comes with their home cultural mind-sets and

76 Abdullah Mahmud, interview at Sogakɔ*f*e zongo, 5th April 2016.
77 Zanibu Mahmud, interview at Sogakɔ*f*e zongo, 14th April 2016.
78 David Bookless, *Planetwise: Dare to Care for God's World*, (Nottingham, England: Inter-Varsity Press, 2008), 50.
79 Abdullah Mahmud, interview at Sogakɔ*f*e Zono, 5th April 2016.
80 Curry, *Ecological Ethics*, 20.

behave according to their cultural self-understanding, creating no room for cultural compromises, integration and mutual respect concerning the environment. Chief Abdullah Muhammad observed that 'They lack one mind about environmental harmony; and wherever this is the case, such a zongo cannot be neat or peaceful.'[81] With the Sogakɔfe urban zongo 'the lingual differences of the Hausa, Frafra, Dagati and Zamramra seem to heighten the non-compromising feelings and absence of mutual respect.'[82] No one cultural group wants to feel inferior and so subordinate to another. The result is development of passive attitudes toward community-level mobilisation of human and material resources to address ecological issues as moral responsibility. Chief Imam of Sogakɔfe, Mahmud Abu Bakar, compares and explains that

> Contrary to what pertains in the villages there is relatively passive ecological attitude and relational behaviours in city zongos. City dwellers live as if they are not owners of their habitation. Everyone does things freely at will. So individuals behave as if asking "why should I be the one to keep city corners clean?"[83]

In other words, because village zongos are relatively and significantly less populous and more homogenous, they are more culturally unified and cohesive than cosmopolitan zongos in caring for creation and sustaining harmonious and peaceful relations in the eco-community. Hajia Hawusatu Eleas who had witnessed such a situation in Nima, a suburb of Accra, believes that it results, among others, from the eco-cultural influences of different ethnic migrants, with cultures that lack good ecological ethos rather being more influential.[84]

The perceived passivity and moral irresponsibleness in caring for creation in a city zongo seems to have another causal dimension – 'the zongo-effect'. It is a possible psycho-social effect on Muslims' self-understanding of belonging to 'zongo'. According to the Sogakɔ*f*e zongo chief, Alhaji Abdullah Muhammad, the Hausa word 'zongo' connotes the idea of a resting place for Muslim strangers on a continuous migratory journey, particularly by trekking. This makes members of a zongo community tend to perceive themselves as strangers, mere visitors, passers-by who are not necessarily part of the town of settlement. Thus, irrespective of duration of stay they tend to distance themselves from the indigenes culturally by referring to them as '*dutɔwo*' (owners of the town); a people

81 Abdullah Muhammad, interview at Sogakɔ*f*e Zongo, 5th April 2016.
82 Imam Alhaji Ali, interview at Dabala Junction, 17th May 2016
83 Imam Mahmud Abu Bakar, interview at Sogakɔ*f*e Zono, 5th April 2016.
84 Hajia Hawusatu Eleas, interview at Sogakɔ*f*e, 12 April, 2016.

to whom the Muslims do not belong by their way of life.[85] Zongo as a place, in their mind, for non-domiciled but 'awaiting and passer-by strangers' does not promote ecological grounding in a land of habitation.

But lack of ecological grounding may not plausibly motivate for moral environmental responsibility, because 'as physical beings we need to be "earthed", "rooted", and "grounded" or we become "dislocated", "uprooted" and "displaced".'[86]

On her part Hajia Sanni Fatti from Sogakɔ*f*e urban zongo blamed apparent ecological unfriendliness in city zongos on lack of an adequate ecologically-minded upbringing as well as daily busyness for survival that leaves no time for personal and environmental care; and sheer laziness.[87] Explaining the meticulous attention that makes her surrounding more strikingly different from others in the same environ she had no doubts that not many Muslims, like other religious people in the urban area, devote time for environmental issues due to economic preoccupations. Economic needs for survival keep them busy and on the move from dawn to dusk. She seemed to echo Seyyed Hossein Nasr.[88] Perhaps busyness for survival limits ecological instincts and ethos by disconnecting the city Muslim and other dwellers from being conscious of daily ecological phenomena. David Bookless explains that 'those who live in large cities, with rapid transport from one man-made environment to another' are not only 'cut off from the cycles of the seasons and changes in the weather,' but also 'lose much of their connection with place.'[89] Yet being connected with a place is 'essential for our psychological and spiritual health as human beings;' as well as 'to have a healthy relationship with the land: the natural environment around us.'[90]

The Way Forward: Pragmatic Implications as Urbanisation of Sogakɔ*f*e Progresses

Muslims are enjoined by the Qur'an to rely on natural instinct to care for creation.[91] However, cosmopolitan life exerts a kind of pressure that makes the Muslim readily compromise his/her *fitra* - instinctual consciousness of our manifold but balanced relations with God and the rest of creation. Significant among the influences of urbanisation

85 Alhaji Abdullah Muhammad, (zongo sarachi), interview at Sogakɔ*f*e, 5 April, 2016.
86 Bookless, *Planetwise*, 50.
87 Hajia Sanni Fatti, interview at Sogakɔ*f*e, 14 April 2016.
88 Nasr, 'Islam, the Contemporary Islamic World, and the Environmental Crisis', 87-93.
89 Bookless, *Planetwise*, 50.
90 Bookless, *Planetwise*, 51.
91 Chishti, '*Fitra*: An Islamic Model for Humans and the Environment', 67.

on practical Islamic environmentalism is the urgency of urban survival through busyness, with little or no time for environmental concerns.[92]

With Muslims in the semi-urban town of Sogakɔ*f*e, I infer that the sense of being zongo dwellers and not belonging to the land of the indigenes, lack of cohesion and cooperation due to cultural heterogeneity, and resisting social inferiority in the urban zongo community constitute an additional urbanisation pressure that indicts an ecologically passive attitude and behaviour. Hajia Hawusatu Eleas lamented that it posed challenges for mobilising and depending on communal spirit in cleaning the environment compared with the situation in rural zongos.[93]

As urbanisation progresses with its consequences on Islamic environmental instinctual consciousness, Nasr's suggestions for environmental education to awaken the *fitra* as a way forward appeals.[94] He calls for both formal and informal ecological education at all levels and academic disciplines in Muslim eco-communities. This includes the *madāris* or traditional training institutes for religious leaders. In his view, the eco-educational curricula or sermons of *imāms* should have objectives and contents that can erase and replace the modern scientific and economic-centred worldview, which underpins sophistication and busyness of life in cities, with the Islamic worldview.[95] Muslim participants in my study at Sogakɔ*f*e hold similar views in agreeing that Islamic environmentalism needs to begin with children in *makaranta* (kindergarten schools), colleges and universities; and as well, it must be preached in *masalachi* (mosques).[96]

In my own contribution, I propose such environmental education to consider an African theocology curriculum, which draws on shared experiences from all three religions in the eco-area - Primal, Islamic and Christian.[97] For, with the progressive urbanisation, it is no longer only Muslims residing in and occupying the religious space in the Sogakɔ*f*e zongo, even though Muslims are the dominant.[98] Patrick Curry encourages resolving ecological challenges best by forging ideological alliances in pluralistic contexts when there is a real potential common ground on a particular issue - care of the environment.[99] Allison Howell

92 Nasr, 'Islam, the Contemporary Islamic World, and the Environmental Crisis', 87-93.
93 Hajia Hawusatu Elias, interview at Sogakɔ*f*e, 12 April, 2016.
94 Nasr, 'Islam, the Contemporary Islamic World, and the Environmental Crisis', 86.
95 Nasr, 'Islam, the Contemporary Islamic World, and the Environmental Crisis, 100-102.
96 Idrisu Ibrahim, interview at Sogakɔ*f*e, 23 April 2016.
97 Ebenezer Yaw Blasu, *African Theocology: Studies in African Religious Creation Care*, (Eugene, OR: Wipf and Stock Publishers, 2020), 234.
98 Adiza Garba, interview at Sogakɔ*f*e, 12 April 2016, narrates a blame-game incidence in which both non-Muslims and Muslims accused the children of each other for messing up a pathway in the zongo with faecal matter.
99 Curry, *Ecological Ethics*, 156.

holds a similar view.[100] African theocology curriculum is pragmatism of Adnan Amin's belief that despite a perceived gap between religions, all faiths share a common ethic based on harmony with nature and care for creation.[101] It celebrates plurality by raising to conscious awareness multiple perspectives regarding God, humanity and planet Earth. All three religions, being in the same riverine ecosystem of the Sokpoe-Sogakɔ*f*e ecological area, share similar holistic views of creation and the role of humans in its care. The only difference to be addressed is in religious ecological practices for sustainability. Consequently, as Allison Howell asserts, emphasis needs to be on meanings rather than forms (symbols and rituals)[102] in the religious eco-practices so as to converge on common approaches or learn from one another to care for the shared environment in the interest of all.

That a collaborative approach is possible is inferable in the responses of participants in the study. For instance, Alhaji Hama, in an interview, explained with great Islamic concern 'if there is any good in the indigenous environmental taboos, and for which even Muslims must obey, then it should be put forward purely as an administrative instrument or measure of the traditional chief, and not by the *trɔ̃nuɔ* (priest of the deity) or pastor.' He meant that Muslims in the ecological area will cooperate with other religious bodies in environmental sustenance efforts provided the ultimate ethical and legal objective of the environmental regulations are what Llewllyn calls 'Masālih al-khalq: *the universal common good*';[103] without any religious undertones.[104] Allison Howell implies that to deepen public awareness about environmental concerns it may be critical to communicate them from their social implications (rather than religious).[105]

It is also possible to learn a way forward from the Zimbabwean Earth keeping projects in response to their deforestation challenges; they innovated ecological rituals that enabled concerted actions based on African religious cosmologies and ethical regulations in the eco-area—primal and Christian.[106]

100 Howell, 'African Christianity and Christian Ministry: Discerning the times', 13.
101 Adnan Z. Amin, 'Preface to Islam and Ecology', xxxiv, echoes this realisation from the United Nations Environment Programme (UNEP), through its Interfaith Partnership for Environment (IPE).
102 Allison M. Howell, 'Researching Gospel and Culture: Tools of Research', *Journal of African Christian Thought*, Vol. 2, No. 2 (December 1999), 22-28 (22).
103 Llewellyn, 'The Basis for a Discipline of Islamic Environmental Law', 193. (Italics in original text).
104 Alhaji Hama, interview at Dabala, 25 May 2016.
105 Howell, 'African Spirituality and Christian Ministry', 14.
106 M. L. Daneel, 'Zimbawe's Earthkeepers -When Green Warriors Enter the Valley of Shadows', in Catherine M. Tucker, (ed.), *Nature, Science and Religion*, (USA: SAR Press, 2012), 202-207.

Conclusion

Theoretically Islam as a religion has some sources that provide impulsion for Muslims in both rural and urban settings to care for creation. These are Islamic theocentric worldviews, the concept of *mizan* (cosmic balance) and the theomorphic understanding of humanity as *khalifat* (vicegerent of God). The Qur'an enjoins Muslims to rely on *fitra* (natural instinct) to care for creation. But a cosmopolitan demand for survival with a busy lifestyle tends to compromise the urban Muslims' ecological *fitra*. For pragmatic purposes the paper analysed the interview responses of Muslim participants in Sogakɔfe semi-urban area to determine their moral impulsions or challenges for creation care in the face of urbanisation. Apart from the characteristic busy urban lifestyle the other factors advanced were 'zongo-mindedness' and cultural heterogeneity, resulting in non-cohesion and cooperation around environmental issues. As a way forward the paper proposes the African theocology curriculum for ecological education at all levels to awaken Islamic environmental *fitra*.

A Primal Vision: Holistic Mission and Care for All Creation

Joshua D. Settles

Abstract

Surveying the scene of African Christianity, one would be hard pressed to miss the nearly relentless focus on evangelism. Churches and parachurch groups regularly organise mission crusades, film shows, rural evangelism projects, and other activities. The urban landscape is littered with signboards and fliers promoting various church programmes, and advertising evangelistic events. The soundscape too resounds with the reverberations of open-air preaching, prayer meetings, and worship, all of which are done with the goal of proclamation the gospel of Jesus Christ. Yet one also may observe, amidst this crowded landscape, open gutters choked with refuse and rubbish of urban life, rivers and streams polluted with run-off from workshops, factories, and mining activities, and air thick with pollutants. These dual realities reveal a disconnection between what many Christians perceive as the evangelistic mandate of the Christian faith, and their understanding of the implications of that faith in relation to environmental concerns.

One of the abiding concerns of Allison Howell was environmental stewardship, which she saw as central to Christian mission. In this essay I explore, through the lens of the primal, the inner connection between holistic mission and creation care. I further explore, through an examination of relevant biblical texts, how the identity and mission of the church, when properly grounded in the primal vision, now fully realised in Christ, informs Christian engagement in environmental concerns.

Introduction

Surveying the Christian scene in Ghana, one would be hard pressed to miss the nearly relentless focus on evangelism and outreach. Churches and parachurch groups regularly organise mission crusades, film shows, rural evangelism projects, and other activities designed to proclaim, quite loudly at times, the good news about Jesus Christ. The landscape of Accra and other urban areas is, literally, littered with signboards, posters, and other religious paraphernalia promoting various church programmes, revivals and evangelistic events. It is not unusual to be accosted in the street by earnest church workers passing out fliers, or to see at major traffic intersections individuals holding placards declaring "Repent" or "Jesus died for you". The soundscape too resounds with the reverberations of open-air preaching, all-night prayer meetings, and vibrant worship services. The ubiquitous mini-buses (*tro-tro*) that ply the traffic-choked streets are not infrequently boarded by evangelistic preachers who turn their fellow passengers into captive, if mobile, congregations. If by chance these proclaimers are avoided, it is less difficult to avoid those who cluster at bus-stops and *tro-tro* stations, using bullhorns and microphones to loudly declare the Lordship of Jesus. All of this is done with the goal of proclaiming the gospel of Jesus Christ.

Yet, amidst this crowded land and soundscape, one also may observe open gutters choked with the refuse and rubbish of modern urban life, rivers and streams polluted with run-off from workshops, factories, and mining activities, and air thick with pollutants, vehicle exhaust, and smoke from burning trash and charcoal fires. The fliers and posters that serve to advertise evangelistic meetings are pasted over again and again until they are unceremoniously dumped into piles of rubbish. Well-heeled churchgoers drop empty water sachets, bottles, and other waste into already choked gutters, and the blaring sounds of Christian evangelistic activity adds one more layer to the cacophonous chaos of urban Ghana, adding stress and doing untold and unmeasured damage to the hearing. These realities reveal a profound disconnection between what many Christians perceive to be the evangelistic mandate of the Christian faith, and their understanding of the implications of that faith in relation to environmental concerns.

Though most Christians would likely agree that Christian faith impels some responsibility towards environmental stewardship, the depth of the disconnection, and the persistence of environmental despoliation despite high levels of Christian adherence indicates some deficiency in the forms of Christianity embraced by most Ghanaians. Allison Howell has noted that 'environmental issues and ecological crisis have tended to remain outside the domain of Christian ministry.'[1] The belief that evangelism is mostly about saving souls has meant that 'Christians have largely

accepted a position in which creation is divorced from Christian ministry and the business of the church.'[2] I contend that this is due, at least in part, to the suppression of the underlying primal vision of the inner connection between Christian mission and creation care, between the redemption of humanity portended by the gospel, and the reconciliation of all things. In this essay, using the primal imagination as a hermeneutical key, I explore these inner connections and, through an examination of relevant biblical texts, demonstrate how the identity and mission of the church, when properly grounded in a primal vision, fully realised in Christ, informs Christian engagement in environmental concerns.

A Primal Vision

Before going further, I wish to clarify what I mean by the term "primal", a term which, though well-known and accepted in some circles, remains unknown by some and contested by others.[3] Suffice it to say that it does not refer to a stage within an evolutionary scheme of hierarchical development of religions, nor is it a substitute for the term *primitive*, in the sense of simplistic or unsophisticated. It rather refers to the 'universal, basic elements of human understanding of the Transcendent and the world'[4], a fundamentally religious or spiritual perspective on reality that is integrated, holistic, and relational. Of this primal sense of interconnectedness, John V. Taylor insightfully observed:

1 Allison Howell, 'African Spirituality and Christian Ministry: "Discerning the Signs of the Times" in our Environment and Community', *Journal of African Christian Thought*, Vol. 20, No. 1 (June 2017), 12-23 (16-17).
2 Howell, 'African Spirituality and Christian Ministry', 18.
3 In his essay, 'The Classification "Primal Religions" as a Non-Empirical Christian Theological Construct', James Cox sets forth the claim that "primal religion" as a term describing a category of religious phenomenon within the academic study of religion cannot be sustained using empirical evidence but is an artificial 'construct employed in Christian theologies of contextualization', and consequently, 'should be removed from the academic study of religion and placed within theology'. James L. Cox, 'The Classification "Primal Religions" as a Non-Empirical Christian Theological Construct', *Studies in World Christianity*, Vol. 2, Pt. 1, 1996, 55-76 (56). While it is true that the term is used theologically by certain Christian scholars, notably Andrew Walls and Kwame Bediako, it is unclear that it can *only* be used in that way. Further, even as he resists it, Cox seems to fall prey to discredited evolutionary theories for he can only conceive of "primal religion" as representing the first in a linear series, moving from lower to greater levels of development, rather than as the core of concentric circles around which all other religious systems develop, with enduring elements that may be taken up into other systems of thought, religious and otherwise, and even become subconscious systems.
4 Gillian Bediako, 'Primal Religion and Christian Faith: Antagonists or soul-mates?' Journal of African Christian Thought, Vol. 3, No. 1 (June 2000), 12-16 (12).

> Not only is there less separation between subject and object, between self and not-self, but fundamentally all things share the same nature and the same interaction upon one another… No distinction can be made between sacred and secular, between natural and supernatural, for Nature, Man and the Unseen are inseparably involved in one another in a total community.[5]

The primal sense of interconnection and holism of which Taylor writes is not, as some might imagine, a feature only of some "primitive" tribal group, or a romantic, quasi-mystical relic of animistic primitivism. No, Taylor's commentary would not be out of place were it to have been written about Christianity, the faith long thought to be the furthest removed from primitive animistic traditions on an ascending scale of religion, 'the highest and most civilised of the monotheistic faiths'.[6] It happens that Christianity and the various primal religious traditions of the world 'have a unique phenomenological affinity',[7] an affinity that emerges not only in the historical record, but in the pages of the Christian scriptures, both Old and New Testament.

There are a number of features that characterise primal religious faith,[8] but 'the primal conception of the universe as a unified cosmic system, essentially spiritual'[9] can be considered the cornerstone of what is termed the primal imagination. Since all of reality is conceived of as spiritual, or as having a spiritual basis, and since the physical acts as a sacrament for the spiritual, there is no firm demarcation between the realms of nature, and the realm of spirit. They are mutual interpenetrating and interconnected realities. Thus, within primal thought there is a 'profound emphasis on the transcendent source of true life and practical salvation',[10] and this true life is not solely, or even primarily, spiritual. Salvation within such a primal vision is holistic and relational and necessarily extends to all facets of human life: physical, mental, emotional, spiritual, and the immediate concern of this essay, environmental. It is unsurprising then that within primal systems, the environment is used, 'realistically and unsentimentally but with profound respect and reverence and without exploitation'.[11] The spirituality of primal peoples is 'characterised by an attitude of reverence for aspects of nature considered sacred'.[12]

5 John V. Taylor, The Primal Vision: Christian Presence amid African Religion, London: SCM Press, 1963, p. 64.
6 Bediako, 'Primal Religion and Christian Faith', 12.
7 Bediako, 'Primal Religion and Christian Faith', 4.
8 See Harold Turner, 'The primal religions of the world and their study', in V. Hayes (ed.), *Australian Essays in World Religions* (Bedford Park: Australian Association for the Study of Religions, 1977), 27-37., for an analysis of six features that characterise the primal.
9 Kwame Bediako, *Christianity in Africa: The Renewal of Non-Western Religion* (Akropong, Ghana: Regnum Africa, 2014), 96.
10 Turner, 'Primal Religions', 32.
11 Turner, 'Primal Religions', 30.
12 Howell, 'African Spirituality and Christian Ministry', 15.

To disrupt, damage, or degrade the natural environment is to risk causing a rift in the interlocking networks of spiritual relationships necessary for the 'true life of man',[13] and therefore 'taboos and rituals [exist] to preserve and maintain the earth on which humans [live]'.[14]

In Christian thought, engagement with the environment is usually discussed in terms of stewardship, with God as owner and human beings as managers.[15] I do not wish to disparage or diminish the legitimacy and potency of this concept in relation to environmental concerns; steward is a scriptural term used by Christ himself, and the sense of responsibility and accountability arising from this concept are important. Nevertheless, stewardship language tends to reduce creation to a resource, with humans 'standing over and against [it], wielding knowledge over it in order to extract a harvestable product'.[16] Not only does the term lend a commodifying and even mechanistic tenor to issues of environmental care, but it also tends to obscure the relational aspects of creation and redemption that are found in the scriptures. Therefore, I wish to press beyond stewardship language to engage the primal vision that underlies and vivifies scripture itself. It is this primal vision of creation and of holistic salvation that enables a proper ethic of environmental care. I begin with the creation accounts in Genesis, which lay the foundation for Christian concern for the environment, and then examine a portion of Colossians that lays out a primal vision of holistic salvation as a basis for holistic Christian mission and creation care.

A Primal Vision of Creation

The two stories of creation have different emphases yet are united in their underlying primal sense of relationship at the heart of the created order. The first account, Genesis 1.1 – 2.4, opens with intimations of Trinitarian presence; the Divine Spirit broods over the primeval waters, followed by a Divine Word that initiates the creative process in a series of distinct but interrelated movements. After each movement of creation, God declares it "good", before moving on to speaking another generative word. On the fifth day, a new element emerges in the divine speech. The Divine Word not only creates and declares "good" but blesses and commands the creatures that he makes. This suggests that these creatures are of a

13 Turner, 'Primal Religions', 31.
14 Howell, 'African Spirituality and Christian Ministry', 15.
15 For example, in scripture land is described as God's possession (see Lev 25.23, Ps. 24.1, 50.12), with human beings as residents with only temporary rights of possession and use (see Lev 25.23).
16 Matthew Philipp Whelan, 'Prefiguring the Salvation of the World: The Eucharist and Agriculture' in Philip Rossi (ed.), *God, Grace, and Creation*, The Annual Publication of the College Theological Society, Vol. 55, (2009), Maryknoll, NY: Orbis Books, 2010), 187 – 200 (190-91).

different kind than those which came before. The creatures that inhabit the sky and the waters (v. 22) are of a kind that can receive blessing, and respond to Divine command, words that suggest relationality. The blessing and the command, "be fruitful and increase",[17] is repeated the following day, this time to the land creatures and to the Man *(adam)* "made in [his] image, in [his] likeness", but the command is modified for *adam* by being broadened to include elements of dominion over other creatures (v. 28). The instructions to *adam* and the other creatures – "everything that has the breath of life in it" – includes provision for their physical sustenance. Though humanity is clearly placed in a privileged position vis-à-vis the rest of creation, it is evident also that creation is a complex web of relationships of which human beings are but a part. There are relationships that exist prior to, and independent of, mankind. Divine provision extends not only to *adam* made "in the image of God" (v. 27), but to the animals as well. They receive from God their own word of blessing and command, independent of what humans receive. Here emerges the primal sense of 'man akin to nature... and brother to the plants and animals which have their own spiritual existences and place in the universe'.[18] Humankind is created 'in an interconnected world based on relationships and community, in which significant roles of land, water and air are established'.[19] It is this fundamentally relational creation that God declares "very good" (v. 31).

The second rendering of creation, Genesis 2.5 – 2.25, is the first of ten "accounts" in Genesis that open with formulaic phrase *'ēlleh tôlᵉdôṯ* (these are the generations/story of) but is the only one in which a personal name does not appear. Personhood is therefore not imputed to the heavens and the earth – a clear resistance to the 'tendency to divinize or personalise the natural order, or to imbue it with any power independent of its personal creator'[20] evident in the naturalistic polytheism that characterised the religious life of the ancient Near East. Nonetheless, the "story" of the heavens and the earth amplifies and extends the relational themes evident in the first story. The Man, now disambiguated from the Woman, is introduced as a creature embedded from the outset in relationships. He is first and foremost formed in relationship with God who moulds and breathes life into him (v. 7). He is, quite literally, a man

17 Unless otherwise noted, all scripture taken from the Holy Bible, New International Version, NIV 2011.
18 Turner, 'Primal Religions', 30.
19 Howell, 'African Spirituality and Christian Ministry', 19.
20 Christopher J.H. Wright, 'The Earth is the Lord's: Biblical Foundations for Global Ecological Ethics and Mission', in Noah Toly and Daniel Block (eds.), *Keepings God's Earth: The Global Environment in Biblical Perspective*, Downers Grove, Il: InterVarsity Press, 2010, 216-241 (220).

of the soil, intimately related to the ground itself, from which he is formed (as are the animals in v. 19). He is related to the environment that he is instructed to work and care for (v.15). He exists in relationship with the animal creation that he names (v. 20), and finally with the woman, the "one-flesh" suitable helper with whom he is to enjoy unashamed relationship (v. 24-25).[21] The idea of dominion introduced in chapter 1 is here clarified as husbandry – the careful tending of the relationships in creation. Chapter 2 closes with a picture of a wholly (and holy) good network of relationships between humanity, God, animals, and the physical world.

Broken Creation

Chapters 3 and 4 of the "story" of the heavens and the earth record the beginnings of the collapse of this wholly good creation, a collapse precipitated by the transgression of God's restriction on the Tree of the Knowledge of Good and Evil (3. 6-7), by the Man and Woman. It is significant that the restriction imposed by God was environmental in nature; it is what might be called a nature taboo, not unlike many that may be observed amongst primal peoples. The promised consequence of this violation was certain death (2.17), yet it is not immediately obvious that death was the result of the Man and Woman's transgression. According to Genesis 5.5, Adam lived a total of 930 years, far longer than almost anyone else in the biblical record. Whatever one makes of this calculation of his age, it is apparent that his death was not immediate, nor even proximate to the transgression itself! His death was not instant, yet when considered from the primal perspective, it does seem to have become inevitable.

The inevitability of death becomes apparent when one considers the collapse of the good creation from a primal perspective. The primal vision of life is not solely or even primarily "spiritual" in the narrow sense but emerges from within a matrix of relationship. Thus, the breakdown of the network of sustaining, wholly (holy) good relationships that existed prior to human disobedience signals the end of life itself as human beings are estranged from the sources of life, both spiritual and material. Relationship between God and humankind (v. 10), between man and woman (v. 16), and between humans and the environment (v. 17-18) are all broken. Animal skins provide coverings for the now

21 Howell has delineated a similar schema of relationships operating within creation, one of which is what she terms 'the emotional or psychological relationship with oneself' based on Genesis 2.25. Howell, 'African Spirituality and Christian Ministry', 19.

shamed Adam and Eve (v. 21), and access to the Tree of Life is barred to them forever. Chapter 4 records the first murder, and the land, already cursed in chapter 3.17, is defiled further through bloodshed. The "story" of the heavens and earth sees the further destruction of human relationships and increasing alienation from creation (v.12) culminating in the vengeful boasts of Lamech to his two wives, the one-flesh union of man and woman in marriage now marred beyond recognition by human sin.

The death that ensued from humanity's disobedience, and in particular the estrangement from the physical creation, is evidence that 'as embodied creatures, no gift is more central to our flourishing than the land and its fruits'.[22] Once the relationship with the physical creation is broken, the earth becomes the site of "painful toil" for human beings that yields "thorns and thistles" (3.17-18) at best, or nothing at all at worst (4.12).

Yet, it is not only humans that suffer from this. Douglas Moo reminds us that the prophetic text of Isaiah 24 'describes the effects of sin in cosmic terms: "the heavens languish with the earth" (v. 4), "a curse consumes the earth" (v. 6)',[23] all of which are the result of human sin and rebellion. Hosea too links human disobedience with environmental destruction:

> There is no faithfulness, no love, no acknowledgment of God in the land. There is only cursing, lying and murder, stealing and adultery; they break all bounds, and bloodshed follows bloodshed. Because of this *the land dries up* and all who live in it waste away; *the beasts of the field, the birds in the sky and the fish in the sea are swept away*. (Hosea 4.1b-3)

Perhaps most critically, Paul states in Romans 8 that creation is itself in bondage to decay, and groans in painful anticipation of its redemption (Romans 8.19-22). The futility into which creation has fallen is the result of human action; 'human sin has led to some kind of change in the nature of the cosmos itself'.[24] Yet Paul does not only point backwards to the negative consequences of the Fall on the environment but points forward as well. As Howell notes, 'God does not, however, leave creation in this disrupted state, for the gospel is a message of hope, restoration and renewal'.[25] This brings me to the next phase of my discussion.

---

22 Whelan, 'Prefiguring the Salvation of the World', 193.
23 Douglas J. Moo, 'Eschatology and Environmental Ethics: On the Importance of Biblical Theology to Creation Care' in Toly and Block, *Keepings God's Earth*, 23-43(30).
24 Moo, 'Eschatology and Environmental Ethics', 29.
25 Howell, 'African Spirituality and Christian Ministry', 19.

The Primal Vision for Holistic Salvation and the Restoration of all things

Given the disastrous consequences of the Fall for humanity and for the created order as a whole, a gospel that is to be understood truly as good news must address not only the disruption of the Divine-human relationship, but also the entire network of wholly (holy) good relationships into which humanity is embedded. Amidst evidence of a broken world characterised by alienation within man, in man's relationship with others, in and within man's relationship to his environment, and ultimately in relationship to God himself, Paul's address to the Colossian church, particularly 1.13-20, is as relevant now as then. In it, the primal vision of holism comes to the fore, for Paul does not limit the scope of Jesus' work to the reconciliation of humanity to its Creator. Paul grounds the identity and mission of the church in a realised eschatological understanding of the cosmic regeneration effected by Jesus' death on the cross and resurrection.

Paul begins his letter as he customarily does with greetings and prayers for the recipients. Although it is clear from 2.1 that the Colossian Christians have no personal experience of Paul, he does not provide any defence of his apostleship as he does in the letters to Corinth and Galatia which suggests that his apostolic authority was not in question among the Colossians.[26] Colossians 1.13-20 lies at the transition point between the opening greetings and prayer, and the body of the letter. The Father, towards whom Paul's prayer of thanksgiving has been addressed, has rescued believers from the kingdom of darkness and translated them into the kingdom of the Son of his love. Already one can perceive the relational emphasis of the salvific enterprise as described by Paul, as Father and Son within the Godhead are both mentioned. Paul's description of this divine deliverance resounds with apocalyptic hope reminiscent of Galatians 1:4 where Jesus is said to deliver, "from this present evil age." The cosmic significance of this act becomes clearer later in the Colossians passage. Verses 13-14 shift the focus from the action of the Father to Christ, in whom redemption is said to be located. This redemption comes through Christ's blood and is specifically defined as the forgiveness of sins. This is not, however, the sum total of what redemption entails, for in verses 15-20, Paul continues with a hymn-like[27]

26 Paul Achtemeier, Joel Green and Marianne Thompson, *Introducing the New Testament: its literature and theology*, (Grand Rapids, MI.: William Eerdmans Publishing Co., 2001), 408.

27 There is some uncertainty about whether Paul in 1.15-20 used an existing Christian hymn or wrote it for the occasion. Peter T. O'Brien, "Colossians" in *New Bible Commentary: 21st Century Edition* 4th ed., ed. D.A Carson, R.T. France, J.A. Motyer, and G.J. Wentham (Downers Grove, Illinois: InterVarsity Press, 1994), 1266.

revelation of Christ, exalting him as the principal agent of creation, as preeminent within the new creation, and as the foundation of cosmic reconciliation.

The apocalyptic hope expressed in 1:13-14 is more fully unpacked in the ensuing verses and begins to answer the claims of the competing Colossian philosophy against which Paul was presumably writing.[28] Apocalyptic thought saw that 'the only way redemption [of the current evil age] could occur would be by means of a new creation, in which the very structures of reality would be altered and a new reality introduced.'[29] Paul sees this new creation realised, "in his dear Son" (1.13) that is, in Christ Jesus.[30] That the new creation is located in Christ is a significant key to understanding Paul's vision of cosmic renewal. In this view, believers, though the "forgiveness of sins" (1:14), become a part of all that has been redeemed at the cost of Christ's blood and are re-embedded into the fabric of relationships torn apart by the Fall.

Christ is described in the first portion of Paul's hymn as the principal agent of creation. The Son is the both the image of the invisible God, *and* the firstborn of creation. The term "firstborn" is not an indication that Christ is the first created being, but rather an indication of his sovereignty of rank[31] and is a likely reference to Psalm 89. The use of the term indicates that all of creation stands in a kind of familial relationship with God. All things in and of creation, including the land itself and the threatening powers are made by and for him (1.16), are sustained by him (1.17), and are intended to exist in wholly (holy) good relationship with him and with each other. The description recalls Genesis 1.6-9 where sky and land are demarcated by God. The position of the Son vis-à-vis the creation and the powers is one of supremacy enjoined by his identity as the agent of creation and of the preservation of creation. It is noteworthy that Christ's supremacy is acknowledged first in terms of his relationship with the non-human creation, including both natural and supernatural elements, as well as mirroring the creational sequence of Genesis 1. This does not diminish humankind but places him in context of all creation and therefore affirms the totality of relationships within the created order, all of which cohere in Christ.

---

28 The precise nature of the false teaching in Colossae remains unresolved, yet it is clear that in whatever case, the Colossians were confronted with a system that involved more than trust in Christ for protection against powerful supernatural forces. Achtemeier, *Introducing the New Testament*, 414.

29 Achtemeier, *Introducing the New Testament*, 295.

30 Paul places significant emphasis here on a "realised eschatology" causing some to question genuine Pauline authorship, as this is not as clearly in focus in other undisputed letters. O'Brien notes that Pauline emphasis on the "already" rather than the "not yet" of salvation may be occasioned by the exact nature of the false teaching Paul is writing to counter. P.T. O'Brien, "Letter to the Colossians," in *IVP Dictionary of the New Testament*, ed. Daniel G. Reid (Downers Grove, Illinois: InterVarsity Press, 2004), 214.

31 Clinton Arnold, *The Colossian Syncretism: The Interface between Christianity and Folk Belief at Colossae*, (Grand Rapids, MI.: Baker Books, 1996), 256.

Verse 18 marks an inflection point in the passage where Christ's pre-eminence within the new creation comes into view. Specifically, Christ, the lord and agent of the original creation, is also lord over the community of the new creation, the church. The human dimension of the new order is more evident than in the previous section as the church, described metaphorically as "the body", is a human community. Christ is the head of this body and as head, 'provides leadership and direction for his people,' and 'is the source of the church's life energy for its growth to maturity.'[32] That the church is part of the new reality brought into being by Christ's blood is indicated by Christ's own position as the "firstborn" from the dead; Christ through his resurrection becomes the pre-eminent founder of a new community as, 'his own resurrection is the harbinger of the great resurrection-harvest of his people.'[33] The resurrection decisively demonstrates the inauguration of the apocalyptic era since the defeat of death signals the end of the current evil age and is the beginning of a new era. In Christ, "all the fullness of God was pleased to dwell" (1:19) so that the church, through participation in the resurrected life of Christ, has already entered this new reality.

That the fullness of God was pleased to dwell in Christ makes Christ the foundation of cosmic reconciliation, for it is through him that God has worked to reconcile all things to himself. Paul is careful to communicate the full extent of Christ's reconciliatory work by noting that the "all things" refers to both things in earth and heaven. 'If "all things," … have to be reconciled to God through him, it follows that all things have been estranged from their Creator,'[34] something clearly seen when the Genesis accounts are read in proper perspective. Creation itself has been "subjected to futility," (Romans 8:20) and therefore must also be included in the scope of regeneration envisioned by Paul. So then both in creation and in reconciliation, Christ's work extends beyond humanity to include all of the created order. Reconciliation is expressed as "making peace"; the totality of relationships that have been broken and distorted since creation are brought back into the harmonious order in which they were intended to function. The primal sense of holistic salvation emerges clearly here, for the salvific enterprise is not, in fact limited to "spirituality" narrowly conceived, nor is it exclusively about human beings. The reconciliation accomplished by and through the cross is much broader than individualised responses to a gospel presentation.

---

32 Arnold, *The Colossian Syncretism*, 259.
33 F.F. Bruce, *The Epistles to the Colossians to Philemon and to the Ephesians*, (Grand Rapids, MI.: William Eerdmans Publishing Co., 1984), 71.
34 Bruce, *The Epistles*, 74.

The primal sense of interpenetration of the physical and non-physical /spiritual realms means that salvation is both spiritual *and* physical, individual *and* corporate, and encompasses both human *and* non-human creation.

The Reconciled and Reconciling Community in Creation

The thrust of Paul's message is that God through Christ has inaugurated a new, or rather a renewed cosmic order; the eschatological longings of Jewish apocalyptic tradition is realised now in and through Christ. The community of the church therefore, as the embodiment of Christ, the second Adam, who is both instrument of creation and firstborn of the new creation, shares in the cosmic reconciliation effected by the blood of the cross. The church likewise participates in the reconciling mission of Christ; a mission which is much broader than the rescue of individuals from condemnation in hell but extends to the repair of the entire web of relationships in, with, and throughout creation. Understood in this way then, the proclamation of Christ as Lord for the church means the declaration that, 'the whole drama that unfolds from creation to consummation… has its climactic center in Jesus Christ. The whole of human history and all of nature stand under God's signature in Christ.'[35] Though the reconciliation and salvation of creation is not centred entirely on the Divine / human relationship, it is clear from the context that the new community of the church, spoken of in the previous verse, is in fact the community of those who have been reconciled to God and who are joined with Christ in the mission of reconciliation. It is an affirmation, borne of the primal imagination, that 'God and man [are] in an abiding relationship which is the divine destiny of humankind.'[36] This abiding relationship encompasses the full array of relationships within creation, and the work of reconciliation is therefore cosmic in scope. Adam is, as it were, restored to his position as husband; his responsibility – to dress and keep the relationships in and with all of creation. Yet this second is more explicitly relational and communal than the first, for here it is a community – the church, people brought into relationship with one another in consequence of their relationship with God through Christ – that is named. This raises intriguing possibilities for the framework of the church's mission particularly in relation to environmental concerns.

35 Bernard Anderson, *From Creation to New Creation*, (Minneapolis: Fortress Press, 1994), 18.
36 Bediako, *Christianity in Africa*, 101.

Firstly, the declaration of Christ's lordship over all creation including the threatening powers of Col 1.16 means that the redeemed community exists in part to remind the world that evil and alienation, whether personal or institutional, are not the final word. Indeed, the church's very identity as a reconciled and reconciling community is a witness against the disruption of relationship that gives rise to such evils in the first place. The church not only acts to deliver individuals from the particular effects of evil that he or she may experience, but also works to address systemic and institutional evils that assail him or her, as well as the broken web of social relationships in which the person lives. For example, the deliverance ministries which are so widespread in the African context, can be broadened to include working against evil systems, addressing familial and social dysfunction, and providing access to mental health resources where appropriate. Additionally, the church may institute programs to promote ethical practices or to address issues of corruption within society.

Secondly, the entire church with Christ as her head must understand its' identity as the community of God's reconciling mission – a fundamentally relational, and not programmatic or organisational, identity. Consequently, the church does not see "missions" as a church program or as the work of certain people within the church, but as the expression of the life of the community. Evangelism becomes an invitation to "be reconciled to God", that is, to enter a restored network of relationships and to participate in the reconciling mission of God as part of God's reconciling community. Relationality is thus placed at the heart of evangelism in a way that resonates with the primal sense of interconnectedness and wholeness. The scope of evangelism is broadened to include more of what has been termed social concerns, as relational wholeness (holiness) is brought to the centre. A person may be invited to participation in the life of the reconciled community and even share in her work even before making a full commitment to Christ. And perhaps most significantly, the whole network of relationship of which a person is part is taken into account in any evangelistic endeavour, including relationship with family, with the broader community, and with the creation itself.

Finally, and of especial concern in relation to the theme of this paper, the church must develop an understanding of itself as part of the community of creation, which includes the non-human environment, and accordingly must do her work in harmony with her physical environment. Everything from land management policy, the use of material in construction, the environmental impact of construction of church facilities, and the cleanliness of her grounds all become seen as means of expressing the reconciling mission of Christ. The church may for example, consider how to promote a non-commodity-based view of land in her preaching and teaching ministries, or ways to advocate for regenerative land use policies in society, or even the purchase of land as a means of environmental preservation in situations where creation is being despoiled and exploited. The increasingly widespread practice of clearing and cementing whole plots of land when building new structures, an environmentally unsound and aesthetically unpleasing practice, may be resisted by churches who when building choose to incorporate natural elements in the design of their buildings and grounds, reserving green space, and shaded areas for prayer, reflection, or simply rest. If the grounds of churches were preserved as a garden spot of beauty and peace amidst the chaos of contemporary urban African life, it would present a silent but potent witness to the world of the holistic nature of salvation.

Conclusion

One of the abiding concerns of Allison Howell has been a holistic response to the broken reality of a world marred by human sin. She expressed this concern in her teaching and modelled it in her practice of life so that the mission proclamation in which she believed was one of both word and deed. Examples of this are found in the *Care for All Creation* calendars she commissioned as a memorial of thanksgiving for God's providence and care in restoring her to physical health after a frightful illness, and in her sponsorship of a community park, Allison's Green, in the community in which she lived. It would be easy to celebrate these "good works" and simultaneously diminish them as a kind of Christian do-gooder-ism unless one understands the deeply primal apprehension of reality that underlie them. In the primal vision, salvation is not about saving souls to go to heaven, but about the repair and restoration of relationships throughout all the created order and is thus inherently holistic in its scope. Christian mission is therefore about the people of God inviting others to step into this restorative process inaugurated in the cross and ultimately fulfilled in Christ. It is about holistic care for *all* creation – human and non-human – so that *all* might be reconciled to him.

African Christianity and the Global Ecological Crisis: An Agenda for Sensitization

Kehinde Olabimtan

Abstract

From the decade of political independence, contemporary study of African Christianity has been exploring the nature and the sociological factors that are shaping the mutation of Christianity on the African continent. In the age of global ecological stress, when religious leaders are being encouraged to contribute to the search for the solution to the crisis by shaping the attitudes of their followers towards the environment, African Christian educators and theologians have a worthy agenda to pursue. Unlike the spontaneous and intuitive reaction to perceived existential threats that informed the indigenization of the faith in the past, the present reality of ecological crisis is yet to dawn on African Christian communities. Theological educators and scholars of Africa's New Religious Movements (NRMs) need to go from trailing the movements to shaping their ecological sensibilities. Happily, Africa's pre-Christian past is at home with this, and Christian movements in the West are already modelling possibilities by rereading the Scriptures and reconfiguring classical doctrines of the Spirit, salvation, and the end in the light of the need of the moment. Much more, individuals and groups are reaching out through denominational and ecumenical advocacies, developing context-sensitive resources for Christian worship and discipleship, and shaping curriculums for theological formation of candidates for ministry. By addressing issues that are germane to their ecological environment, African Christians can stand in solidarity with the rest of humanity in ensuring "our common future" in a world God loved.

Keywords: creation, ecology, culture, development and ethics

Introduction

This paper is my fitting tribute to Professor Allison Howell. I had originally intended to write along my familiar path of African mission history, but I decided to shelve that idea for two reasons. First, my current learning in eco-theology is opening-up for me a new vista in contemporary missiological concern, and that is the ecological crisis now plaguing our planet. This is where my thought is presently active, and it is only natural to continue to plumb the depth of this hyphenated study in continuing reflections. The second reason is because I have been privileged to do a missiological study of the environment under the tutelage of Professor Howell during her March 2011 biennial seminar at the Overseas Ministries Study Center (OMSC), New Haven, Connecticut, in the United States. That experience gave me my first inkling that my past training in the built environment might still be useful for my fledgling academic theology.

Professor Howell further gave me a boost when she invited me, the following year and in 2015, to come alongside to teach the course "Studies in Transformational, Integral and Sustainable Development" at Akrofi-Christaller Institute of Theology, Mission and Culture (ACI) in Akropong-Akuapem, Ghana. Two things happened on the two occasions I participated in that experience with her. I was exposed to the history and rudiments of global environmental concerns, especially climate change and poverty. Then I learned in her presentations the connection between culture and ecology. I did not know at the time that I would pursue a degree program in eco-theology, but time proved that Providence was at work in this tutelage. For four years now, I have been learning to steady my feet on the road she set me; and in my recent exploration of ecological education in North American theological institutions, I have come to appreciate how far-sighted Professor Howell's initiative at ACI was for mission studies in West Africa.

At the time I was learning to understand the connections between theology, culture, and the environment, I was invited in September 2012 to teach the course Africa religion in the newly established Department of Religious Studies of a Christian university in southwest Nigeria. The university is sited on the old grounds of a mission-founded teachers' college. Southwest Nigeria is a Yoruba country, and it lies in the tropical rainforest that is rich in diversity of flora and fauna. However, the semi-urban population of the university town, like other settlements in the country, has taken a bite of the modernist pie of commodification of nature. With amazement, I watched loggers enter the school and drove deep into its drying river valley to fell the remaining few trees there, cart them away for commercial use through the university gate unchallenged. Evidently, it was considered a normal activity.

As a school still *developing* physically, I saw the same process at work in the official infrastructural expansion. Grounds were cleared without reference to the forestry department of the Faculty of Agriculture. There was no input from that department in the physical planning and conservation of the environmental resources of the institution. An attempt to publish a code of ethics for the university community, which contained provisions on the harvesting of plants and game for food and medicine, was coolly rebuffed. Officially and unofficially, the emerging learning environment was daily shorn of its lungs in what the catholic theologian Leonardo Boff calls ecocide.[1]

Still raising my gaze, I saw the same process at work as I shuttled weekly the road between Lagos and the university town, via Ibadan. Christian religious campsites were emerging steadily, and they began with intense clearance of new sites. Ogere, a location along the Lagos-Ibadan expressway, remains till date the site for loading into containers for shipment abroad logs harvested from around the Ijebu country. The same rape of nature can be seen at strategic locations along major routes across the country where sellers trade in roasted and fresh games indiscriminately harvested from the forest as "bush meat".

The ongoing quiet but steady rape is not peculiar to southwest Nigeria. It can be seen across the West African subregion: in the logging going on in the Ashanti Region and the "galamsey" mining in southern Ghana; the violation of the hills and mounds in Ekiti State, Nigeria, in the search for "solid minerals"; and the illegal gold-mining that is currently at the roots of banditry in Zamfara State of Nigeria, reminding one of the late 20th century "blood diamonds" of Sierra Leone. Still, the same environmental carnage is unabatingly playing out in the Democratic Republic of Congo where one of the densest tropical forests of the world is being laid bare through commercial logging[2] and hard-crusted illegal mining that has plagued the region in decades of regional wars and political instability. Other more visible aspects like the oil exploration in

1 Leonardo Boff and Mark Hathaway, "Ecology and Theology of Nature," in *Concilium*, Linda Hogan, João Vila-Chã, and Agbonkhianmeghe Orobator (London: Hymns Ancient and Modern, 2018), 44.
2 Wangari Maathai, *Replenishing the Earth: Spiritual Values for Healing Ourselves and the World* (New York: Doubleday, 2010), 37–41.

the Niger Delta are well known for their mega-pollution, and they have been subjects of international advocacy. These and more are aspects of the ecological destructions quietly ravaging the continent where religion is an everyday affair.

It is ironical that the reason for the exploitation of nature's resources in Africa is to meet human need, but the accompanying human cost of pollution and exposure to harmful chemicals tends to negate the material gains from these activities. They eventually impoverish the communities where the intense extractions of resources are taking place and leave them worse off in health. This eventual consequence of the short-term gain from disrupting the ecological balance of the environment are proofs that human beings are an integral part of the ecological environment. Yet modern society, through the influence of science-as-ideology, still mistakenly think the environment is something outside there and with which we can tinker at no risk to ourselves.[3]

The Challenge

The present worldwide ecological distress has been a subject of concern from the mid-twentieth century. Although segments of global interests deny the reality and some remain indifferent, the increasing awareness of the crisis is forging alliances across ideological divides – political, economic, religious and non-religious. It is believed that the desired change to remedy the situation will come not only from improved technology but essentially through attitudinal change in people towards the environment. This was the substance of the appeal of two eminent scientists to religious leaders of the world in 2014. It is not a strange expectation for religious functionaries to be invited to contribute to the solution to our ecological crisis, since many people's perception of the world around them have been shaped by religious traditions, especially beginning with their myths of creation. Religious cosmogonies are at the roots of human spirituality, and they provide the lenses through which we first see the natural world as sacred.

In Africa, the different expressions of the indigenous religion are founded on this understanding of the sacredness of the world around us. However, beyond the emphasis modernity places on the material dimension of that world, African religion and philosophy is also conscious of the spiritual aspect and hold both material and non-material realities in balance.

3 Wendell Berry, *Sex, Economy, Freedom, and Community: Eight Essays* (New York: Pantheon Books, 1993), 34.

Both the physical and the non-physical dimension of our planet interact symbiotically. Harold Turner discussed this integral understanding of reality in the African religio-cultural environment in his "Six-Feature Analysis of Primal Religions" indicating that holism is natural for the primal African mind.[4]

By miscarriage of purpose, the coming of Christianity into the African environment challenged this prevailing precolonial ethos. This is not so much because the African mind holds a holistic view of the universe, but because of its method of using the material as the medium for engaging the metaphysical world, hence the qualification of the indigenous religion by the misnomer: idolatry. Enlightenment Christianity understood African religion as worshipping creation rather than God. From the early 20th century, African converts have intuitively been resetting this form of Christianity on the continent to answer the quest of their rustic forebears for life in its abundance through the indigenous religion.[5] Sharing their holistic understanding of the universe, these African converts to Christianity are at home with the phenomena recorded in the Christian scriptures which enlightenment Christianity labours to comprehend.

Nevertheless, the continuing traction of modernity on the African continent through (mis)education and the media continues to ensure respectively the secularization of society and the perversion of Christianity in material centeredness. From whichever direction one sees the ongoing rape of nature in Africa, whether as expressed by the *agbegilodo*[6] in the university town or the government of Nigeria exploring oil in the Niger Delta or the gold mining in Ashanti and Zamfara, the destruction of the environment is an affront to the primal sensibility of Africa. And in fact, it is through these intense extractions of nature's resources to service industries in the rest of the world that we in African make our own detrimental contributions to the global ecological crisis.[7] With the prevalence of poverty on the continent and the continuing effects of climate change being witnessed in stiff competition for resource control, oftentimes leading to war and social violence, it is time to appraise the role religion, particularly Christianity, can play in redeeming the present situation on the continent.

4 Harold W. Turner, "The Primal Religions of the World and Their Study", in *Australian Essays in World Religions*, edited by Victor C. Hayes (Bedford Park, South Australia: AASR, 1977), 27–37.

5 Laurenti Magesa, African Religion: The Moral Tradition of Abundant Life (Maryknoll, NY: Orbis, 1997).

6 This is Yoruba word for lumbermen.

7 See: Ivan R. Mugisha, "DR Congo Entry into EAC Will Be a Game Changer," *The East African*, June 15, 2019. https://www.th-eeastafrican.co.ke/news/ea/DR-Congo-entry-into-EAC-will-be-a-game-changer/4552908-5158402-barl6d/index.html (accessed June 25, 2019).

The Study of African Christianity

So far, the study of new religious movements (NRMs) in Africa has been trailing the development of African Christianity, with the aim to understand the mutating configuration of the faith of the Church on the continent. Pioneering studies of Harold Turner, Bengt Sundkler, Andrew Walls, John Peel, Godwin Tasie and other academics centred on the emergence of the grassroot movements – *Aladura, Sumsum asore,* Zionists – and other creative appropriations of Christianity by largely unlettered African convert-evangelists. The thrust of their works was on the indigenous appropriation of Christianity such that the seemingly foreign faith became intelligible to the masses of their people. This form of Christianity produced an unprecedented large following in the threatening colonial environment of the first half of the twentieth century.[8] The success of these evangelists derived from their drawing from the local resource of lively spiritual awareness, which the European missionary could hardly appreciate, but which they fused with Christianity to make the faith theirs.

The successive scholarship of African NRMs presently being championed largely by African academics places emphasis on the sociological influences of education, economics, and globalization as the forces driving religious change among African middle class. The largely uncritical study has succeeded in explaining the phenomenon without shinning the light on its soft underbelly. The social media across Africa is currently feasting on the emerging cacophonies of money, power, and scandals dogging the movements.

Nevertheless, it is important to understand that the current movement is operating by the same mental map of the universe as that of the previous movement. The differences between them derive essentially from their horizons. The former movements, led by the hardly literate African evangelists, operated within the limited horizon of African indigenous society. Their successor movements have been influenced by western education and its accompanying cultural fermentation of modernity. This is visible in their use of the metropolitan languages of the former colonial powers, particularly English; their use of mass media to spread their messages and influences over a large swath of people, far and near;

8 The "strange" laws of the colonial powers and the existential trauma of wars and diseases in the first half of the 20th century provided the challenging environment that motivated African Christians to reach back into their past to create a form of Christianity that answered their need for security. On the other hand, the colonial powers feared the resultant mass movements as potential seedbeds of nationalist rebellion.

and their global network with similar religious movements in the West. Modernity sets them apart from the previous movement, and it is at the roots of their consumer culture.

A New Agenda

The first wave of Africanization of Christianity was intuitive, and it emerged spontaneously in response to perceived existential threats. Its ethos of African-ness presupposes the continuing understanding of the precarious nature of the ecological environment. Like precolonial Africa, the movement did not have to contend with the challenges of population explosion that eventually came with continuing improvements in life expectancy facilitated by modern medicine and health management. Hence, the ecological balance of the environment could not but be taken for granted as in the pre-Christian past. It was not an issue in the first wave of Africanization of Christianity.

Africa's NRMs are flourishing in a different ecological situation, and the need for African Christianity's contribution to stemming the tide of the growing crisis will not proceed without deliberate efforts at recovering latent resources of indigenous knowledge system. This is to say that African academics and theologians can no longer be trailing NRMs on the continent in romantic studies; it is time to be involved in the theological formation of their protagonists towards *Our Common Future*. This is a tall order, because the current form of this popular Christianity on the continent is colonial in mindset, being largely influenced by the American consumer culture, part of which belligerently denies climate change.[9] It is still challenging because the commodification of nature's resources through the influence of modernity now runs deep and wide in African society so much that the social memory of the people on the traditional understanding of the sacredness of the environment is almost lost. It can also be added that with the pervasive demonization of many things traditional to African society, ecological education of African Christians must proceed with the congruent understandings of the ecological environment in both African tradition and in the Christian scriptures.

9 The African situation is doubly worse because whereas the churches in the American environment are somewhat accountable to society, those in Africa are untethered. Nigeria is a foremost example.

The Environment in Primal Africa

Precolonial African societies do not have abstract notions of the environment as an entity from which human beings are detached. Rather, they understand the integral relationship between all beings cohabiting the universe, seen and unseen. They believe that all have their places of mutual usefulness when they function within their nature appointed strengths and limits. While these forebears developed sophisticated skills in exploring the environment, they also recognized their limits and vulnerabilities, hence their religious attitude towards the world around them, physical and non-physical. The environment is therefore both moral and ecological.[10] Religion, which served the dual purpose of drawing spiritual resources for human survival as well as serving as an instrument of social control, binds together in the human mind the moral and the ecological understanding of the African environment.

At the mundane level, the ecological environment furnishes communities self-understanding as peoples in diverse climatic environments. The wisdom, proverbs and anecdotes of the elders are distilled from their observations of the natural world around them with its wonders, mysteries, and the rhythm of times and seasons. It has been said of indigenous peoples worldwide that they conceive the environment as land, and Africa is no exception. Land here is more than the physical, geographical landscape; it includes all the life-forms that are active in it, both human and non-human. It also includes the natural features of water bodies, hills and mountains as well as the spirits of the ancestors who earlier trod it and are interred in it. The land is thus seen as a single matrix in which all these elements of living humans, dead ancestors, coming generations, spirits of animals and natural objects interact as one reality.[11] This "kinecentricity" is the reason behind the deference indigenous peoples pay to those sentient beings with which they share the environment.[12]

By implication, the land, as a place in indigenous conception, is more than its "cartographic location" in a three-dimensional space but includes all the active relationships that create the sense of place for all the sentient

10 Scholars of African religion have developed these themes in their works. See: John V. Taylor, *The Primal Vision: Christian Presence amid African Religion* (London: SCM Press, 1963); John S. Mbiti, African Religions and Philosophy, 2nd ed. (London: Heinemann, 1990); *Introduction to African Religion*, 2nd ed. (Long Grove, IL: Waveland Press, 2015); Laurenti Magesa, *African Religion: The Moral Tradition of Abundant Life* (Maryknoll, NY: Orbis Books, 1997).

11 Fikret Berkes, Mina Kislali Oglu, Carl Folke and Madhav Gadgil, "Exploring the Basic Ecological Unit: Ecosystem-like Concepts in Traditional Societies," *Ecosystems* 1, no. 5 (1998), 412.

12 Nancy Turner and Pamela R. Spalding, "'We Might Go Back to This': Drawing on the Past to Meet the Future in Northwestern North American Indigenous Communities," *Ecology and Society* 18, no. 4 (2013): Article 29. Ecology and Society. http://www.ecologyandsociety.org/vol18/iss4/art29/ (accessed May 28, 2019).

beings that interact there.[13] It is also more than a commodity that can be measured and parcelled out; rather, it is an invaluable heritage to which the spirit and soul of its occupiers, animate and inanimate, are closely tied. Consequently, in virtually all traditional societies of the world, the land, as an essential part of the natural environment, is at the heart of peoples' identities and the conception of their universe.[14]

At the spiritual level, through the remedial incantations that follow diagnoses, Africa's indigenous religious functionaries make cases for physical, moral, and spiritual redresses of personal and social dysfunctions by appealing to the integrity of creation. By orally recollecting mythical stories of creation along with other formulas by which they temporarily share sacred time with the divinities, they make their appeals to the metaphysical realm through what Mircea Eliade calls the "myth of eternal return".[15] Theologians today will acknowledge this phenomenon in the wake of the discoveries of quantum physics as a demonstration of the inextricable entanglement of mind and matter.[16] African sages believed this verbal recollection is potent to recreate the past in the present and infallibly vindicate their quest for the redress of the anomaly at hand. Hence, nature and their understanding of cosmology furnish their mystical jurisprudence.

In recognizing the value of the ecological environment for human wellbeing, primal Africa, like other primal societies, appreciates the need to uphold its integrity. To this end, taboos are instituted for social control and their violations are quickly remedied for the healthy perpetuation of society. Local divinities, understood as intermediaries between humans and the creator God, are reverenced as traditions stipulate. And traditions laid down by forebears are sustained, not so much in their details but in their essences, through changing times.[17]

13 Sarah King, "Context Matters: Studying Indigenous Religions in North America," *Religion Compass* 7, no. 11 (2013): 500. Doi: 10.1111/rec3.12066; Meera Baindur, "Nature as Non-terrestrial: Sacred Natural Landscapes and Place in Indian Vedic and Puranic Thought," *Environmental Philosophy* 6, no. 2 (2009), 45.

14 Sarah King, Jane Hubert, "Sacred Beliefs and Beliefs of Sacredness," in *Sacred Sites, Sacred Places,* edited by David L. Carmichael, (London: Routledge, 1994), 16.

15 Mircea Eliade, *The Sacred and the Profane: The Nature of Religion,* trans by Willard R. Trask (New York: Harcourt, Brace and World, 1963), 104-07.

16 Theologians consider the development in quantum physics apophatic in that it questions the certitude of materiality and acknowledges that reality is an inextricable entanglement of the material and the subliminal in nature such that they "are iteratively reconfigured through each intra-action, thereby making it impossible to differentiate in any absolute sense between creation and renewal, beginning and returning, continuity and discontinuity, here and there, past and future." See: Karen Barad, *Meeting the Universe Halfway: Quantum Physics and the Entanglement of Matter and Meaning* (Durham, NC: Duke University Press, 2007), ix.

17 The strong temptation of tradition is to freeze ancestral stipulations, but there had been situations where traditional functionaries understood changing times and saw the need to modify tradition. Alafin Atiba at Oyo did this in 1854 in the troubled Yorubaland of West Africa. Although it renewed the social angst of the age in the eventual destruction of Ijaiye in 1862, it was one instance where the ultimate custodian of an African tradition of kingship saw the need to update tradition in a changing cultural environment.

However, precolonial Africa was not a romantic garden of Eden occupied by the noble savage. From time to time, it had its own share of destructive warfare and ecological challenges that called for remediations. But these are often on relatively small scales since population was far behind available resources. The widening horizon of society through systematic contact with Europeans and Arabs from the 16th century gradually put pressure on indigenous African values until the situation reached the tipping point in the nineteenth century long-drawn, fratricidal wars. The *Mfecane* in Southern Africa, the Ashanti wars in the Gold Coast, and the Yoruba wars are notable examples.

Still, the esoteric nature of indigenous African priesthood that makes much of the ecological environment is also its Achille's heel. As a human system, it was dogged by the frailties that tend to come with aging and sheer opportunism of priestcraft.[18] Even in precolonial times, there were make-believe religious cults that were set up to exploit the masses of the people, and some of the implosions of society, as in the case of the Yoruba people of southwest Nigeria in the nineteenth century, have been adduced to the collapse of the religious institutions that held society together.[19] The glitters of modernity in the aftermath of colonization continue to soften the environment for an unremitting decadence, not only of the cults but also of the noble values of restraint and ecological sensibility they fostered. The inability of the old system to hold its own in the face of modernity calls for the appropriation of its successor faiths towards the ecological redemption of society. Happily, virtually all religions of the world today have their perspectives on the ecological environment and Africans who have embraced them will do well to understand these perspectives and apply them towards a sustainable future for the continent. However, this should be done in congruence with African primal vision if the efforts will be intelligible and fruitful.

A Case for Involvement

The converts who appropriated Christianity early in the nineteenth century did so intuitively. They were coming from a cultural matrix that appreciated spiritual dynamics of the world around them and saw the value of the new faith for themselves and its congruence with the

18 Bolaji Idowu, *African Traditional Religion: A Definition* (London SCM Press, 1973), 173.

19 Samuel Johnson, *The History of the Yorubas: From the Earliest Times to the Beginning of the British Protectorate* (Lagos: CMS, 1921), 188; Brodie Cruickshank, *Eighteen Years in the Gold Coast of Africa Including an Account of the Native Tribes and their Intercourse with Europeans*, vol. 2 (London: Hurst and Blackett, 1853), 324-28; Francis L. Bartels, *The Roots of Ghana Methodism* (London: Cambridge University Press), 55-59; Anene E. Afigbo, "The Aro Expedition of 1901-1902. An Episode in the British Occupation of Iboland," *Odu* (New Series) 7 (April 1972), 3-27.

essential aspects of their ancestral faith, particularly the integral nature of mind and matter. They had no problem bridging the two, because it was not only desirable; the new is a continuity of the old shorn of its non-essentials and imbued with new value of unfeigned generosity and goodwill towards society. For several reasons, the current need to appropriate Christianity in Africa for the ecological healing of society in the twenty-first century will not come by instincts. It will have to be deliberate.

First, the awareness of the ecological changes going on all over the world is still not intelligible to the masses of our people. They see unusual flooding, erosion of coastal settlements, and disastrous winds; but they hardly link these intense changes in climate to the uncontrolled utilization of environmental resources both at home and far away. Moreover, the educational curriculum of many countries in Africa has not taken seriously the need for ecological education and attitudinal change. Another formidable challenge is the dominion-centred Christianity that promotes consumer culture in the name of material success. This form of Christianity, based on a certain interpretation of the text of the Christian scripture Genesis 1:28, is the most widespread form of Christianity on the African continent among young people. It is appetizing to their cultural taste and ambition of upward social mobility.

On the African continent, Nigerian new churches are the principal propagators of this doctrine, from West Africa to East and Southern Africa.

Second, the situation for African Christianity is complicated by the changing theological emphasis in the mission churches in the bid to survive the real threat of mass movement of their young people to the new churches. The pulpits of these first-generation churches are increasingly being occupied by young preachers who are projecting the prosperity messages of the NRMs to their people to stem the drifting. Even their theological institutions remain primarily focused on the agenda of their denominations, and that is to train ministers for the continuous perpetuation of their institutions. This is often done without considering regular innovations in the training curriculums to prepare their candidates for the challenges of the contexts of their ministries. And so, the subtle competition for survival between the old and the new movements continues.

Third, when placed in the context of the permissive attitude of the multilateral institutions of the United Nations, addressing the African ecological situation become more challenging. The notion that Africa, along with the people of global South, is a victim of the consumer culture of the affluent North indulges African governments in their indifference to the ecological degradations going-on on the continent. All the legal and illegal extractive activities highlighted above constitute the foundations on which the economies of many African countries are built, and they significantly contribute to the global ecological crisis. A country like Nigeria that has not been able to get its acts together in generating power for her citizens but runs on hundreds of thousands of private generators to power domestic and industrial activities contribute in no small measure to the effluents being pumped into the atmosphere.[20]

The bottom line is that the present lack of awareness in African Christian communities of the ecological degradations going on, the aggravating doctrinal position being peddled around by African NRMs, and the environmentally unfriendly foundations on which African economies are built today all call for the education and awareness of the people. A classical heritage of Christianity is service for the common good. African Christian communities need to wake up to the ecological need of the hour in the spirit of this heritage.

Christian Ecological Theology Today

At the roots of the emerging theological discourse on the environment is the question of how Christians are to see and appropriate the bounties of nature in a world in which human consumption of resources has become unsustainable. The need to take a position has been heightened by the increasing ecological stress impinging particularly on vulnerable peoples and other sentient beings in the environment which is also threatening the planet. In response to the development, the philosophical bellicosity between religion and science are thawing and the Christian constituency is making progress in reformulating theology. This profound influence of ecological awareness on the teachings of the Church is being seen as "an opportunity and a challenge for renewal and reformation".[21] Phyllis Tickle called it "Emergence Christianity".[22]

20 Consider the several thousands of generators that constantly power for 24 hours the telecommunication transmission points across the country.

21 Ernst M. Conradie, "Ecumenical Discourse on Pneumatology and Ecology," *Journal of Reformed Theology* 6, no. 3 (January 2012), 189.

22 Tickle saw the emerging Christian response to the ecological challenges as consistent with her perceived half-millennium cycles of theological renewal of the life of the Church in human history. Phyllis Tickle, "Emergence Christianity," https://www.youtube.com/watch?v=aG-GNvDeFV8 (accessed June 3, 2017).

The perceived kinship between the Christian faith and the natural environment is not just being discovered and confessed. Church traditions that are founded on sacramental understanding of life and reality have always acknowledged it in their liturgies. While the term "sacrament" has been used largely to describe church rituals and ceremonies, the application has been extended to various experiences of encounter with the divine in the ordinariness of everyday life. As a divine creation and matrix of God's self-revelation, John Hart calls the natural world a "sacramental universe" and its diverse flourishing ecosystem "sacramental commons,"[23] both of which "express complementary perceptions of divine immanence in, and engagement with humanity through, the created cosmos."[24]

It is noteworthy that Hart, as other contemporary Christian thinkers,[25] does not formulate in isolation of science his theology of creation, which he ascribes to "the dynamic realization of divine imagination."[26] Rather, for him, the continuous emergence of the universe over billions of years in all its complexities and in conformity with the laws of sciences – physics, chemistry and biology – has been "periodically stimulated and enhanced by contingent events or by the Spirit's creative power."[27] Implicitly, for Hart, the discoveries of science do not nullify the ascription of creative intelligence to the Spirit of God while the doctrine of the latter does not necessarily negate discovered scientific laws. Rather, it is within this scientific evolutionary process and workings of the Spirit that we may understand in the liturgies of sacramental church traditions – Orthodox, Catholic, Anglican and Lutheran – the epithets ascribed to God as the creator, sustainer and redeemer of the universe.

What light does the renewed understanding of the environment as a creation sustained and redeemed by God through his Spirit shed on the old confession? It is that while the different elements of nature are bound together by specific ecological parameters so that they function in their nature-allotted, complementary roles, they receive life from the Spirit. The sciences have discovered many of the laws and dynamics that hold them together in their stable ecological interactions, but they have not been able to explain the source of their "living-ness".

23 John Hart, *Sacramental Commons: Christian Ecological Ethics* (Lanham, MD: Rowman and Littlefield Publishers, 2006), xiii-xviii.
24 Hart.
25 Denis Edwards, *Ecology at the Heart of Faith* (Maryknoll: Orbis books), 8-14.
26 Hart, Sacramental Commons, xiii.
27 Hart, 3.

Stephen Hawking expressed this much.[28] Christian theology ascribes that life to the divine Spirit, *rua'ch* in Hebrew.[29] In acknowledging the sciences, Christian thinkers in the twenty-first century are making Christian theology and science intellectual allies, moving them towards a mutually nutritive juncture in contemporary understanding of the environment as a divine-scientific reality.[30] This holds three implications, at the least.

First, the understanding is leaving behind the hard-crusted dichotomy between the realm of nature and the realm of the Spirit, especially as posited by the nineteenth century theologian Albrecht Ritschl.[31] Second, it means the acknowledgement of the sustaining presence of the Spirit in creation goes beyond the traditional perceptions of indigenous religions of the world which tend to put primacy of sacredness on the pristine. It also goes beyond places designated as sacred for religious worship.[32] Rather, it follows that if the empirical discoveries of the sciences in understanding nature is a true revelation within its own genre, the technological products derived from those discoveries can be no less sacred. In fact, they may be regarded as manifestations of the divine Spirit's continuing activity in creation if they are produced with an eye on their ecological soundness. Third, the believed continuing presence of the Spirit in creation paradoxically makes creation the nexus of the two attributes of God as both immanent and transcendent.[33] The former inevitably implies panentheism (God filling all creation) and the latter God's sovereignty over and above creation.

Sensitizing African Christians

Instituting change tends to begin with those who see beyond the crowd, and religious change is not exempted from this dynamic. If the required attitudinal change will occur among African Christians in respect of the ecological challenges of our time, those who shape the thoughts of the masses of the people must see the road ahead. This is to say that

28 Stephen Hawking submitted that "Even if there is only one possible unified theory [for scientists to describe the universe], it is just a set of rules and equations. What is it that breathes fire into the equations and makes a universe for them to describe? The usual approach of science constructing a mathematical model cannot answer the questions of why there should be a universe for the model to describe." *The Illustrated a Brief History of Time*, updated and expanded ed. (New York: Bantam Books, 1996), 232.

29 Denis Edwards, *Ecology at the Heart of Faith*, 31; Council for World Mission and Evangelism – World Council of Churches (CWME-WCC), "God's Transforming Spirit: Reflections on Mission, Spirituality and Creation," *International Review of Mission* 101, no. 1 (April 2012), 61.

30 Philip Kariatlis, "An Examination of the Theological-Ethical Contributions of Archbishop Stylianos (Harkianakis) of Australia to Creation Theology and Environmental Issues," *Phronema* 31, no. 2 (2016), 24.

31 Cf. Kirk Wegter-McNelly, "Difference within Theology of Nature: The Strategies of Intelligibility and Credibility," *The Journal of Faith and Science Exchange* (August 2012), 241, https://hdl.handle.net/2144/3984 (accessed May 2, 2019); Jonathan R. Wilson, *God's Good World: Reclaiming the Doctrine of Creation* (Grand Rapids: Baker Academic, 2013), 116-17.

32 John Hart, Sacramental Commons, xiv.

33 Philip Kariatlis, "An Examination of the Theological-Ethical Contributions", 25.

the theological formation of Christian leaders, lay and clerical, need to weigh in on the matter. Local churches and ecumenical bodies can, through their informed leaders and institutions that interface with the public, re-educate society towards sustainability.

At the basic level, the theological re-formation of Christian leaders can begin with the reformulation of, at least, three cardinal doctrines of the church in the light of the ecological changes in the world today. They are the doctrine of the Spirit (Pneumatology), the doctrine of salvation (Soteriology), and the doctrine of the end (Eschatology). A quick literature review of these doctrines shows that Christian scholars are already rereading the scriptures in the light of the crisis of our age to hear again what the biblical witness has to say on these doctrines. Happily, they by no means contradict Africa's primal vision of the world but affirm it.

The Doctrine of the Spirit

The doctrine of the Holy Spirit is at the heart of Christian theological rethinking going on today on the ecological environment. The confessed presence of the Holy Spirit in creation highlights the significance of that presence as active, sustaining, and redemptive. Hitherto, mainline churches have confessed the active presence of the Holy Spirit in the world, especially in reference to Christian missions, social change, and the providential ordering of history. On the other hand, traditions that emphasize the charism of the Holy Spirit have championed immediacy of the presence of the Spirit at worship through verbal and non-verbal demonstration of that presence, especially through the workings of miracles. This latter understanding presupposes the suspension of the natural laws for human benefits as in the phenomenal practices of indigenous religions.

Beyond these two broad traditions are other shades of perspectives in the understanding of the presence of the divine in the natural environment. To this end, Ernst Conradie has identified among Christian theologians in the last two decades the development of pneumatology in conjunction with ecology;[34] and, in recent years, many more perspectives have been brought into the combined study. In his words,

> They come from diverging perspectives, including liberation theology, process theology, ecofeminism, the legacy of Teilhard de Chardin, new age mysticism, neo-pagan practices, indigenous

34 Ernst M. Conradie, "Ecumenical Discourse on Pneumatology and Ecology", 190-91.

> theologies and various forms of creation spirituality".[35] Others "seek to retrieve the vision of classic Christian theologians such as Basil of Caesarea ... and Gregory of Nazianzus.... Yet other contributions are situated within the context of ecumenical dialogue on Faith and Order or Life and Work".[36]

Conradie's reference to ecumenical dialogue comes from the study document that emerged from the Athens 2010 Mission and Spirituality Consultation of the Working Group of the Council for World Mission and Evangelism (CWME) of the World Council of Churches (WCC) in cooperation with the Climate Change Programme of WCC and the WCC Indigenous Peoples Project. Characteristically, the document liberally draws from contemporary theological movements from below, particularly conceiving the presence of the Spirit of God, *rua'ch,* in creation in the feminine gender with its associated character of fecundity, nurture and vulnerability in an overwhelmingly patriarchal world.[37]

Current developments in perspectives, sources, and methods in pneumatology are still diverse and need coherence and alignment with other teachings of the church.[38] Nevertheless, the theological emphasis on the presence of the Holy Spirit in creation is still akin to its classical understanding in the mainline churches, but it now provides the basis for redemptive action in the age of ecological stress. Pneumatology in this wise also follows in the trail of African understanding of the active presence of the metaphysical in nature.[39] Yet it is different in that while the belief in the presence of elemental spirits in nature serves as the motivation for magic in indigenous religions, that is the manipulation of phenomena for private ends, the renewed understanding of the presence of the Holy Spirit in creation invites Christian people to tread softly in God's holy "temple" by living in harmony with God's design for creation. This contrast is essential as pneumatology in the context of ecology is being misconstrued in conservative Christian circles as sacralising nature, hence neopaganism.[40]

---

35 Conradie, 191-92.

36 Conradie, 192.

37 CWME-WCC, "God's Transforming Spirit", 63-4. The encyclical of Pope Francis, *"Laudato Si,"* carries the same feminine ethos in its reference to creation as "sister" and "mother earth". See: "Encyclical Letter *Laudato Si* of the Holy Father Francis on Care for Our Common Home", http://w2.vatican.va/content/francesco/en/encyclicals/documents/papa-francesco_20150524_enciclica-laudato-si.pdf (accessed September 10, 2018).

38 Ernst M. Conradie, "Ecumenical Discourse on Pneumatology and Ecology", 193-94.

39 I call it a misnomer because the people do not see themselves as worshipping nature. Rather, they reverence the spirits believed to inhabit and energize natural elements like trees, water bodies, land, sky, and other natural phenomena. They believe these spirits are more powerful than human beings and can hurt or help them, depending on their approaches.

40 See: Cornwall Alliance for the Stewardship of Creation, https://cornwallalliance.org/ (accessed June 25, 2019).

The Doctrine of Salvation

In his 1984 encyclical, "Reconciliation and Penance", John Paul II ascribed the growing ecological challenges facing the world to human sinful nature. According to him, "Since by sinning man [sic] refuses to submit to God, his internal balance is also destroyed, and it is precisely within himself that contradictions and conflicts arise. Wounded in this way, man almost inevitably causes damage to the fabric of his relationship with others and with the created world."[41] More positively, however, the Pope wrote two years later that:

> The Incarnation of God the Son signifies the taking up into unity with God not only of human nature, but in this human nature, in a sense, of everything that is "flesh": the whole of humanity, the entire visible and material world. The Incarnation, then, also has a cosmic significance, a cosmic dimension. The "first-born of all creation," becoming incarnate in the individual humanity of Christ, unites himself in some way with the entire reality of man, which is also "flesh" and in this reality with all "flesh," with the whole of creation.[42]

Catholic and Protestant theologies will agree on this spiritual root of contemporary ecological challenges as well as on the significance of the incarnation for our value of the natural world. Yet, for too long, the anthropocentric understanding of salvation, especially in the Protestant tradition, produced an otherworldly-oriented spirituality that denigrates the material world in which human beings and other sentient beings coexist.[43]

And although the Christian proclamation affirms the spiritual reign of God in the world and, as the Pope implies, the incarnation put the lie on the comparative inferiority of the material to the spiritual, the doctrine of salvation in Christianity did not place premium importance on the comprehensive nature of redemption until the recent decades of global ecological challenges. Consequently, it was easy for Christians to acquiesce to the rabid consumption of nature's resources that is leaving behind ecological imbalance.

---

41 John Paul II, "Post-synodal Apostolic Exhortation Reconciliation and Penance of John Paul II to the Bishops, Clergy, and Faithful on Reconciliation and Penance in the Mission of the Church Today," 1984, http://w2.vatican.va/content/john-paul-ii/en/apost_exhortations/documents/hf_jp-ii_exh_02121984_reconciliatio-et-paenitentia.pdf (accessed March 12, 2019); Pope Francis, *"Laudato Si"*.

42 John Paul II, "On the Holy Spirit in the Life of the Church and the World," 1986, http://w2.vatican.va/content/john-paul-ii/en/encyclicals/documents/hf_jp-ii_enc_18051986_dominum-et-vivificantem.pdf (accessed March 12, 2019).

43 Mary E. Tucker, *Worldly Wonder: Religions Enter Their Ecological Phase* (Chicago: Open Court, 2003), 44-5; Stratford Caldecott, "At Home in the Cosmos: The Revealing of the Sons of God," *Nova et Vetera,* English Edition, 10 (2012), 106; Dave Bookless, "A Famine of Hope: Christian Mission and the Search for a Sustainable Future," *Global Connections Occasional Paper* 26 (Summer 2007), i-ii; Ilsup Ahn, "Deconstructing Eschatological Violence Against Ecology: Planting Images of Ecological Justice," *Cross Currents* (June 2017), 458-75; Douglass J. Moo, "Nature in the New Creation: New Testament Eschatology and the Environment," *Journal of Evangelical Theological Society* 49, No. 3 (September 2006), 451.

If the incarnation laid the groundwork for the belief in the intrinsic value of the natural world, the doctrine of salvation in the age of ecological distress is rooted in the belief in the active presence of the Holy Spirit in creation, saving and redeeming it from corruption. In this wise, creation is understood as the totality of all beings that share life together on the planet and not just humanity.[44] Inevitably, as responsive agents to the workings of the Spirit, the road to ecological salvation lies in human beings exercising social justice among themselves, in their consumption of nature's resources, and in ways that "ensure the health of the natural world for present and future generations."[45] Implicit to this expanding awareness of the comprehensive nature of salvation is a call to reconceive the mission of God in the world and not to discard the earth "once our souls are saved, but … also to be transformed through the *ru'ach's* grace".[46] Drawing on the exhortation of John Paul II, Stratford Caldecott sees this transformation of humanity as central to the salvation of the ecological environment as he writes that:

> The healing of the world around us depends on a re-ordering and a healing of the inner world of [human] imagination, intelligence, and will. Man [sic] was intended to be the mediator of creation, the one in whom all things connect, through whom all things are reconciled, the image of the invisible God (Col. 1:15–20). This high calling is fulfilled in Christ, the new Adam, into whom we are baptized when we receive the Holy Spirit.[47]

Making the salvation of the present ecological environment contingent on human "imagination, intelligence, and will" is, however, problematic. Can a "wounded" humanity that inflicted so much damage on the environment still be its means of salvation? This question leads to the doctrine of eschatology as it is being reformulated with respect to the present global ecological crisis.

The Doctrine of the End

The Christian doctrine of the end of history is another field on which ecological theology is currently playing out. The destiny of humankind and the end of history have received attention from Christian thinkers but, again, with human beings as the focus of redemption and eternal

44 CWME-WCC, "God's Transforming Spirit", 76–7.
45 Nancy G. Wright, "Christianity and Environmental Justice," *Cross Currents* 61, no. 2 (June 2011), 169.
46 CWME-WCC, "God's Transforming Spirit", 77; Dave Bookless, "A Famine of Hope", ii.
47 Caldecott, "At Home in the Cosmos", 108.

reward. On the other hand, and in contrast to the sanguine hope expected to herald the final redemption of saved humanity, popular Christian spirituality denigrates the present material world believed to be reserved for conflagration. In the age of ecological stress, the silent ecological aspects of the Christian scriptures, both the obvious and those that are less so, are shinning out and are receiving attention. Theologically, however, the development of eschatology in the light of the fate of the earth is tied to hope.[48]

Through much of human history, hope has been considered essential to human survival and wellbeing in the world. In view of the present human ecological dysfunction – evident in unmitigated economic imbalance and the festering of poverty, diseases and disabilities – contemporary, postmodern world is growing ambivalent of hope.[49] The level of degradation that has been meted out to the ecological environment and the ideological resistance to its amelioration by the powerful also trump the hope of restoring ecological balance.

Moreover, the diverse conflicting attitudes of denial, unbelief and self-seeking by interested persons and groups make hopeless the possibility of realizing healing, especially when hope is anchored "closely to moral motivation and end-setting action."[50] Where such end-setting appear unrealizable, moral motivation takes flight with hope. Still, the contention over perspectives between advocates of anthropocentric, eco-centric and theocentric views of nature add to the brewing sense of hopelessness.[51] However, present theological thinking on ecology is nuancing the concept of hope, making a distinction between the glib uses of the word and its essential understanding[52] while also arguing its theological foundations and value for life.[53]

Christian theology of hope arises in the context of doubt and uncertainty.[54] It was developed by Jürgen Moltmann in the twentieth century as a fitting response to the despair that followed the two major wars of the

48 Caldecott; Willa Swenson-Lengyel, "Beyond Eschatology – Environmental Pessimism and the Future of Human Hoping," *Journal of Religious Ethics* 45, no. 3 (August 2017), 431.
49 Oliver Burkeman, "This Column Will Change Your Life: The Case Against Hope," *The Guardian* – International Edition, https://www.theguardian.com/lifeandstyle/2014/apr/12/change-your-life-case-against-hope (accessed March 20, 2019).
50 Willa Swenson-Lengyel, "Beyond Eschatology", 431; Hermen Kroesbergen, "Ecology: Its Relative Importance and Absolute Irrelevance for a Christian: A Kierkegaardian Transversal Space for the Controversy on Eco-theology," *HTS Theological Studies* 70, no 1 (November 2014), 1-8.
http://dx.doi.org/10.4102/hts. v70i1.2719.
51 Dave Bookless, "A Famine of Hope", i.
52 Caldecott, "At Home in the Cosmos", 109-12; Willa Swenson-Lengyel, 413-30.
53 Benedict XVI, *Spe Salvi* [On Christian Hope] https://w2.vatican.va/content/benedict-xvi/en/encyclicals/documents/hf_ben-xvi_enc_20071130_spe-salvi.pdf (accessed March 20, 2019)
54 Willa Swenson-Lengyel, "Beyond Eschatology", 431.

century and the continuing threats of human self-destruction during the cold-war era. The theology is founded on the premise that God suffers with humanity and, through the resurrection, offers humanity hope. Much more, the cosmic Christ who was raised bodily from death presents creation the ultimate model and hope of final renewal, and not destruction.[55]

A critique of Moltmann's theology of hope observes that he links hope "exclusively to eschatology" without addressing the ethical concomitant in the here and now. Ilsup Ahn complemented his "future-oriented" theology with a "future-directed" ethics of settling account as in Jesus' parable of the talents:

> Christians' present struggle toward the full realization of ecological justice in an anticipation of God's eschaton becomes their ethical responsibility. Indeed, the future-directed motif of anticipation helps us have a better understanding of our ethical responsibility and ecological justice. To be more specific, in anticipation of the full realization of ecological justice, Christians are to organize their actions to bring it to concrete realization step by step. In this respect, we can say that the development of ecological eschatology and the enhancement of ecological justice are in fact deeply interconnected.[56]

This ethical emphasis on human agential role in the restoration of creation to its primal wholeness is a retrieval of the pre-Fall mandate to humanity as its "mediator"[57] of nurture, misunderstood as license to oppressive dominion as it turned out to be. This retrieval is a common denominator, understood as the ethical concomitant, in the different approaches to Christian theology of the environment.[58] Yet, the brewing culture of hopelessness about the situation challenges the value of human engagement with creation towards transformation. The solution to this impasse may lie in Caldecott's entwinning of eschatological hope with faith in God's promised redemption and love for his creation; that is, ecological conversion.[59] The trinity of faith, hope and love is, therefore, the potential motivation to believe that wounded but healed humanity can meaningfully engage in their vocation to tend the blighted garden of God through a "future-directed" ethics of environmental stewardship.[60]

---

55 Ilsup Ahn, "Deconstructing Eschatological Violence", 461.
56 Ahn, 471.
57 Caldecott, "At Home in the Cosmos", 106-08.
58 Ilsup Ahn, "Deconstructing Eschatological Violence", 464; Folarin George, "From Primordial Curse to Eschatological Restoration: Ecological challenges from Genesis 3:14–20 and Romans 8:18–25," *Verbum et Ecclesia* 32, no 1 (September 2011). https://verbumetecclesia.org.za/index.php/ve/article/view/492/799. (accessed April 2, 2019), doi: 10.4120/ve.v32i1.492.
59 Caldecott, "At Home in the Cosmos", 110-11.
60 The various movements to this end through education, religious awareness, various alliances, and more efficient technologies can be regarded as efforts to recover the vocation.

A call for the rereading of the scriptures and reformulation of the Church's cardinal doctrines in the light the growing ecological crisis is no radical invitation. It has been the pattern in the theological development of the Church. Theologies have evolved in response to the developments in society, including the indigenous response of Africans to the burdens of colonialism and existential threats that provoked African indigenous Christianity earlier referred to. Despite the accompanying risks of accommodating the convenient and the permissive, the ever-growing understanding of the need to make the gospel relevant to the concern of every generation is an instinctive acknowledgement of God's eternal contemporality with his creation, human and non-human. For the present scholars of African NRMs, it is time to stop trailing the movements uncritically for what they preach and promote; it is time to be involved in the reshaping of their values through education.

The main challenge of the African NRMs is their resentment of intellectual values and considerations, coupled with their belligerent confidence of theological correctness. Hence, the theological institutions of the erstwhile mission churches are potential places to begin as Allison Howell ventured in 2012 and 2015; they too have in various ways adapted to the African cultural environment despite their imported liturgies and formularies. Since the WCC has gained the trust of some of the first-generation indigenous churches, they are placed in the position to fruitfully engage their theological development to make them ecologically compliant. Happily, the continental body, Organization of African Instituted Churches (OAIC), run two regional institutions: Good News Theological College and Seminary, in Accra, Ghana, and Zion Bible College of Swaziland in Manzini, Swaziland. These are potential institutions to further the sponsorship of ecological education.

A silver lining appears to be emerging in the horizon for the ecological education of Pentecostal movement. Time will tell if more voices will be raised like that of David Bookless.[61]

61 David Bookless, "Earth, Wind and Fire: A Pentecostal Approach to Creation Care," A Rocha International (Planetwise Blog), https://blog.arocha.org/en/earth-wind-and-fire-a-pentecostal-approach-to-creation-care/ (accessed June 27, 2019).

Promoting Ecological Ethics

As theology in search of praxis, Christian ethics is drawing from the emerging theological formulations to make its contribution to the necessary Christian response to the ecological crisis of our time. Of all the Christian intellectual disciplines, ethics remains the foremost in directly interfacing with the secular society.[62] As public theology in the West, it is arguing from various perspectives for responsible engagement with the environment.

Christian ecological ethics is premised on "environmental virtues" or "virtue ethics"[63] that are cultivated through habitual practices, the result of which constitutes ecological conversion: a sense of "solidarity with the creatures that make up our planetary community."[64] To this end, and like Caldecott, Blanchard and O'Brien have coupled four classical virtues of prudence, courage, temperance, and justice to the trinity of faith, hope, and love.[65] In the rough world of contention between ideologies, and where ecological degradation calls for "preservation, restoration and conservation,"[66] Christian ecological ethics seek to equip Christians and their communities for the long-haul attention presently required by global ecological degradation.

However, John Chryssavgis offers an ethical response of "in-action or mere awareness" towards ecological reclamation. By this he means a pause that allows us to contemplate on the harm that has been done and "gain new 'in-sight' into our world, … abandon the urge for unbridled expansion and focus on the sustainability we so desperately need".[67] This is the Orthodox method of theological discourse that places premium importance on contemplation as foundational to ethics. By no means advocating passivity, contemplative approach to eco-justice is a personal or collective discipline that seeks to gain insights into the crisis at hand with the aim to arrive at the knowledge of appropriate redemptive actions.

Speaking of redemptive actions, it was the Kentucky lay Christian farmer, poet, and environmentalist Wendell Berry who said "[T]he world cannot

62 I use the word "secular" not with respect to irreligion but as plurality of religions and ideologies.
63 Kathryn D. Blanchard and Kevin J. O'Brien, *An Introduction to Christian Environmentalism: Ecology, Virtue, and Ethics* (Waco: Baylor University Press, 2014), 12; Ronald L. Sandler, *Character and Environment: A Virtue-Oriented Approach to Environmental Ethics* (New York: Columbia University Press, 2008).
64 Denis Edwards, Ecology at the Heart of Faith, 112.
65 Blanchard and O'Brien, An Introduction to Christian Environmentalism, 12.
66 John Hart, Sacramental Commons, 204-06.
67 John Chryssavgis, *Three Perspectives on the Sacred: Healing Wisdom from the Desert, the Mountain, and the Cosmos* - The Augustana Distinguished Lectures (Camrose, Alberta: The Chester Ronning Centre for the Study of Religion and Public Life, 2015), 38.

be discovered by a journey of miles, no matter how long, but only by a spiritual journey, a journey of one inch, very arduous and humbling and joyful, by which we arrive at the ground at our own feet, and learn to be at home."[68] This is the experience of our African forebears and we need to retrace it in active and responsible Christian discipleship as we tread the earth. Thankfully, good beginnings have been made in theological education institutions like the Akrofi-Christaller Institute of Theology, Mission and Culture (ACI) and Trinity Theological Seminary (TTS), Legon, in West Africa, and in some other theological institutions in East and Southern Africa. However, these need to percolate down to the local churches and Christian faithful. In this respect, African Christians can draw from the models of emerging ministries in the churches of the West where local churches, Christian denominations, and ecumenical bodies are waking up to make their modest contributions to ameliorating the ecological crisis of the age. A few examples may not be out of place.

The younger, church-founded universities in North America are incorporating environmental education into their programs, and this may be instructive for the newly founded church universities across the African continent. One of such schools in Canada states clearly the aim of its program in this respect:

> The goal of the Environmental Studies program...is to develop godly leaders who possess solid scientific and technical skills and are actively growing in their creative, problem-solving, and thinking abilities. We believe that these skills are best developed within the context of a Christian liberal arts education, in which a biblical perspective on the environment will help future leaders offer innovative and effective solutions to the challenging task of creation stewardship.[69]

Various church groups and associations are also contributing to the need of the hour through advocacy, outreaches and development of age-graded worship and discipleship resources for ecological orientation. Ecumenical bodies and various church traditions have also developed resources for facility design and management to ensure their church buildings are energy efficient and that old structures are retrofitted to be equally environmentally compliant.

68 Wendell Berry, "A Spiritual Journey," in *The Collected Poems of Wendell Berry, 1957-1982* (New York: North Point Press, 1987).
69 Trinity Western University, https://www.twu.ca/environmental-studies/program-overview (accessed April 5, 2019).

As in Africa, theological institutions in the West are far behind in giving attention to the ecological need of the hour, but good beginnings are also being made through a specialized network like the Green Seminary Initiative (GSI).[70] Can the initiative at ACI and TTS be amplified through West African Association of Theological Institutions (WAATI), Association of Evangelicals in Africa (AEA), and All Africa Conference of Churches (AACC)? Since resource persons may still be scarce, these networks may fruitfully facilitate the education and orientation we need to make significant contributions to this need of the hour.

A European, evangelical mission organization, A Rocha, is promoting the culture of creation care in the field of agriculture and conservation in Africa, but it is still early to pronounce the viability of its efforts.[71] An earlier model of Marthinus Daneel among the Shona people collapsed after his exit from Zimbabwe.[72] African Christians and churches need to develop their own resources and engage in advocacy, based on the identified areas of need such as uncontrolled logging, ecologically destructive mining, bush-burning, game hunting, building development, waste management, and clean energy generation and conservation. Since these areas are particularly sensitive to the economy of society, no foreign interest can authentically carry out the advocacy. African Christians also need to address the excessive commodification of environmental resources that has become the default means of achieving the so-called national development, but which actually impoverishes the people through individual criminality, communal conflicts, and state sponsored violence.

70 The Green Seminary Initiative (GSI) is hosted by Green Faith, a United States based, interfaith coalition on the environment (https://www.greenfaith.org/) and the Theological School at Drew University. It is presently being assisted by the Forum on Religion and Ecology (FORE), Yale University, and the Luce Foundation. Cf. Green Seminary Initiative, https://greenseminaries.org/# (accessed May 2, 2019).

71 A Rocha International, https://www.arocha.org/en/ (accessed June 28, 2019).

72 Daneel mentioned the collapse at Boston 2010 conference in celebration of the centenary anniversary of World Missionary Conference of 1910 at Boston University, Massachusetts. See also Marthinus L. Daneel, *African Earthkeepers: Wholistic Interfaith Mission* (New York: Orbis Books, 2001).

Conclusion

Contemporary ecological crisis is a public issue that calls for Christian thoughts on the environment. In response, Christian thinkers have been bringing to bear on the crisis the doctrines of salvation, Holy Spirit, and the end, among others.[73] There are two ways to interpret the development: application or reformulation of old doctrines. The former perceives the development as a broadening of perspective on doctrines that have been exclusively applied to humanity, to the extent of losing perspective on the bigger ecological environment in which humanity functions. This is a rehabilitative understanding. The latter takes the ecological environment as its starting point in reformulating theology and recognizes the emergence and flourishing of humanity as integral to the emergence and flourishing of the cosmos. This latter understanding is no less rehabilitative; but it is revolutionary in that it makes humanity and other beings in the cosmos joint heirs of redemption. It is a radical shift in Christian consciousness and African Christians will do well to re-orientate themselves to this development and respond accordingly. This is because it is consistent with Africa's primal past and longing, and it anticipates the full realization of Pauline teaching on the ultimate redemption of all creation.

73 Apart from the major doctrines of the church, recent academic works have also advanced covenantal and agapeic approaches to the environment while stewardship remains the theological staple in Evangelical tradition.

PART FOUR

BIBLE TRANSLATION AND INTERPRETATION

Appreciating the Complex Identity of Women in Christian Mission among a Cosmopolitan Society: The Case of Lydia in Acts 16:14

Vellah Temko Ngaina

Abstract

Although Lydia only appears briefly in Acts, this article examines how the multi-faceted lives–and practices of cosmopolitan women reflect the plurality of interpretation of their complex identity within the Christian scholarship and the world today. The article will demonstrate how various complex identities and social contexts of the cosmopolitan Greco-Roman world were understood against the cultural, economic, political and religious contexts. I will interrogate the complex identities of women in a cosmopolitan New Testament society using the case of Lydia from Acts 16:14. This text provides an engaging introduction to Lydia and reveals her four complex identities that are consistent with the ancient Mediterranean cultural and social contexts such that we can appreciate this special figure with her social world.

To explore this topic, I conduct a comparative exegetical analysis of Acts 16:14 using an interdisciplinary method. From this I draw meanings from *Biibilya Nyēē Tiliil* (BNT), the Sabaot translation, and several commentators on the book of Acts while comparing them with the Greek text as preserved in Nestle-Aland.

From the findings implications are discussed for African Christian women who find themselves in a similar cosmopolitan society and churches. It offers a renewed understanding of what could be a contribution of African Christian women to a cosmopolitan society or church.

Introduction

The rise of new ways of international or intranational migration today affects every day experiences, dynamics and has consequences for identity. Migration not only has an economic, political and religious impact, but also reshapes the demographic, social and cultural characteristics of both the host society and those being hosted.[1] Thus, the identity of people living in these migrant societies is distinguished by a dynamic interplay of varying factors. For example, within multicultural or cosmopolitan societies, people come from multiple origins. They have socio-economic differences; some are ethnic migrants or are from minority groups. There are also social class divisions and multi-religious formations.

Women in cosmopolitan societies may be involved in extensively diverse religious and social compositions and associations. As it seems, society generally expects women to juggle local and multiple identities naturally whether as a woman, wife, worker, citizen, non-citizen, custodian of their indigenous cultures and religions while maintaining the broader identity of the cosmopolitan community. Migrants are to co-exist, adapt, and interpret the cosmopolitan society depending on the cultural context in which they find themselves, despite the diversity of religious beliefs and practise.

This article aims at examining how the complex identity of women in the cosmopolitan Greco-Roman world was understood in terms of the cultural, political, economic, and religious contexts. It will also discuss implications for women in Christian mission in Africa and reflect on the complex identity of Allison Howell, as woman missionary in Africa. These objectives will be approached with a comparative exegetical analysis of Acts 16:14 using an interdisciplinary method. I shall draw meanings of the text as suggested by *Biibilya Nyēē Tiliil* (BNT), the Sabaot translation, and several commentators on the book of Acts while comparing them with the Greek text as preserved in Nestle-Aland.

Background

We cannot underestimate the role Lydia plays in the growth and spread of the early messianic Christian community. Unfortunately, commentators only mention the story in passing to validate or describe the doctrine of baptism or feminist acknowledgement of Paul's treatment of women.[2]

1 Youna Kim, *Transnational Migration, Media and Identity of Asian Women; Diasporic Daughters* (New York: Routledge, 2011), 48.
2 See David Lertis Matson, *Household Conversion Narratives in Acts: Pattern and Interpretation* (Sheffield: Sheffield Academic Press, Ltd, 1996), 136; see also Richard S. Ascough, *Lydia: Paul's Cosmopolitan Hostess* (Collegeville: Liturgical Press, 2009), 1.

However, we must study Lydia's story in its own right for the major role she plays in early Christian mission through the spread of Christianity among the Gentiles and specifically in Macedonia.[3] Rackham highlights that even though Macedonians were akin to Greeks, they were unique people. He describes them as being "a simple, rough, hardy people, who in the glorious time of Greek history had been looked upon by the Athenians as almost barbarians."[4] However, at the time Paul and his contingent came to Macedonia, their religious life was complex sharing affinities with the Greeks, Romans, and Thasians.

Philippi, one of the four districts and cities, is important in this discussion for it is the geographical location that Paul begins his mission in Macedonia and the residence of Lydia.[5] Philippi was strategically positioned at the borders of Thrace and Macedonia. Originally called Datos, Crenides or Krenides, meaning a place 'with many springs', it was inhabited by Thracian tribes.[6] Although located within the limits of ancient Thrace and a Thracian city, Thracians colonised and occupied the privileged site because of its fertile land, gold and silver.[7] Philippi, therefore, became a powerful and strategic location for political, economic, religious, and inter-cultural growth, especially because of its cosmopolitan nature and it was strengthened further by the Romans.

Complexities Underlying the Ambiguous Identity of Lydia

After a description of the marginal setting of the episode in terms of the place (outside the gate) and participants (women) involved in Acts 16.13, this verse explores the complex identity of one of the converts. The verse provides finer details and results on what happened after Paul and his

---

3 See Matson, Household Conversion Narratives in Acts, 136; see also Ascough, Lydia, p.1; M. B. Hatzopoulos, 'Macedonia and Macedonians', in Robin J. Lane Fox, *Brill's Companion to Ancient Macedon: Studies in Archaeology and History of Macedon 650 BC- 300 AD* (Leiden: Brill, 2011), 43-50 (43). Hatzopoulos describes Macedonia as a geographical term of the land that was inhabited or ruled by the Macedonians from the time the kingdom was founded in the year 700 BC until when they were suppressed by the Romans in the year 168 BC.

4 Richard Belward Rackham, *The Acts of the Apostles: An Exposition* (London: Methuen & Co, 1901), 279.

5 Richard N. Longenecker, 'The Acts of the Apostles' in *The Expositor's Bible Commentary, Volume 9* (Grand Rapids: The Zondervan Corporation, 1981), 207- 573(479).

6 See Chaido Koukouli-Chrysantaki, 'Colonia Iulia Augusta Philippensis', in Charalambos Bakirtzws & Helmet Koesler (eds.), *Philippi at the Time of Paul and After His Death* (Eugene: Wipf & Stock, 1989), 5-36 (5). Koukouli-Chrysantaki explains that earlier writings show that the same city bore the name Datos and its King Philip of Macedon renamed the city after himself; see also Lilian Portefaix, *Sisters Rejoice: Paul's Letter to the Philippians and Luke-Acts as Received by First-Century Philippian Women* (Stockholm: Almqvist & Wiksell International, 1988), 60, Portefaix shows that the first time Philippi is mentioned was during the Persian invasion in 490 B.C by Herodotus who narrates that Xerxes marched and passed by Pangaion, a place where the Thracian tribes had possession of gold and silver mines; Herodotus 7:112. William Smith, *Dictionary of Greek and Roman Geography Volume Two* (Boston: Little, Brown and Co., 1854), 923; Smith defines Satrae as a Thracian people who occupied a portion of the Pangaeus, between the Nestus and the Strymon. Herodotus states that they were the only Thracian tribe who had always preserved their freedom; a fact for which he accounts by their country, - a mountainous region, covered with forests and snow – and by their great bravery; R. C. H. Lenski, *The Interpretation of the Acts of the Apostles* (Columbus: The Wartburgh Press, 1994), 652.

7 See F. F. Bruce, *Commentary on the Book of the Acts: The English Text with Introduction, Exposition and Notes* (Grand Rapids: W. M. B. Eerdmans Publishing Company, 1960), 330; Bruce notes that, Philippi "received its name from Philip of Macedon, who seized the gold-mines in the vicinity and fortified what had formerly been the Thasian settlement of Crenides." Longenecker, 'The Acts of the Apostles', 479; Koukouli-Chrysantaki, 'Colonia Iulia Augusta Philippensis', 7.

companions spoke to the women (v.13). Luke reports the response of one of the women towards the message of Paul. The narrator does not only give the background of the woman, but also allows the reader to glean her social position through the explicit and implicit information provided. Luke, therefore, details the woman's identity by providing four crucial but difficult descriptions as follows: discussed below

Lydia's Name

In the Greek text, Lydia is first introduced and described by the phrase τις γυνὴ ὀνόματι Λυδία 'and a certain woman named (by name) Lydia'. Unlike several women in the Bible who remain nameless, Luke gives

this woman an identity, which raises questions that mostly relate to her background or status. Scholars have suggested that this phrase denotes either a proper name[8] or simply a place of origin.[9] Those arguing for the latter suggest it was an ethnic appellation describing her place of origin.[10] From this viewpoint, the name in its original form is most probably contracted from Thyatira, an ancient kingdom of Lydia before it was incorporated into the Roman province of Asia.[11] As a result, the phrase should be read as 'the Lydian'. The proposition further endorses the thought that Lydia was possibly a freedwoman or a freed slave, for slaves bore geographical names.[12]

Besides the geographical factor, her occupation as a trader points to Lydia's status as a free woman. Pervo, for example, states that "Lydia represents one important type of early Christian convert: a possible former slave who operates a business."[13] He, therefore, ties and bases his argument on freed slavery to her trade and Lydia as a geographic region. Sarah Pomeroy indicates the type of trade when she notes that, "Freedwomen, since they often came from the East, frequently sold

8 See Ernst Haenchen, *The Acts of the Apostles: A Commentary* (Philadelphia: The Westminster Press, 1971), 494; Haenchen indicates that it is a personal name since ὀνόματι has been used; see also Ben Witherington, *The Acts of the Apostles: A Socio-Rhetorical Commentary* (Grand Rapids: Wm. B. Eerdmans Publishing Co., 2001), 491.

9 Matson, Household Conversion Narratives in Acts, 143.

10 Ascough, *Lydia,* 6; see also I. Howard Marshall, *The Acts of the Apostles: An Introduction and Commentary* (Downers Grove: InterVarsity Press, 1983), 267; Justo L. Gonzalez, *Acts: The Gospel of the Spirit* (Maryknoll: Orbis Books, 2001), 189; Richard I. Pervo, *Acts: A Commentary* (Minneapolis: Fortress Press, 2009), 403. Wayne A. Meeks, *The First Urban Christians: The World of the Apostle Paul* (New Haven: Yale University Press, 1983), 203, Meeks points out that, "The author does not tell us that Lydia was a freedwoman, but her name, properly a place name, perhaps is a relic of servile origin"; Rackham, *The Acts of the Apostles,* 282; Bruce, *Commentary on the Book of the Acts*,331; Luise Schottroff, *Let the Oppressed Go Free: Feminist Perspectives on the New Testament* as translated by Annemarie S. Kidder (Louisville: Westminster John Knox Press, 1991), 132.

11 Longenecker, 'The Acts of the Apostles', 461.

12 See Shelly Matthews, *First Converts: Rich Pagan Women and the Rhetoric of Mission in the Early Judaism and Christianity* (Stanford: Stanford University Press, 2001), 86; see also Ascough, *Lydia*, 6-7; Ascough upholds that "if it is an ethnic appellation it would indicate that at one time Lydia was a slave who had been freed."; Pervo, *Acts,* 403; Meeks, *The First Urban Christians*, 24; Rackham, *The Acts of the Apostles*, 282-283.

13 Pervo, *Acts,* 403.

luxury items or exotic merchandise, such as purple dye or perfumes."[14] Several inscriptions suggest that some traders in purple-dyed clothes were ex-slaves.[15] Conversely, even though the inscriptions attest to this notion, it does not prove that Lydia was one of the freed slaves; therefore, some considerations have to be made.[16]

To start with, those who argue that Lydia was a freedwoman assume that the naming follows the Roman practice. Verses 11-12 suggest that the story is retold from a Greek background; besides the narrator mentions the home city of Lydia, Thyatira in Asia Minor. This confirms that Lydia was a Greek woman and may or may not have followed the Roman naming practices. In essence, the presence of colonialists in their region did not erase their most important practice. If it had followed the Roman practice, Teresa Calpino observes that Lydia would have been referred to by the traditional double name used for higher status Roman women and not a singular name.[17] Usually, Roman women were never called by their names or nicknames but rather their family's cognomen. Witherington comments, "That Lydia is called by her personal name suggests she is of Greek extraction, and it probably also indicates she is a person of some status and standing."[18] However, in the same inscriptions existing in the first and second centuries, there have been recordings of women of status who bore the name Lydia.[19] The name Lydia was popular with women as attested in the frequent use by Horace.[20] The Lukan account depicts Lydia as having control of a household. This therefore means that she was a free person, whether a freed slave or not.

14 Sarah B. Pomeroy, *Goddesses, Whores, Wives, and Slaves: Women in Classical Antiquity* (New York: Schocken Books, 1995), 200.

15 See G.H.R Horsley, *New Documents Illustrating Early Christianity: A Review of the Greek Inscriptions and Papyri Published in 1977* Vol. 2 (AHDRC; Sydney: 1982), 27; Horsley uses the Latin Vulgate translation of purpuraria for 'purple seller' and admits that there was no single Latin word that could properly translate it. He further cites numerous Latin inscriptions from Rome that mention people who participated in this kind of trade as found in CIL (Corpus Inscriptionum Latinarum) 6.2.9843-9848, of special interest though is CIL 6. 4.3 that reports of one Veturia Fedra, a *purpuraria*, who set up the inscription by herself, her *patronus conlibertus* who lived with her for twenty years and a *libertus*. He therefore concludes in the following words: "One feature of these texts is that several people involved in this business are explicitly designated as ex-slaves. This may well be the most appropriate category in which to locate Lydia; that she is of freed status would be consonant not only with her occupation, but also with her name; see also G.H.R Horsley, New Documents Illustrating Early Christianity: A Review of the Greek Inscriptions and Papyri Published in 1978 (AHDRC; Sydney: 1983), 54; Horsley admits that sometimes the name Lydia has been explained as an ethnic appellation or an ethnic slave name.

16 Ivoni Richter Reimer, *Women in the Acts of the Apostles: A Feminist Liberation Perspective* translated by Linda M. Maloney (Minneapolis Fortress Press, 1995), 108.

17 See Teresa J. Calpino, *Women, Work and Leadership in Acts* (Tubingen: Mohr Siebeck, 2014), p. 198; see also Witherington, *The Acts of the Apostles*, 491.

18 Witherington, *The Acts of the Apostles*, 491-492.

19 See Ascough, *Lydia*, 6-7; see also Horsley, *New Documents Illustrating Early Christianity*, 54, Horsley cites recent attestation of inscriptions of these kinds of women that include Julia Lydia of Sardis (L. Robert, BCH 102 [1978] 405; Julia Lydia Laterane of Ephesos, a high priestess and daughter of Asia (SEG 869; 857).

20 Horace, Carmen, Book 1:8.1;1:13.1;1:25.8; 3:9.6-7 in the W.E. Gladstone, *The Odes of Horace*, translated into English (London: John Murray, 1894), 11,17, 30 and 91.

Nevertheless, the introduction of Lydia's name using the dative ὀνόματι 'called' intimates a personal name and not appellative.[21] BNT seems to have this understanding when it introduces Lydia using the Sabaot conventional way of introducing a character in an episode or story. In most cases, if the name of the character were known, the storyteller would provide the name and a further description of whether it is man or woman, old or young. For example, *Kimii :murēēt ake nyēē /kikēēkuurēē Chēēbkōōk*, 'there was a certain man who was called *Chēēbkōōk*'.[22] Therefore, the phrase is rendered as *Kimii :cheebyoosyeet ake yooto nyēē /kikēēkuurēē Liitya* 'There was another woman there who was called Lydia'.

Also, the use of the phrase πόλεως Θυατείρων 'of (the) city of Thyatira' comports better with the idea of Lydia's citizenship status.[23] BNT uses proper name qualifiers in translating the phrase πόλεως Θυατείρων as *Kichōōnēē :cheebyoosyaanaa kirinkēēt ake nyēē /kikēēkuurēē Tyaatiira* 'that woman came from a town called Thyatira'. Having considered all factors and in line with the fluidity in the naming process outside Roman citizens, inscriptional evidence, presence of geographic names for women and the addition of 'City of Thyatira' to her name, we can conclude that Lydia was an immigrant to Philippi and not necessarily a former slave.[24]

Lydia's Profession

Second, Luke identifies her specific occupation/profession as a πορφυρόπωλις[25] 'a seller (dealer in) of purple-dyed garments' or 'a specialist in purple goods'; to distinguish her from the general cloth merchants. Essentially, πορφύρα can either mean 'the purple fish', the purple dye for wool obtained from the shellfish or murex. However, here it indicates the garment made from the dye of the shellfish, also known as the purple fish.[26] The use of the colour purple connotes royalty. Imperial monopoly of the trade is anterior-to the writing of this letter. That may explain the difficulty implied in the profession assigned to Lydia.

21 Lenski, The Interpretation of the Acts of the Apostles, 656.
22 Such introductions of characters in Sabaot stories are common, whether as major or minor characters. Some of the examples are exemplified in the collections of Sabaot stories in K. Kigai, P.B. Mang'esoy & Iver Larsen (eds.) *Kī Tuuyēch: Mākoonkōōk Kēny* (Nairobi: Bible Translation and Literacy (E.A.), 10, 23, 24. *chēēbto nyēē /kikēēkuurēē Chēēsiro*, 'a girl who was called *Chēēsiro*', *Kimii :murēēt ake nyēē /kikēēkuurēē Chēēbkōōk*, 'there was a certain man who was called *Chēēbkōōk*' */Kikēēkuurēē choorwaanaa bo Chēēbkōōk Araab Cheeseebe*. 'The friend of *Chēēbkōōk* was called *Araab Cheeseebe*'.
23 See Lenski, The Interpretation of the Acts of the Apostles, 656.
24 Calpino, Women, Work and Leadership in Acts, 198.
25 This term is only used here in the New Testament.
26 See William F. Arndt & F. Wilbur Gingrich (eds.), *A Greek-English Lexicon of the New Testament and Other Early Christian Literature* (London: The University of Chicago Press, 1957), 700; see also Fredrick W. Danker & Walter Bauer (eds.), *A Greek-English Lexicon of the New Testament and Other Early Christian Literature 3rdEd (BDAG)* (Chicago: The University of Chicago Press, 2000).

There has been much scholarly debate about the descriptions of Lydia's profession. This has implications for her social status and not her profession.[27] Matthews points out that "the disagreement stems in part from conflicting views concerning the respectability of merchants in antiquity."[28] Typically, there have been three stereotypical views from scholars about Lydia's profession. Some argue that Lydia was a person of means, for she needed a substantial amount of wealth and capital to deal that trade.[29] The kind of cloth she handled was highly prized and mostly reserved for emperors and upper classes of society.[30] Scholars who argue this position, assume that Lydia was of high social status because of her profession, ability to offer hospitality to the missionary team and being in charge of a household.

On the contrary, others hold the view that Lydia's purple dyeing profession was considered a low-status job requiring little wealth from the elite class,[31] probably because of its abhorrent process and the products used in dyeing.[32] They argue that just because Lydia was a handler of expensive material meant for the ruling class, this did not mean she shared their status. Reimer uses the writings of Cicero to demonstrate how people viewed the profession as lowly and therefore concludes the trade possibly occurred outside the city gate because people considered it filthy.[33] That said, Lydia is described as a 'seller', 'merchant', 'trader' and sometimes a 'dealer' and not a producer of purple dye products. Even if she operated both, the employees were expected to do both and not the owner.[34] Therefore, the argument that Lydia's profession involved a process that was 'dirty' and therefore low status does not hold.

---

27 See Reimer, *Women in the Acts of the Apostles,* 99; see also Matthews, *First converts,* 86. Matthews admits that the dispute among the scholars is how to interpret Lydia's status in respect to the modifiers attached to her name.

28 Matthews, *First converts,* 86.

29 See Matthews, *First converts,* 86; see also Haenchen, *The Acts of the Apostles*, 494; R. J. Knowling, 'The Acts of the Apostles' in *The Expositor's Greek Testament* (London: Hodder & Stoughton, 1990), 345; Lenski, *Interpretation of the Acts of the Apostles,* 657; Lenski highlights that Lydia's profession required large capital and possibly she was a widow who carried on with her husband's business. However, there has been inscriptional evidence indicating that there were wealthy and influential women in the society in Lydia's time. Some of the fragmentary Latin inscriptions from Philippi appear to refer to dealers in purple CIL 3.664.1 and CIG 2519 use the feminine form πορφυρόπωλις that confirms that women were involved in the profession; W. M. Ramsay, *St Paul the Traveller and the Roman Citizen* (New York: G.P. Putnam's Sons, 1896), 214; Ramsay concurs with Lenski's thought that she must have possessed a large amount of capital and since the husband is not mentioned then probably she was a widow; Patterson, Dorothy Kelly & Rhonda Harrington Kelley (eds.), *Women's Evangelical Commentary: New Testament* (Nashville: B & H Publishing Group, 2011), 317; Kelley acknowledges that Lydia's kind of business and her ability to house the group of missionaries demonstrated that she had wealth.

30 See Matson, *Household Conversion Narratives in Acts*, 143-144; Lenski, *Interpretation of the Acts of the Apostles,* 657, mentions that the purple dye was considered to be a royal garment worn by rich Romans, prominent ladies, state officials and emperors; Kelley (eds.), *Women's Evangelical Commentary*, 317;Harold E. Will, *Will's Commentary on the New Testament Including a Contemporary Rendition: Volume 5-Acts* (Grafton: 1995), 272.

31 See Matthews, *First converts,* 86; Pervo, *Acts*, 404; Pervo mentions that Lydia was practicing an unpleasant profession and that would have probably earned her a low status in the society.

32 Jason T. Lamoreaux, Ritual, Women, and Philippi: Reimagining the Early Philippian Community (Eugene: Wipf & Stock Publishers, 2013), 103.

33 See Reimer, *Women in the Acts of the Apostles*, 105-107; See also Cicero, De Officiis. 1.42, Translated by Andrew P. Peabody, *Cicero De Officiis; Translated with and Introduction and Notes* (Boston: Little, Brown and Company 1887), 42-43; Schottroff, Let *the Oppressed Go Free*, 132.

34 Schottroff, Let the Oppressed Go Free, 132.

Still, others hold a middle position that Lydia was not necessarily of high status in the society, but rather her profession earned her a quasi-elite status.[35] The concession is based on was that the occupation being smelly, yet it brought wealth and prestige to the city. Pervo proposes that by ancient standards Lydia would not be considered as rich although early Christians may have regarded her so.[36] Parsons argues that Lydia's position, as a householder, was enough for her to be considered successful. However, his description of her as "of low status but (relatively) high income" places her in this middle position.[37]

BNT renders this description with the phrase *nyēē kyooltootē sirooychēē ki ārroonēch chēbo āliisyēēt nyēbo barak miisin* 'who used to sell dresses/clothes that were red of very high/much price'. As it is, *nyēē kyooltootē* 'who used to sell' is to emphasise that Lydia was a seller. A trader is known by the Sabaot indigenous term *cheemung'aaryaanteet* 'businesswoman or businessman' from the noun *mung'aareet* 'trade', to mean 'one who practices trade'.

Lydia's Cosmopolitan and Geographical Position

Luke skilfully and carefully adds the third description of Lydia as being an indigene of the urban city of Thyatira[38] when he uses the phrase πόλεως Θυατείρων. Technically both cities (Thyatira and Philippi) had experienced the two dominant cultures, a situation in which Lydia found herself. In this light, Ascough best describes Lydia as 'cosmopolitan' which, in this case, means "one who is at home in diverse contexts."[39] Lydia can, therefore, be said to be an immigrant of Macedonia either as a resident or as just travelling for business and an indigene of Asia Minor. This information thus confirms her identity, which some scholars explain as European.[40] It corroborates her professional links and helps provide evidence of the roots of her purple-dye business.

---

35 Matthews, *First converts*, 86.
36 Pervo, *Acts*, 403.
37 Mikeal C. Parsons, *Acts* (Grand Rapids: Baker Publishing Group, 2008), 230.
38 See Craig S. Keener, *Acts: An Exegetical Commentary, Volume 1, Introduction and 1:1-2:47* (Grand Rapids: Baker Academic, 2012), 2395; Keener details some of the aspects of this urban city as follows: first, its own imperial cult; second, the coins depicted the local tutelary deity, Apollo Tyrimnos…holding the emperor's hand; third, the city had a Jewish community; fourth, it was known for its craftspeople and merchants who belonged to strong guilds; fifth, these guilds worshipped the emperor; sixth, this city was strategically positioned geographically for trade, and seventh, it was famous for dyes and dyer guilds as attested in seven inscriptions (CIG 3496-98).
39 Ascough, *Lydia,* 14.
40 Several biblical scholars have designated the region of Paul's mission as being to Europe. Some even express that Lydia was the first convert in Europe, which technically makes her a European. It should be appreciated that Luke is writing in a context and the use of this designation was not used in the first century unless it is for a specific reason for which it should be acknowledged. See also Pervo, *Acts,* 389-390; Matson, *Household Conversion Narratives in Acts*, 136, 139,141-142,150,151 and 153; Charles H. Talbert, *Reading Acts: A Literary and Theological Commentary on the Acts of the Apostles* (Macon: Smyth & Helwys Publishing, Inc, 2005), 138; Bruce, *Commentary on the Book of the Acts,* 331; Lenski, *The Interpretation of the Acts of the Apostles*, 657; Spencer, *Acts*, 162-164.

Thyatira city was celebrated and famous for the skill of making purple-dyes and trade of purple-dying.[41] A special guild of dyers existed, and inscriptional evidence points to this fact.[42] During the Roman Empire, dye works and clothing manufacturing was established, but this trade was well known prior to this time in Thyatira.[43] However, the Thyatiran purple might be classified as an 'imitation' purple because of the materials used. Keener explains that Thyatiran purple, known today as "Turkey red", is "from the root of the local madder plant rather than the murex shellfish."[44]

Nevertheless, the above two descriptions of Lydia give details on her economic status and geographical position. As a purple-dye trader, whether as an independent seller or an agent of her native city, whether the cloth was imitation or first-class, Lydia is known for her kind of profession and not her status in the society. Some factors may have contributed her kind of profession, which include the fact that Philippi could have provided the necessary market for her products because of the presence of both retired and active Romans in service in the city as earlier mentioned. Also, the position of Thyatira situated at the crossroads of four major roads to Magnesia, Pergamum, Sardis and Smyrna created the necessary link and therefore made it a centre of trade and industry.[45] It was common for traders, artisans, and people, in general, to move from one city and settle or work in another city. These groups of people would live by the "laws and customs of the host city, with specific liabilities and privileges according to the individual situation."[46]

---

41 See Lenski, *The Interpretation of the Acts of the Apostles*, 656-657; see also Ramsay, *St Paul the Traveller*, 214; Bruce, *Commentary on the Book of the Acts*, 331; G.H.C MacGregor & Theodore P. Ferris(eds.), 'The Acts of the Apostles' in The Interpreter's Bible (Nashville: Abingdon Press, 1954), 219; Marshall, *The Acts of the Apostles*, 267; Matson, *Household Conversion Narratives in Acts*, 143; Longenecker, *The Acts of the Apostles*, 461; Longenecker points out that this trade was famous in the Thyatiran city and further mentions that most of these activities were carried out by women at home; Homer, Iliad 4.141-142; Keener, *Acts*, 2395.

42 See Ascough, Lydia, 18; Keener, Acts, 2395-2396; Lenski, The Interpretation of the Acts of the Apostles, 656-657; Ramsay, *St Paul the Traveller*, 214; C.K. Barrett, *A Critical and Exegetical Commentary on the Acts of the Apostles: Introduction and Commentary on Acts 15-28* (London: T & T Clark Ltd, 1998), 782. Some of the Latin Inscriptions from Philippi that mention dealers in purple include CIL 3.664.1 that uses pu]rpurari[us or i], which honours a purple dyer from Thyatira; ND 2.27 has examples from somewhere else; CIG 2519 uses the feminine form πορφυρόπωλις to confirm the activity of women in this trade. There are other inscriptions from other places like Thessalonica in IG 10.2.1.291 that mention a purple dealer from Thyatira in Macedonia; this gives a connection of Macedonia and Asia Minor in this business.

43 See Reimer, *Women in the Acts of the Apostles*, 100; see also Abiel Abbott Livermore, *The Acts of the Apostles with a Commentary* (Boston: James Munroe and Company, 1844), 228.

44 Keener, *Acts*, 2396.

45 Ramsay, *St Paul the Traveller*, 214.

46 John E. Stambaugh& David L. Balch (eds.), *The New Testament in Its Social Environment* (Philadelphia: The Westminster Press, 1986), 41. Schottroff, *Let the Oppressed Go Free*, 133.

Fourth, Luke uses another problematic identifier that points to her religious standing when he describes Lydia using the phrase σεβομένη τὸν Θεόν that means God-fearer or worshipper of God.[47] The BNT seems to have adapted the second meaning when they describe her as ānkikutunkyinē *Yēyiin* 'was kneeling before God'. Thus, the intransitive verb *kutuny* meaning 'kneel' is used; in this case, the action was done repeatedly by Lydia. However, it can also be translated using a descriptive equivalence in the phrase *iywēye Yēyiin* 'fearer of God or fears God'.

That said, this problematic identification has generated considerable scholarly debate. Some scholars assume that the technical term 'God-fearers' commonly referred to by the Greek, Latin and Hebrew as σεβόμενοί τὸν Θεόν, *metuentes* and *yir'êshamayim* 'fearers of Heaven' to mean 'Gentiles'.[48] Others refer to them as 'polytheists 'or 'sympathisers' attracted to the Israelite religion but have not become proselytes;[49] thereby subscribing to a kind of hybrid worship which Ramsay describes as "half Jewish, half pagan."[50]Some scholars challenge this theory and instead propose that the technical term refers to pious Jews and not to Gentile God-fearers.[51]

Scholars such as A.T. Kraabel deny the existence of σεβομέη τὸν Θεόν and instead advance that it is a Lukan literary invention for his theological purpose and no such corresponding class or group of people existed in history.[52] In response to this, some scholars have been able to present varied evidence for the existence of 'God-fearers' from Greek and Latin inscriptions, intertestamental literature, LXX, works of Philo and Josephus, rabbinic literature, NT, and patristic literature of other

47 BDAG, 746. Arndt (eds.), *A Greek-English Lexicon of the New Testament*, 753.

48 This can be traced from the Midrash Rabbah on Deuteronomy, and it is used to describe a Gentile who had accepted the truth of the Jewish religion but had not been circumcised.

49 See J. PaulPollard, 'Women in the Earlier Philippian Church (Acts 16:13-15, Phil. 4:2-3) in Recent Scholarship', in Caroll D. Osburn, *Essays on Women in Early Christianity* (Eugene: Wipf & Stock Publishers, 1993), 261-280 (268); see also Witherington, *The Acts of the Apostles*, 493; Barrett, *The Acts of the Apostles*, 783, Barrett uses the designation 'sympathiser' and concludes that Lydia should be understood as 'a devout woman'; Reimer, *Women in the Acts of the Apostles*, 93; Reimer also uses the word 'sympathiser' but adds that this description should be understood within the context of the synagogue and Sabbath.

50 See Ramsay, *St Paul the Traveller*, 215; see also Ralph Marcus, 'The Sebomenoi in Josephus', *Jewish Social Studies*, Vol. 14. No. 3 (July, 19520, 247-250 (247).

51 See Marcus, 'The Sebomenoi in Josephus', 247, This idea has been propagated by Feldman and Kirsopp Lake who use the writings of Josephus, Antiquities 14.110 to demonstrate that Josephus reports of the presence of God-fearing Jews all over the world including those in Asia and Europe who were contributing gifts to the temple in Jerusalem; see also F.J. Foakes Jackson & Kirsopp Lake (eds.), *The Beginnings of Christianity: The Acts of the Apostles* (Eugene: Wipf & Stock Publishers, 2002), 85; Feldman, 'Jewish, Sympathizers in Classical Literature and Inscriptions', *Transactions of the American Philological Association*, Vol. 81(1950), 200-209.

52 See A.T. Kraabel, 'The Disappearance of the 'God-Fearers'', *Numen*, Vol.28, Fasc.2 (December, 1981), 113-126 (120). Kraabel points out that the absence of inscriptional references to either God-fearers or God-worshippers from the archaeological remains of the six Diaspora synagogues is evidence that the use of these terms in Acts was Lukan creation. k

world religions.[53] Louis Feldman draws his evidence for the existence of God-fearers from literary and epigraphic sources.[54] Reynolds and Tannenbaum also unearthed inscriptional evidence from the synagogue at Aphrodisias that corroborates the use of the term θεοσεβής for its members.[55]

Building on this discovery, Levinskaya argues that the inscription gives the strongest rebuttal of Kraabel's doubts for it validates the "widespread interest in Judaism attested during the first century."[56] Moreover, while responding to Wilcox and Kirsopp, Lake interprets σεβομέη τὸν Θεόν as referring to the pious in the Jewish community without necessarily making a distinction.[57] She points out that words have a technical meaning when they are used in a particular context, otherwise it has a more general meaning.[58] It, therefore, behoves the author to determine and distinguish how the word is used. Kraabel uses this evidence to suggest that the inscriptional evidence only refers to pious Gentiles' contribution to the synagogue. Probably Matthews is a more persuasive critique of Kraabel's argument on the non-existence of σεβομέη τὸν Θεόν. He notes that historical reality of their existence is one issue and literary construction by Luke is another.[59] These scholars reconstruct and analyse the evidence concerning God-fearers, and the possible terms used and establish that there existed a group of 'sympathisers' or 'semi-Jews'.[60] Even though they may not have been a well-defined group of people, they historically existed, thus illustrating a grey area where boundaries were not clear and defined.

53 See Pollard, 'Women in the Earlier Philippian Church', 268. Some of the Greek and Latin early writers include: first, Petronius who makes a distinction between those who eat pork and adopt monotheism as 'sympathizers' while those who undergo circumcision are full-fledged Jews. Second, Epictetus makes a distinction between a sympathizer and a Jew by virtue of baptism. Third, Juvenal, Satires 14.69 describes the progression of a sympathizer from observing Sabbath, accepting monotheism, abstaining from pork, and finally becoming a fully-fledged Jew by undergoing circumcision. Fourth, Dio Cassius reports of execution that took place after some members had affiliations with Judaism; see also Josephus, *Antiquities,* 11:85,14:110, Philo, *De Virtutibus,* 179.

54 Literary evidence includes evidence from the Hebrew Bible, the Septuagint, NT, Greek, and Latin authors, Jewish authors (Josephus and Philo), Talmudic and Midrashic sources while epigraphical evidence is from synagogue inscriptions found in Diaspora Israelite religion and mostly in Asia Minor.

55 Joyce Reynolds & Robert Tannenbaum (eds.), *Jews and Godfearers at Aphrodisias* (Cambridge: Philological Society, 1987), 65. θεοσεβής appears in the Aphrodisias inscription three times and in all places, it is used in connection to a proper name. Most importantly, the inscription is dated to the early third century CE.

56 See Stephen Llewelyn, *New Documents Illustrating Early Christianity, Vol 9: A Review of the Greek inscriptions and Papyri Published in 1986-87* (Grand Rapids: Wm. B. Eerdmans Publishing Co., 2002), 79; see also Irina A. Levinskaya, 'The Inscription from the Aphrodisias and the Problem of God-Fearers', *Tyndale Bulletin* Vol. 41, No. 2 (1990), 312-318 (316). The Aphrodisias inscription that was discovered most likely in the third century, lists and includes the God-fearers as an official group of people and further traces rules, they abide by.

57 See Matthews, *First Converts*, 56-57; see also Lake (eds.), *The Beginnings of Christianity*, 88; Wilcox uses Luke 1:50 a verse from the Magnificat as a strong indication that 'God- fearers' is not an exclusive signifier of Gentile synagogue affiliates while Lake cites Acts 13:43a for the same argument since it is paired with proselytes, a technical term for Jewish converts.

58 See Lake (eds.), *The Beginnings of Christianity*, 88; Lake argues that the terms σεβομέη τὸν Θεόν and σεβόμενοιτον Θεόν describe the non-Jews who believed in monotheistic God of the Jews and possibly attended the synagogue but that does not mean they could not be used to describe the pious Jews; see also M. Wilcox, 'The "Godfearers" in Acts: A Reconsideration', *JSNT*, Vol. 13 (1981), 102-122. While using the Inscription from Miletos (CIJ 2.748), he translates and prefers reading the term as pious Jews and further relates that to Acts 13:16 to the piety of Israelite men. He concludes by suggesting that the term refers to the 'pious' amongst the Jewish community whether Jew or Gentile, proselyte or 'adherent'.

59 Matthews, *First Converts*, 56

60 Pollard, 'Women in the Earlier Philippian Church', 268.

In my opinion, the use of the terms "Jews" and "Gentiles" by modern scholars seems to aggravate the misunderstanding. These two words have always been used to either refer to Jews and Greeks or Judeans and Greek. Malina and Pilch point out,

> Judeans were people who practiced the customs of Judea, while Greeks were people who practiced the customs of Hellenists, a broad configuration of 'civilized' Mediterranean peoples characterized by their use of the common Greek language. Taking the phrase "Judean and Greek" to mean Jews and Greeks, or worse, Jews and Gentiles, is simply erroneous, as well as anachronistic and ethnocentric.[61]

The debate has been on whether to translate the term Ιουδαιος as 'Jew'[62] or 'Judean'[63] or even use the two interchangeably.[64] Yet others propose that none of them is a satisfactory translation and therefore problematic. The contention is whether this term refers to a particular or any other ethnic group, area, or religion.[65] The term as used in Palestine, emphasises geography while in the Diaspora it appealed to religion. Eric Orlin's explanation is quite helpful when he says,

> The idea that God fearers were Gentiles who selectively and partially worshipped the god of Israel without fully converting to Judaism depends on defining Jews primarily by "religion." It may be more productive to think of ancient Mediterranean Jews as an *ethnos*, like Romans, Egyptians, Celts and others, defined more by various shared practices (language, foods, marriage, funerals, worship) and beliefs (in common ancestry, homeland), and so forth. Joining the Jewish *ethnos*, then, would have required more than adopting, particular religious practices. So, too, the notion of Godfearers presumes an ancient norm of full practice, imagined to have been in force throughout the Greek and Roman Mediterranean, but usually derived from rabbinic paradigms.[66]

In essence, there was a porous line between the culture and the religion of the people and therefore the use of this term was a deliberate

61 Bruce J. Malina & John J. Pilch (eds.), *Social-Science Commentary on the Letters of Paul* (Minneapolis: Fortress Press, 2006), 4.

62 Scholars who propose that this term should be translated as 'Jew' recognize that even though 'Judean' was the most preferred term before the second century BCE its use shifted in the development of the history of Judaism especially during the Maccabean period and gradually, they were known as 'Jews'.

63 See Malcolm Lowe, "Who Were the IOUDAIOI?" *Novum Testamentum* 18 (1976), 101-130 (130); see also Steve Mason, 'Jew, Judaeans, Judaizing, Judaism: Problems of Categorization in Ancient History,' *JSJ* 38 (2007), 457-512 (510-511); Shaye J.D. Cohen, "Ioudaios: 'Judaean' and 'Jew' in Susanna, First Maccabees, and Second Maccabees." In H. Cancik, H. Lichtenbeger & P. Schafer (eds.), *Geschichte – Tradition – Reflexion: Festschrift fur Martin Hengel zum 70. Geburtstag: Volume 1: Judentum.* (Tubingen: Mohr Siebeck, 1996), 211-220 (212); Shaye J. D.Cohen, *The Beginnings of Jewishness: Boundaries, Varieties, Uncertainties* (Berkeley: University of California Press, 2001), 14-15.

64 Josephus is a good example of a writer who uses both 'Judean' and 'Jew' interchangeably of course with an understanding that one refers to the geography and religious where necessary.

65 Lowe, "Who Were the IOUDAIOI?", 102-103.

66 Eric Orlin, *The Routledge Encyclopaedia of Ancient Mediterranean Religions* (New York: Routledge, 2016), 372.

separation of the two in reference to the religion and not the culture possibly from rabbinical sources. Orlin articulates, "people in the ancient Mediterranean often venerated the gods of others in diverse ways (festivals, fasts, gifts), without necessarily giving up their own prior practices, or identifying themselves wholly or in part with those other groups."[67] Therefore, there is a possibility that Lydia had embraced the Jewish religion and practised Sabbath worship, probably a practice that she had adapted from her home country even before coming to Philippi.[68] For Josephus reports that in the time of Antiochus IV, about two thousand Jewish families were transported from Mesopotamia to Lydia and Phrygia.[69] Alternatively, she might have accepted the Jewish religion in Philippi while still maintaining her indigenous religious practises. That said, the ambiguity of Lydia's identity is quite significant; she cannot be identified either as Roman or Jewish, Macedonian or a European, wealthy or poor, free or ex-slave, married or not. She has a mixture of identities in her ethnic, economic, religious, and social position placing her among the most unique converts of the first century Christianity.

Conversion of Lydia

Despite her complex identity and ambiguous status, Luke reports that Lydia ῄκουεν ῆς 'was listening'. Significantly, the use of this imperfect indicates a repeated or continuous hearing in which finally ὁ κύριος διήνοιξ εν τὴν καρδίαν 'the Lord opened the heart'. This phrase is a fulsome description of a Hebrew form of speech that is reminiscent of 2 Maccabees 1:4 of Lydia's divinely inspired response to Paul's teaching. In this episode, the three actors are active: Paul speaks, Lydia listens, and finally, the Lord 'opens' Lydia's heart. Lydia's response in faith is therefore ascribed to divine activity, and it does not come because of a one-time event but rather after a repeated conversation with Paul, an action attributed to the Lord.[70] The reference to Paul and his companions going back to the prayer place in v.16 attests to this fact. Joel Green intimates that when Luke uses this metaphor it emphasises her transformation, which is 'deep-rooted and multifaceted, a transference of orientation and allegiance.'[71] This manifests in the practices she

67 Orlin, *The Routledge Encyclopaedia of Ancient Mediterranean Religions*, 372.
68 Longenecker, *The Acts of the Apostles*, 461.
69 Josephus, *Antiquities of the Jews* 12:147-153.
70 See Parsons, *Acts*, 230. Parsons emphasises on the divine nature of the conversion; see also Marshall, *The Acts of the Apostles*, 267; Marshall says, "conversion is due to the action of God who opens the hearts i.e. the minds, of men and women to receive his Word." Witherington, *The Acts of the Apostles*, 493.
71 Joel B. Green, "She and Her Household Were Baptized' (ACTS 16:15): Household Baptism in the Acts of the Apostles' in Stanley E. Porter & Anthony R. Cross (eds.*), Dimensions of Baptism: Biblical and Theological Studies* (New York: Sheffield Academic

performs in the next verse. BNT rendition has this understanding but omits the phrase διήνοιξεν τὴν καρδίαν 'opened the heart', instead it renders the metaphorical language with a non-metaphor as follows, *Kiyey :Yēyiin cheebyoosyaanaa kōōyēnchi ng'aleekaab Bāwulō.* 'God made that woman to respond/accept the words of Paul'.

Nida et al. recommend combining the two verbs διήνοιξεν 'opened' and προσέχειν 'pay attention to' as consequent actions and this explicates why the rendering of the phrase 'opened the heart' is not explicit. They propose,

> In some languages it is important to combine opened her mind with the phrase pay attention to as being two subsequent actions---for example, "caused her to be receptive to what Paul was saying and to believe it."[72]

The last sentence, therefore, is broken down into two subsequent actions that are 'caused her to be receptive' and 'believe'. BNT has the two verbs as follows: *Kiyey* from the transitive verb *yey* that means, 'to do or create'. The same root word is used regarding *Yēyiintēēt* 'God' as the creator. Thus, if the action is ascribed to God, then it would make sense in the Sabaot understanding. The other verb προσέχειν is *kōōyēnchi* from the transitive verb *yēn* that means, 'to respond favourably to'. This means a positive response that has a connotation of accepting the message as presented by Paul. That said, καρδίαν is a seat of physical, spiritual and mental life. Therefore, it is the centre and source of the whole of the inner life that includes thinking, feeling, and volition. In this verse, the 'heart' designates of the inner awareness and therefore, should be understood as the seat of thought.[73]

The Greek metaphor 'opened the heart' can be problematic even though the 'heart' can be translated using *mukuulēyto* an equivalent in Sabaot. However, the understanding of 'heart' in the context of this metaphor can be paralleled in Sabaot to other body parts such as *mooyēēt* 'stomach' which supersedes the emotional aspect of the heart. Normally an idiomatic expression *kiityaach mooyēēt* (literally 'the stomach was untied or released' like a prisoner) can be used to express this thought. Sabaot

Press Ltd, 2002), 72-90 (88).

72 Nida (eds.), A Translator's Handbook on the Acts of the Apostles, 314.

73 See BAGD; see also Jeff A. Benner, *New Testament Greek to Hebrew Dictionary* (College Station: Virtualbookworm.com Publishing Inc., 2010), 6. The noun in Hebrew has the meaning of mind but is also seen as the seat of thought. Besides the Hebrew equivalent of καρδίαν has two nouns *ley-vav* that mean mind, literally the vital organ which pumps blood, but, is also seen as the seat of thought. The mind and *leyv* that means heart, literally, the vital organ which pumps blood, also seen as the seat of thought; the mind. The noun used in this argument is *ley-vav.*

use the expression when a person's mind is 'shut or closed' to something, thought or opinion. When it is 'released or untied' or has a positive attitude towards the same, then, it can be said to be open.

Implications for Women in Africa

Drawing on contributions from Lydia, a cosmopolitan woman, the article looks at several implications of Luke's description of her identity and the commentators varied interpretations attached to it. When Luke reveals Lydia's identity in Acts 16:14, he does so with the sole purpose of giving his readers a description of a significant woman of faith and in Paul's missionary activities in first-century Greco-Roman world. However, the varied interpretations by Biblical scholars tend to focus on her social status, citizenship and religious standing rather than her personality or character. The descriptions of her identities are based on the stereotypical views from the elite class demonstrating her kind of stratified society or even the different theological positions held by religious leaders and commentators from the Greco-Roman world.

Wayne Meeks, for example, highlights some of the indices a person of higher status in Roman colonies and provinces like Philippi displayed include Roman citizenship compared with resident aliens, being a city councillor, having wealth more preferably inherited rather than worked for, investment in land rather than trade, family and origin.[74]

Lydia is presented as possibly a single woman, who could not attain a high position in the social hierarchy in terms of sexual identity, yet her profession probably posed a fair amount wealth and a relatively high economic status but its production was considered low in status. Besides, she was involved in trade rather than land, which belonged to the elite class. Nonetheless, the description acknowledges her wealthy profession as a trader rather than her status. Her name does not indicate whether she is a slave, freedwoman or freeborn and therefore her overall status cannot be known.

Unlike several women in the Bible who remain nameless, Luke gives this woman identity in her context. Even though σεβομένη τὸν Θεόν may not have been a well-defined group of people, they historically existed, thus illustrating a grey area where boundaries were not clearly defined. Nevertheless, the universality of Jesus Christ and Christianity

74 Wayne A. Meeks, *The Moral World of the First Christians*, (Philadelphia: Westminster John Knox Press, 1986), 34.

that transcends any language, ethnicity, social class or nation completely transforms her life, home and community when the Lord opens her heart.[75] Her contested religious standing becomes the 'preparatio evangelica' for the Gospel of Jesus Christ, just as the pre-Christian past of the African cultures and religions have become the part of the longstanding tradition of the (early) Church.[76]

Although the article is about Lydia, I believe that we can link her complex identity to Allison M. Howell, a woman missionary, born in Africa, who returned to Africa, and for whom we honour in this Festschrift. The efforts, ministry and life of Howell as a woman, Christian worker and a migrant from Australia to Ghana for over decades reveals how she was/can integrate in a multi-ethnic and religious society while maintaining her connections and identity with her indigenous roots. As a worker, she is not just an academic theologian, but a Church woman who used her intellectual gifts and previous training to serve the church and communities she finds herself in. She invests her time and gifts in learning languages and cultures in countries and places where her indigenous language (English) and cultures are considerably different from her own.[77]

Economically, Howell empowers and raises funds for institutions she is engaged with (including Akrofi-Christaller Institute of Theology, Mission and Culture), community projects and transforming women's lives.

She gets herself involved in dealing with the challenges of women and men in a cosmopolitan society such as Accra where she used to live and at ACI where students struggle to juggle as parents, researchers, Christian workers and migrants. She can achieve this because she is equipped, empowered and can use her training in anthropology which informs her approach of dealing with people from such cosmopolitan societies.[78] Her deeper religious convictions and faith in Jesus Christ enable her to

reflect, interpret and apply Scriptures to the different situations that face her, her community and her environment. She has championed these convictions in her teaching ministry, community projects and care for the environment. All the above descriptions of Howell's identity and

75 Kwame Bediako, *Jesus in Africa: The Christian Gospel in African History and Experience*, (Carlisle, Cumbria, UK: Editions Cle, and Regnum Africa, 2000), 24.

76 Bediako, *Jesus in Africa*, 26.

77 See Allison M. Howell, *A Daily Guide for Culture and Language Learning* (Accra: AmaraZaane Consulting Services Limited, 2014), v; see also Andrew F. Walls, 'Foreword', in Allison M. Howell, *The Religious Itinerary of a Ghanaian People: The Kasena and the Christian Gospel* (Achimota: Africa Christian Press, 2001), vi.

78 Walls, 'Foreword', vi.

achievements make her a household name in communities where she has taught, worked and lived.

Even though the African cosmopolitan societies and churches may offer some kind of escape from the inbuilt traditional social stratification and identity, the host society may even increase the pressure on women to conform because they too have their own multiple identities in which they have to adapt. For example, gender roles (identities) in most African societies traditionally define the female as a homemaker and the male as a financial provider. However, it may seem that systems and institutions in the cosmopolitan cities today have shifted and transformed these identities and in response, more women are providing financial stability to their families while men fill the roles of homemakers and caregivers.

Therefore, as African Christian women of once locally defined cultures emigrate and venture into cosmopolitan contexts, they understandably seek to retain some aspects of their traditional ancestry and identity that include language, dressing, cuisine and religion. Most of them form associations to reinforce their local or national identities where they can meet, eat and drink together, venerate their deities and even assume the responsibility of giving 'proper' burial of their fellow indigenes in the foreign land or even taking them home.

Conclusion

Migration and Africa's colonial history destabilised some of the local or ethnic identities including Sabaot, yet there have been concerted efforts to preserve some of them, a responsibility mostly enforced by women. However, cosmopolitanism should be able to promote global universality and not new social hierarchies that reconfigure society and church missions into new inequalities and particularities; thus, there is a need for balance. This is only achievable when African Christian women and leaders are properly trained, empowered socially, mentally and economically and also encouraged to appreciate their own indigenous cultures and languages. Lydia's mixture of identities in her ethnic, economic, religious, and social position places her among the most unique women converts of the first century Christianity, a model that can be replicated and used to encourage the struggling cosmopolitan African Christian woman and workers today seeking to be understood.

Translation of 'Visiting the Iniquity of Fathers upon Sons...' (Exodus 20:5) into Kinyarwanda[1]

Gabriel Akimana

Abstract

God's second commandment contains what appears to be a threat, 'a jealous God visiting the iniquity of fathers upon sons up to the third and fourth generation'. This sounds embarrassing in the ears of modern-day readers and interpreters. In some Bible versions, a reader may understand that God punishes innocent children, grandchildren and great-grandchildren because of the sins of their parents. Some other passages, like Ezekiel 18:20, however, emphasize individual accountability and this raises questions about an apparent contradiction. The source of misunderstanding stems from the interpretation of the phrase 'vising iniquity'. Many Bible versions render the Hebrew participle *pōqēd* 'visiting' as 'punishing' or 'taking revenge'. All the four current Kinyarwanda Bible versions translate in that sense as *guhana* 'to punish' or *guhora* 'to revenge''. The present paper traces and discusses the history of translation and interpretation of that phrase in the context of the second commandment and argues for the use of the verb *kugenza* 'to investigate' in Kinyarwanda translation. This contribution is made in honour of Allison Howell who has raised concern about the need of the Bible translated into indigenous languages and interpreted in the light of the context of local communities.

1 The issue was briefly discussed without details by Gabriel Akimana, 'Translation Issues in an Inter-confessional Bible Version: An Evaluation of Bibiliya Ijambo ry'Imana through A Hebrew-Kinyarwanda Analysis of Selected Passages' (Unpublished Thesis, Akrofi-Christaller Institute of Theology, Mission and Culture, Akropong-Akuapem, 2016), 219.

Introduction

Lamin Sanneh has demonstrated that in order to achieve successful evangelisation, the Gospel should be translated into the culture and worldview of the people.[2] In that respect, the Bible as the basis of Christian beliefs and teachings has to be faithfully translated into indigenous languages and interpreted in the context of the reading communities. In her ministry, Allison Howell has raised concern about translation of the Gospel in general and of the Bible in particular. She has stressed the need for Bible commentaries to be composed and written in indigenous languages and reflect their contexts rather than translating Bible commentaries from Western languages and contexts.[3] The present paper on the translation of a Biblical passage into one of the African languages is written in her honour.

Part of the rationale of the second commandment (Exod. 20:5.6; Deut. 5:9) literally reads: 'for I, the Lord your God, am a jealous God, visiting the iniquity of fathers upon sons up to the thirds and fourths, to my haters'. Reading some Bible versions, some may interpret this as God punishing innocent children, grandchildren and great-grandchildren because of the sins of their parents. One may wonder—and it has always been so—how and why a merciful God of justice could punish innocent children because of the sins of their parents or ancestors. The misunderstanding is mainly based on the interpretation of the phrase 'visiting iniquity'.

Many Bible versions render the Hebrew participial phrase *pōqēd* 'visiting' as 'punishing' or 'taking revenge'. All the four current Kinyarwanda Bible versions have inherited from foreign languages versions[4] the translation of the Hebrew *pōqēd* as 'punishing' or 'taking revenge". This is problematic because the ideology of the (so-called) punishment of innocent descendants due to the sins of their ancestors is one of the weapons used by genocide ideologists and perpetrators. Moreover, such a reading is potentially dangerous in a post-genocide context as it entertains the spirit of retaliation. The present paper traces and discusses the history of translation and interpretation of the statement and suggests an alternative Kinyarwanda rendering that could contribute to the education of post-genocide generations in Rwanda.

2 Lamin Sanneh, *Translating the Message: The Missionary Impact on Culture*, Maryknoll: Orbis Books, 2009.
3 Allison Howell, 'Beyond Translating Western Commentaries in the Commentary Writing in African Languages', *Journal of African Christian Thought*, Vol. 13, No.2 (December 2010), 21-33.
4 *Bibiliya Yera* (BY), *Bibiliya Ntagatifu* (BN) and *Bibiliya Ijambo ry'Imana* (BII) are based on English and French Bible versions cross-checked with the originals. *Bibiliya Ubuhinduzi bw'Isi Nshya* (BUIN) is based completely on The New World Translation. For the history of the Kinyarwanda versions see Akimana, Translation Issues, 92-124.

Pōqēd as Taking Vengeance or Punishing

The most widespread interpretation and translation of the Hebrew participle *pōqēd* is 'punishing' or 'taking vengeance'. The tradition can be traced back to the LXX's *apodidous* ('giving back') followed by the other early Greek versions of the Old Testament[5] and other languages which depended on the LXX in translation.[6] In the LXX, the sins of the fathers are 'given back' to the children until the third and fourth generation. This implies that those who are punished are guilty, but it is more likely that the fathers are not included among those who are punished. The supplement of the word 'generation' which is not in the Hebrew became a source of complication in later translations. However, the LXX carefully avoids confusion by reproducing the Hebrew preposition *l^e^* with the dative 'to those [who hate me]' instead of 'of those [who hate me]'. By so doing, the reader would understand that the generations of the progeny are also part of those who hate the Lord.

Latin speaking interpreters generally use the various forms of *reddo* 'to give back' and other synonyms like *retribuo*. While 'giving back' appears in translations, 'punishing' is used as its parallel or synonym in commentaries. Interpretation details in that category vary about whom, when, how and why God punishes. Writing to Paula to comfort her about the death of Braesilla, a twenty-year old, brilliant woman with fervent faith, Jerome (c. 347-420) raised questions about God's justice, especially the prosperity of the wicked and the misery of the righteous. He questions why the wicked have wealth and good health and live long enough to blaspheme God while innocent children and untutored young people die early. Referring to the contradictions in the Bible, for example, 'the soul that sins is the one that will die' (Ezekiel 18:20), on the one hand, and the countless sins of an old man being avenged upon a harmless infant (Exodus 20:5), on the other, he concluded that God is unfathomable and sovereign in his judgements. Therefore, any believer of Christ must rejoice in all his judgments no matter the circumstances.[7]

Quoting Dionysus, Eusebius relates how Macrianus, the General and advisor of Valerian who was also the Chief of the synagogue of the Egyptian gods, induced Valerian to persecute Christians with whom

5 So Theodotion, Simmachus and even Aquila who is notorious for being literal. Origen, Hexapla, Text edited by Fredericus Field, *Origenes Hexaplorum, Tomus I: Genesis-Esther* (Oxonii: Typographeo Clarendoniano, 1875), 115.

6 The Ethiopian Ge'ez translates this word in the same way. Acknowledging my ignorance in that language, I am thankful to Seblewengel Daniel and Agizachew for their help.

7 Jerome, Letter XXXIX. Ad Paulam de Morte Blesillae, Text edited by Isidore Hilberg, I., Sancti Eusebii Hieronymi Epistulae, Pars I: Epistulae I-LXX, Scriptorolum Ecclestiasticorum Latinum, Vol. LIV (Vindobonae: F. Tempsky, Lipsae: G. Freytag, 1910), 297-298.

previously he had been friendly. As a result of Macrianus' advice, Valerian attacked Syria, but he was defeated and killed. Macrianus took over from him and he gave power to his two sons Queitus and Macrianus. Quietus was killed in Syria, Macrianus (father and son) were also killed in the West by pretenders. Eusebius interpreted the word of God saying 'I am he who renders the sins of fathers upon children up to the third and fourth generation of those who hate me' as being fulfilled upon Valerian and Macrianus. In his argument, Eusebius uses the Greek *apodidomi* or *antapodidomi* which the Latin translations render with *retribuo*.[8]

In Tertullian's view, the statement means that innocent children are punished with their sinning fathers. But he argued that that law had become obsolete with the coming of the apostolic era.[9] In the same line, an anonymous author appended to Tertullian argued that in former times God used to punish (*reddere*) the fathers and guiltless infants as he did it to humanity in the deluge and to the people of Sodom and Gomorrah, but with His great zeal of love, the same God sent His son Jesus to offer his blood and cleanse the whole world.[10]

Citing Exodus 20:5, Origen (c. 184-c.253) kept ἀποδιδοὺς [11] and Rufinus faithfully translated him into Latin using *reddens* 'giving back'.[12] Origen cited Exodus 20:5 among other passages in the Old Testament which according to the 'heretics' came from the mouth of another god different from the God of the New Testament. The heretics had argued that the God of Jesus Christ cannot exert the punishment of the fathers upon innocent children. Further in his *Against Celsus*, Origen argued that the text should be interpreted figuratively, since there are other passages which affirm that punishment should fall only on the sinner. However, he notified the reader that it was not yet time to go further.[13]

What the above interpreters share is the interpretation that the vengeance of God falls upon innocent children because of the sins of their parents. Except for Eusebius who applied the statement to the Pagans, the other early Church Fathers were troubled by that Old Testament statement. Some regarded the law as outdated. Others interpreted the statement figuratively. For Rabbinic interpreters, however, the children are

8 Eusebius, Ecclesiastical History, Book vii, Chap. 10. Migne, Eusebii of Pamphilii II, Patrologia Graecae, Vol. 20 (Paris: Vilgo d'Enfer, 1857), 661-62.
9 Tertullian, De Monogamia, Chap. Vii. Migne, Tertulliani, Vol. 2, (Paris: Vilgo d'Enfer, 1879), 979-1008 (987).
10 Anonymous, Adversus Marcionem Libri Quinque. Migne, Tertulliani, 1135.
11 Origen, 'De Principiis' . Redepening, Origenes De Principiis, (Lipsiae: in Bibliopolio Dikiano, 1836, 54.
12 Redepening, *Origenes De Principiis*, 337.
13 Origen, Against Celsus, Paul Koetschau, *Origenes Werke: Zweiter Band, Buch v-viii Gegen Celsus*, (Leipzig: J.C. Hinrichs'sche Buchhandlung, 1889), 254.

punished if they continue with the sins of their fathers. Some Christian interpreters also held the same position.

Like the LXX, the Aramaic targums supplied the word *dar* but in the construct state 'the generation of [those who hate me]'. However, to clarify the matter, the translators amplified the text indicating that the offspring are sinning as their fathers did.[14] The Pseudo-Jonathan Targum does alike with *wmtp̱r'* 'and returning'.[15] The Talmud cites the Hebrew text as 'visiting' but in commentary uses 'to [be] put to death'. Furthermore, it argues in the same direction; the children are punished if they hold fast to (literally: 'hold in their hands') the sins of their parents, or if they had power to restrain their fellows from evil but did not do so.[16] This means that some generations may be strong enough to break the sinning tradition and convince their parents to repent. The Targums and the Talmud became the reference and standard for most rabbinic interpretations.[17] On the model of the Targum, Umbro Cassuto, a contemporary Hebrew commentator, amplifies the text to stress that the punishment falls upon the progeny if they are part of those who hate the Lord.[18]

From a Christian perspective, Clement of Alexandria (c.150-c.215) argued that God is good, showing mercy to those who love him but also punishing those who hate him. He stressed that the aim of God's reproof is the salvation of those who are reproved. Even though he textually quoted from the LXX, it seems that he regarded those punished as guilty and deserving punishment. [19]

Preaching on Matthew 23:29-30, John Chrysostom (347-407) stressed repeatedly that Jewish leaders would be punished because their behaviour was worse than their fathers who killed the prophets. He used Ex. 20:5 to support his argument and stated,

> And this is what God says elsewhere: "Giving back the sins of fathers upon children, upon the third and fourth generation of those who hate me." Not as if for the crimes committed by others one were

14 Each Targum has its own way of putting it.
15 *Mikraot Gedolot*, http://mg.alhatorah.org/Full/Shemot/20.1#e0n6.
16 Sanhedrin, 27b, https://www.torah-box.com/torah-pdf/pdf/talmud_sanhedrine_27b.pdf?i=1.
17 See for example Rabbi Shelomo Yitzchaki (RASHI), Midrash Aggadah Buber, Tovia ben Eliezer, Shemuel ben Meir, Shabtai Bass, and Judah Loew of Prague. Mikraot Gedolot, http://mg.alhatorah.org/Full/Shemot/20.1#e0n6.
18 Umbro Cassuto, *A Commentary on the Book of Exodus*, Jerusalem, 1951; translated by Israel Abrahams, (University of Capetown, 1967), 242-43.
19 Clement of Alexandria, 'Paedagogus', Book 1, Chapter 8. Text edited by Nicolai Le Nourry, *Clementis Alexandrini*, Tomus Prior (Paris: Vulgo d'Enfer, 1857), 336.

> to suffer punishment, but as long as they who, after many have been sinning and have been punished, yet have not been better, but have committed the same offenses, are justly worthy to suffer their punishments also.[20]

In Augustine's view, only the guilty are punished for their sins. Primarily, he understood the sin in question as the original sin in which every human being is born. Second, the offspring shall suffer the double punishment if they persist in their parents' sins. Referring to Exodus 20: 5, he argued that those who imitate their fathers suffer not only their own punishment but also of those they have imitated.[21] Augustine understood the sin in question as the original sin transmitted from parents to their children. He cited Exodus 20:5 among other passages to support his argument related to the reality of the original sin. He stressed the use of the singular 'iniquity' which is passed upon all men. For him, "I shall render the iniquities of the fathers upon the children"[22] certainly applied to the children before they came under the regeneration of the new covenant, that is through Baptism as it was prophesized in Ezekiel 18:2.[23]

To the question 'why does God who is said to be just threaten to render the sins of the children up to the third and fourth generation?', Ambrosiaster (4th c) answered: 'The Lord neither does nor says any injustice, whoever doubts it is out of his mind.'[24] In his view, God punishes the fathers who persevere in their iniquity and their children who imitate them in idol worship. The same way he rewards the descendants of a righteous person who are righteous themselves with the double glory for a thousand years.[25]

Similarly, Aquinas held the same opinion that only the sinners and not the innocent are punished. Citing Exodus 20:5 alongside with Psalm 61:13 and Romans 2:7-8, he argued that humans, unlike things, have the right to do what is good and be rewarded or to do what is bad and get punished. Though he used the verb *visitare* in the citation he used it in the sense of *poenire* in his comment that God punishes or rewards everyone according to his (her) work.[26]

---

20 John Chrysostom, Gospel According to Saint Matthew, Homily LXXIV.2, Migne, *S.P.N. Ioannis Chrisostomi*. Tomus VII. Patrologiae Graecae, Vol. 58, (Paris: Vulgo d'Enfer, 1862), 681.
21 Augustine, 'Enarratio in Psalmum CIX', Section 15. Migne, J.-P. *Sancti Aurelii Augustini, Tomus Quartus, Pars Altera* (Paris: Vulgo d'Enfer, 1865), 436-37.
22 *Reddam peccata patrum in filios.*
23 Augustine, Enchiridion ad Lorentum, C. XLVI, Text edited by Herm. Bruder, *S. Aurelii Augustini de Doctrina Christiana Libri Quatuor et Enchiridion ad Laurentium*, (Lipsae: Smtibus et Typis Caroli Tauchnitii, 1838), 200-201.
24 *Nihil iniuste dominum facere aut dicere qui dubitat insanus est.*
25 Ambrosiaster, Questio XIIII [sic], Text edited by Alexander Souter, *Peudo Augustini Questiones Veteris et Novi Testamenti CXXVII* , Scriptorolum Exxlestiasticorum Latinum, Vol. L, (Lipsae: G. Freytag, 1908), 39-40.
26 Aquinas, Contra Gentiles, lib. 3 cap. 140 n. 9, https://www.corpusthomisticum.org/scg3111.html.

According to Luther, the threatening is part of the chief commandment, it equally applied to a person breaching any of the other commandments.[27] In Luther's perception, God cannot leave it unavenged if men turn from Him and trust and believe anything but Him. His anger cannot cease until the fourth generation, even until they are exterminated.[28]

Matthew Henry (1706-1772) regarded 'visiting iniquity' as meaning 'punishing it severely'. He argued that the punishment falls upon the children if they follow the tradition of 'idolatry' as inherited from their fathers. God is patient and forbears an idolatrous people up to the fourth generation. Punishment may consist of the total ruin of families and can also be executed upon the children after their parents are dead. But it becomes more severe and heart breaking if the parents live long enough to witness their children of the third or fourth generation perishing by the sword, carried away as captives or being enslaved.[29]

Some contemporary interpreters support the 'punishing' meaning and emphasize the importance of the individual responsibility. Victor Hamilton bases his argument on a statistical count of the use of the verb *pāqăd* in the Bible. He concludes that the verb means 'to visit' when is used without a preposition and 'to punish' when used with the preposition *b*ᵉ or *'al* as it is the case in Exodus 20:5. He acknowledges cases in the Ancient Near East and in the Bible where the innocent offspring could suffer punishment because of the sins of their fathers. For him, the Bible gives examples of both corporate and individual accountability even in the same prophecy of Ezekiel. But he still maintains that in the case of Exodus 20:5, 'those who hate me' applies also to the children.[30]

According to Peter Craigie, 'punishing iniquity' means that the false worshipping of the Lord had consequences on future generations because of lack of proper instruction concerning the covenant. It could affect the prosperity of the covenant community for more than one generation.[31] Similarly, John Borton points out that "The harshness of the threat in 5b-6 has to be evaluated in the light of far stronger community feeling than is normal with us. The worship of a god could not be an individual matter: the whole extended family shared in the sin-and therefore in the punishment."[32] Patrick Miller and Adam Clarke hold a similar position

27 In the Catholic and Lutheran traditions, the first commandment goes from vv. 2-6.
28 Luther, Large Catechism. *The Book of Concord*, 265-67. https://bookofconcord.org/pdf/TrigBOC.pdf.
29 Matthew Henry, *Commentary on the Whole Bible, Volume I (Genesis to Matthew Henry Deuteronomy)*, (Grand Rapids, Michigan: Christian Classics Ethereal Library), 529. http://www.ccel.org/ccel/henry/mhc1.html.
30 Victor Hamilton, *Exodus: An Exegetical Commentary* (Grand Rapids: Baker Academic), 2011, 473.
31 Peter C. Craigie, *The Book of Deuteronomy* (Grand Rapids, Michigan: Eerdmans), 1976, 130-31.
32 John Barton, *The Oxford Bible Commentary* (Oxford: Oxford University Press, 2001), 81.

among others.[33] Ryken and Hughes clearly express this position when they state,

> This is not to deny individual responsibility. God holds each one of us accountable for our own sin. The Bible says, "The soul who sins is the one who will die. The son will not share the guilt of the father, nor will the father share the guilt of the son" (Ezek. 18:20a). God never condemns the innocent but only the guilty. Here it is important to notice something in the second commandment that is often overlooked—namely, how the threat ends. God says that he will punish three or four generations "of those who hate me" (Exod. 20:5). It is not only the fathers who hate God but also their children. People who struggle with the fairness of this commandment usually assume that although the father is guilty, his children are innocent. But the children hate God as much as their father did (which, given the way they were raised, is not surprising). Therefore, it is fair and just for God to punish them for their sin and for their father's sin.[34]

Pōqēd as Remembering

In the Targum of Jonathan, the use of the verb *pāqăd* is in the sense of 'remembering, recalling'. Unlike Onkelos and Neofiti who used *sʿr* 'to visit, to inquire', Jonathan used *dḵr* 'to remember, to recall' in parallel with *prʿ* 'to return, to pay'. This seems to have influenced Rabbi Abraham Ibn Ezra and subsequently other rabbis to elaborate on the theme of 'remembering' in their commentaries. For him, 'The Name' cannot raise his anger against the son if he is among those who love Him; this would be in contradiction with Jeremiah 29:51 and Ezekiel 18:20. He portrayed his understanding of *pqydh* 'visit' as *zkyrh* 'remembrance' in the following statement,

> The meaning of *pqydh* is to be equated to *zkyrh*, for The Name will wait [to see if] the wicked would return from his sin and that he would bear a son who is better than him. And behold, if he walks in the ways of his father and also the third generation, and also the fourth generation, The Name will not lengthen his nose to the fourth, for otherwise he would lose the memory of everything. The Name will recall what the father did, and what the son did, and the son's son, and he will not relent beyond the fourth [generation].[35]

33 Patrick D. Miller, *Deuteronomy* (Louisville: John Knox Press, 1990), 77; Adam Clarke, *Clarke's Commentary: Genesis-Deuteronomy* (Wesleyan Heritage Publications, 1998), 547.
34 Philip G. Ryken and R. Kent Hughes, ed., *Exodus: Saved for God's Glory* (Wheaton, Illinois: Good News Publishers, 2005), 567-72.
35 *Mikraot Gedolot*, http://mg.alhatorah.org/Full/Shemot/20.1#e0n6.

Subsequent rabbinic interpreters refer to Ibn Ezra or stress some aspects of his argument with supporting biblical illustrations such as Deut. 24:16; Isaiah 14:20; Genesis 15:16; Numbers 14:18; Deuteronomy 5:14; and Amos 2:15. Some insist that the punishment at the fourth generation consisted of the extermination of the whole family line from the surface of the earth.[36]

From a Christian perspective, Jerome who had shown perplexity about the justice of God punishing innocent infants for an old man's countless sins had another answer to the question. In a letter, he warned Sabinianus, a deacon who had misbehaved in many respects, and urged him to repent and not persist in his sins, even though God is slow to anger and relents from avenging sin. God expected this ~~it~~ from him. Jerome wrote,-

> It is therefore that he renders (*restituit*) the sins of the fathers in the children unto the third and fourth generation; he would not want to punish (*punire*) those who sin at once but relents first and condemns last. For if he were to avenge the iniquity immediately, the church would lose many; and certainly would not have the apostle Paul.[37]

Pōqēd as Inquiring

Ezekiel Hopkins (d. 1690) interpreted *qanah* to mean 'inquiring', related to the jealousy of God. For him, jealousy had two characteristics: ~~it is~~ on the one hand, distrustful and suspicious, and on the other searching and inquisitive. Therefore, God had a vigilant eye on his people, like a husband on his wife, ready to avenge with anger any kind of infidelity. As for the types of punishment, he distinguished between temporal and eternal punishments. The eternal punishment was never given to repenting or reforming children, that is, those who did not follow the footsteps of their fathers in sinning. Eternal punishment was consistent; no sinning individual would escape. But as for temporal punishment, it could fall upon the children whether imitating or repenting. He cited the Amalekites who were punished four hundred years after the sin was committed by their ancestors (1 Sam 15:2).[38] He regarded temporal punishment as never consistent. Hezekiah was a good example of the son of a wicked who became prosperous.[39]

---

36 Chezekiah ben Manoach, Ya'akov ben Asher, Ovadiah Seforno, Chayyim ben Atar, Meir Leibus Weiser. *Mikraot Gedolot*, http://mg.alhatorah.org/Full/Shemot/20.1#e0n6.

37 Jerome, Epistula CXLVII. Ad Sabinianuji Diaconum Cohortatoria de Paenitentia, Text edited by Isidorus Hilberg, *Sancti Eusebii Hieronymi Epistulae, Pars III: Epistulae CXXI-CLIV*, Scriptorolum Exxlestiasticorum Latinum, Vol. LVI, (Lipsae: G. Freytag, 1918), 317

38 Other examples he cited included were from 2 Sam 12:4 and Matt. 23:35.

39 Ezekiel Hopkins, *An Exposition of the Ten Commandments* (New York: The American Tract Society, 2004), 126-164, thildebrandt@gordon.edu.

Prior to Hopkins, John Calvin (1509-1564) found the meaning of 'inquiring' in *pqd* itself. He translated the participle *poqed* with its literal Latin equivalent *visitans* 'visiting'[40] and he further commented: 'To visit iniquities, (*visitare iniquitates*) is equivalent to inquiring (*inquirere*) into them, or taking cognizance of them, in order that punishment should be inflicted in proportion to the crime.'[41]

Calvin thought it was absurd that God punished innocent children because of the sins of their parents. He stated,

> But when God declares that He will cast back the iniquity of the fathers into the bosom of the children, He does not mean that He will take vengeance on poor wretches who have never deserved anything of the sort; but that He is at liberty to punish the crimes of the fathers upon their children and descendants, with the proviso that they too may be justly punished, as being the imitators of their fathers.[42]

Pōqēd Explained and Applied to Kinyarwanda

The thorough study of G. André is very helpful in understanding the verb root *pqd*. The root appears in other Semitic languages in various forms,[43] most generally with the primary meaning: 'to visit, to search, to seek, to examine, and similar meanings'. In the Old Testament, it means checking presence, sometimes with the negative result as in to miss; mustering an army especially checking those fit for military service or checking how many have been killed; taking a census; taking an interest in a person or to inquire about someone. In that sense it is also used in parallel with *zāḵ*ăr 'to remember'. The interest may disadvantage the person and in that case the verb would mean 'to condemn'. In the hif'il and sometimes in qal, it means to commission, to appoint. When God is the subject, it means 'to pronounce or execute judgment' which could be negative or positive. Therefore, the expression *pāqăd* 'āwôn *'al* means 'to condemn, to punish'.[44] André concludes,

> Although *pqd* seems to be a word with a double meaning in Hebrew, one must assume the presence of a basic meaning that is then construed differently in different contexts. One such basic meaning might well be "examine closely," whereby the judgment or decision issuing from such examination is included.[45]

40 John Calvin: Commentarium in Quinque Libros Mosis, Pars II. Guilielmüs Baum, Edüardus Cünitz, Eduabdüs Reüss, ed., *Ioannis Calvini*, Vol. XXIV. (Brunsvigae: C. A. Schwetschke et Filium, 1882), 375. https://archive-ouverte.unige.ch/unige:650.
41 Calvin, 380.
42 Calvin, 381.
43 G. André, 'פָּקַד paqad' in *Theological Dictionary of the Old Testament*, Vol. 12, Translated by Douglas W. Stott, (Grand Rapids, Cambridge: Eerdmans, 1974), 50-63 (50-51).
44 André, 'פָּקַד paqad', 50-60.
45 André, 'פָּקַד paqad', 50-51.

André's invaluable input deserves some additional comments. First, none of the identified Semitic languages has 'punishing' as the primary meaning of the verb. Second, the primary meaning of the verb is 'to visit', that is, 'to be present at the very place'. By extension, depending on contexts, the verb could cover the motivation of visiting, the purpose, the result, the decision and/or the issuing action. The motivation could be the interest in the person to visit. The purpose of visiting could be to inquire, to seek, to search, to monitor, to inspect, or to oversee. The result of the inquiry could be that somebody or something is missing or to be found or to be searched for (nif'al). The action could be to take care of, to judge, to condemn, or to vindicate. One could appoint or be appointed or commissioned to take the above actions. Therefore, any translator of the verb should bear it in mind and use as much as possible the verb that expresses the primary idea before going to the purpose, the result or the decision.

For the sake of application to the subject matter, the primary idea is that God visits his people. The motivation is that He is interested in the people because they are chosen and they are connected by a covenant, on the analogy of a husband-wife relationship. With an inquisitive eye of a jealous husband, the purpose of the visit is to inquire, investigate whether the wife may not be misbehaving. Though the more expected result might be negative; as the parents are unfaithful, He prolongs His investigation upon the children until the third and fourth generations. The more expected decision is to punish or take vengeance but also to bless, in case a generation is repenting or reforming. The four aspects of visiting, inquiring, remembering, punishing or blessing would depend on the result. Looking at the various translations and interpretations of the statement under study, one may argue that many of them are limited.

The current Kinyarwanda versions have shortcomings at two levels. First, they seem to have ignored the primary meaning which is to 'visit' and have taken the decision that the meaning is 'to punish, to take revenge'. Second, they translated 'those who hate me' as a genitive which excluded the guilt of the progeny and made God's judgment unfair. *In Bibliya Ubuhinduzi bw'Isi Nshya* (BUIN)[46] and *Bibliya Yera* (BY)[47] the punishment is

46 …*mpanira abana icyaha cya ba se kugeza ku buzukuru b'abanyanga* 'I punish children for the sin of their fathers up to the grandchildren and the greatgrandchildren of those who hate me'.
47 …*mpora abana gukiranirwa kwa ba se, nkageza ku buzukuruza n'ubuvuvu bw'abanyanga* '…I take vengeance on the children for the iniquity of their fathers, and I do it up to the great-grandchildren and the great-great grandchildren of those who hate me'.

clearly extended to the innocent progeny of the sinning forefathers.[48] But it is not clear in both versions whether the fathers are included or not. Explicitly, *Bibiliya Ntagatifu* (BIN) states, '…*ihanira icyaha cy'ababyeyi mu bana babo kugeza ku gisekuruza cya gatatu n'icya kane cy'abanyanga*' ('…punishing the sin of the parents in their children up to the third generation and the fourth of those who hate me'). However, it is not clearly stated whether the progeny are innocent or guilty. What confuses the matter in this version is the use of the phrase 'generation of' which is ambivalent in Kinyarwanda. *Bibiliya Ijambo ry'Imana* (BII) reads: 'I punish those who hate me, and their children, and their grandchildren and their great-grandchildren'[49]. Thus, the version clearly states that the God-hating fathers are punished with their offspring, but again it is not clear whether the grandchildren and great-grandchildren are innocent or guilty.

In Kinyarwanda, the primary idea can be expressed by the verb *gusura* 'to visit'. Unfortunately, this verb cannot cover the four levels of meanings of the statement in question. The most fitting alternatives are the various stems of the verb *kugenda* 'to walk, to go': the applicative intensive stem *kugenderera* 'to visit', the causative *kugenza* 'to investigate' and the causative reversive with the intensive or repetitive meaning *kugenzura* 'to inspect, to monitor, to evaluate, to audit'. *Kugenderera* is preferably used for persons and would not go with an abstract object *icyaha* 'sin'. *Kugenzura* is more open and used in many aspects of human activities. It may be acceptable because the level of suspicion is low, but the aspect of rewarding is more highly intensified than that of punishing or vindicating. *Kugenza* is the best alternative; being generally used in legal matters the aspects of punishment or vindication are highly intensified depending on the results of the investigation. Therefore, an alternative translation of the passage would be: *kuko Uwiteka Imana yawe ndi Imana ifuha, ngenza icyaha cy'ababyeyi ku bana babo kugeza ku buzukuru n'abuzukuruza banyanga* 'for I the Lord your God am a jealous God, investigating the sin of the parents upon their children up to the grand-children and great-grandchildren hating me'.

48 BUIN puts the grandchildren and the great grandchildren while BY has the great grandchildren and the great-great grandchildren.

49 ..*mpana abanyanga n'abana babo, n'abuzukuru babo, n'abuzukuruza babo* 'I punish those who hate me, and their children, and their grandchildren, and their great-grandchildren'.

Conclusion

In Biblical times, people believed that innocent children could be punished because of their fathers' sins and some Biblical stories relate such cases. Some calamities befalling the nation of Israel, the wicked and the innocent, could be interpreted as receiving punishment from God. In the context of strict monotheism, everything good or ill was believed to come from God. On the other hand, from life experience, the misbehaviour of some people may have negative consequences on humanity including innocent people. However, that is not what is expressed in the rationale of the second commandment even though some interpretations and translations including the current Kinyarwanda versions point to that sense.

The phrase 'visiting the sin' covers primarily the sense of patient cross-generational investigation with a threat of punishment or promise of reward depending on the decisions based on the findings, whether the generations are imitating or repenting from the sinful traditions of their fathers. I have argued that the verb *kugenza* 'to investigate' is better for carrying the meaning of the Hebrew *pqd* in the context of Exodus 20:5. The aim of the alternative translation as faithful as it may be is not to solve the problem of the justice of God. Questions about the prosperity of the wicked and the suffering of the innocent still remain. Nevertheless, the statement has confessional and pedagogical values. The God we believe and trust is a just and merciful God. He does not leave injustice unpunished, and He delights in repentance and transformation. Karol Meyers calls it 'the language of the hyperbole' intended to warn the people against the cross-generational consequences of the sin of idolatry and the immensity of the everlasting blessings promised to those who keep trust and faith in the Lord.[50] In the Rwandan post-genocide context, the statement is a warning, more than ever before, against the transmission of evil ideologies from parents to their children. It is a call upon the younger generations to part company with old ethnic and genocide ideologies.

50 Meyers, Carol L., *Exodus: The New Cambridge Bible Commentary* (Cambridge, New York, Melbourne, Madrid, Cape Town, Singapore, Sao Paulo: Cambridge University Press 2005), 171-72.

EPILOGUE

Ode to an Angel

Alex Asiedu

Tucked somewhere on the northern fringes of Accra is an estate called Palm Valley. Mid-sized and middle class, it is one of several dozen residential estates dotting the outskirts of Ghana's capital. A short drive down to the western wall bordering the estate shows the neatly arranged bricks and mortar give way to a lovely expanse of green, streams and some bird life. The lovely little oasis is called Allison's Greens.

The Park, Allison's Greens in Kuottam Palm Valley Estates, Oyarifa, Accra

The Park may have had a different name. Allison Howell, who it was named after, did not want her name on it. But the community, grateful for her foresight and generosity would not have it any other way. Allison, singlehandedly, thought up the idea of the park and resourced funds to develop it.

The official signage on the park

If the park's name is unlikely, its existence is even more unlikely. Palm Valley is a cluster of middle-class houses carved out of an area that was all wooded just over a decade ago. Housing developments like these have provided homes for many Ghanaians but the unplanned nature has created an environmental disaster for Accra. There are houses built on waterways, green spaces that have been concreted over and trees that are dispensed of with reckless ease. The result, a city, much like large parts of urban Ghana, that is drowning under its own environmental mess, frequently flooded, covered in plastic waste in and stripped of much of its flora and fauna.

The original state of the park

The story of the park and how it came into being mirrors the story of Allison's life and how she has lived it. Warm, resilient and self-effacing she was able to convince the owners not to develop the strip of land on which it sits and did not give up until they gave in. Generous and humble she raised the funds for the project and still resisted having her name on it.

Even when she was going through treatment for cancer, she showed grace and dignity in her pain, capturing pictures of birds on her morning walks and putting together a lovely picture calendar from the images. True to her core she gave most of them out as gifts to her community and friends. Patiently optimistic, she held out hope that the mass of shrubs and waste could turn into a place of natural, vegetative beauty and stuck to the task until her vision turned into reality.

2018 Calendar created by Allison with photos of rare species of birds found in Oyarifa

Sadly, these may be attributes that are slowly being eroded in modernity's self-absorbed rat-race. Her story is a timely reminder that one person can still be a force for good to bring about change and stem the tide that threatens to sweep away our values and our planet.

Allison has many more wonderful traits. But perhaps her most striking is her quiet ability to live out Christ's values without judging others. An Australian who chose to serve in the Kasena area of Northern Ghana, she immersed herself in their culture while sharing the gospel. She did the same in Akropong and at Palm valley, sharing with us, eating with us, dancing with us, mourning and celebrating with us.

Allison with her neighbours on the park

She became like us. Almost like the Master did 2000 years ago. There is no higher calling than that - sharing the gospel in a simple, practical, loving way and accepting others without compromising one's values.

Thank you, Allison. Your light still shines here.

The writer and Allison

CONTRIBUTORS

INI DORCAS DAH (PhD) is a lay preacher of l'Eglise Protestante Evangélique du Burkina Faso. She is the founder and president of l'Association Evangélique Sowtaa (Association Evangélique pour la Joie et le Développement de la Femme, Burkina Faso). She is also a Professeur Associée (Visiteur) of l'Institut Pastoral Hébron (IPH), Bouaflé, Côte d'Ivoire and an Adjunct Research Fellow at the Akrofi-Christaller Institute of Theology, Mission and Culture (ACI), Akropong-Akuapem, Ghana from where she received a PhD. She has published Women Do More Work Than Men: Birifor Women as Change Agents in the Mission and Expansion of the Church in West Africa [Burkina Faso, Côte d'Ivoire and Ghana] (Regnum Africa: 2017 and Wipf and Stock 2018), and articles on women in Christian mission, theology, human need and environment, and spirituality and hope in Africa. Her research interests are Christian history, Gospel and Culture and Holistic Mission and Development.

EBENEZER YAW BLASU (PhD) is a Research Fellow at the Akrofi-Christaller Institute of Theology, Mission and Culture, (ACI), Akropong-Akuapem, Ghana. He is a researcher in living theological issues, particularly religious cosmological and ecological praxis, and holistic missional and transformational development through Christian higher education. He is the author of African Theocology: Studies in African Religious Creation Care (2020), Physiologic Link Between Nutrition and Reproduction (2014), and The Messiah is Coming Again (2002). He is a contributing author to the Journal of African Christian Thought and the Evangelical Review of Theology.

RUDOLF K. GAISIE (PhD) is a Research Fellow at the Akrofi-Christaller Institute of Theology, Mission and Culture at Akropong-Akuapem, Ghana and serves as Director of the Institute's Centre for the Study of Early African Christianity (CESEAC). He is a Methodist layperson. His research interests include Early Graeco-Roman and (North) African Christianity, Christianity and Culture, Mother Tongue Biblical Studies and African Christian Leadership.

ANDREW F. WALLS (of blessed memory) was an Honorary Professor, University of Edinburgh and University of Aberdeen; Professor of the History of Mission, Liverpool Hope University; Emeritus Professor,

Akrofi- Christaller Institute of Theology, Mission and Culture and University of Aberdeen.

ROBERT ADDO-FENING (PhD) is a historian and former Acting Head of the Department of History at the University of Ghana. Legon. He has twice been a Fulbright Scholar and has been an active contributor to the national life of Ghana through his membership of numerous boards and committees and in his role as Chairman of the Boards of Directors of Ghana Post from 2001 to 2008. In addition to his publication on Akyem Abuakwa 1874-1943: from Ofori Panin to Ofori Atta (Trondheim, 1997), he has also published numerous articles in refereed journals on both Ghanaian and Indian history.

ANTHONY O. BALCOMB (PhD) is Senior Research Associate in the School of Religion, Philosophy, and Classics at the University of Kwazulu-Natal. He is the author of two books and sixty published articles in peer reviewed journals. He was a pastor in a Pentecostal denomination in South Africa for fifteen years and his special interests are around what happens at the interface of the encounter between African and Western epistemologies and world views.

BENHARDT Y. QUARSHIE (PhD) is the Rector of the Akrofi-Christaller Institute of Theology, Mission and Culture (ACI), Akropong-Akuapem, Ghana and a minister of the Presbyterian Church Ghana. He holds a PhD from Princeton University in the field of Biblical Studies.

GABRIEL AKIMANA (PhD) is an ordained minister of the Presbyterian Church in Rwanda. He is also a Lecturer, teaching Biblical Hebrew and Old Testament at the Protestant Institute of Arts and Social Sciences (PIASS), Huye, Rwanda, and an Adjunct Research Fellow at the Akrofi-Christaller Institute of Theology, Mission and Culture (ACI), Akropong-Akuapem, Ghana from where he received a PhD. His research interests are Translation and Contextual Interpretation of the Bible.

EMMANUEL ALEX Y. ASIEDU is the Managing Director of STANBIC Investment Management Services. He is currently the president of the Ghana Securities Industry Association, the umbrella body for capital market operators in Ghana and President of the CFA Society, Ghana. He also chairs the national advisory board of Impact Investment Ghana. Alex is involved in a number of social-impact programmes and activities that aim at creating positive health and educational outcomes. He lectures as an adjunct at Ashesi University, a leading Ghanaian university and works with the Share Foundation, a local not-for-profit that supports the educational needs of Ghanaian children. He is a Trustee of the Gaede Foundation supporting local communities with educational and health grants and providing start-up funding for micro-businesses. He also serves on the international advisory board of the West African Centre for Cell Biology and Infectious Pathogens (WACCBIP) and is a member of the management committee of the School of Social Sciences, University of Ghana, Legon.

ANGELA DWAMENA-ABOAGYE (PhD) is the Executive Director of The Ark Foundation, Ghana, a Christian Mission NGO which established the first Domestic Violence Shelter in Ghana in 1999. The Ark Foundation has been involved in addressing issues of violence against women and children through direct services provision, policy and legislative advocacy, training and public education. Angela holds a Bachelor-of-Laws (LL.B) degree from the University of Ghana, and a Qualifying Certificate to practice law (B.L) as a Barrister and Solicitor (1989). She also has a Masters-in-Law (LL.M) degree from the Georgetown University Law Centre, Washington D.C, USA (1995), a Master-of-Arts (M.A) degree in Theology (2006), a Master of Theology (MTh) degree in African Christianity (2013) and a Doctor of Philosophy (PhD) Degree (2018), from the Akrofi-Christaller Institute of Theology, Mission and Culture, Ghana. She has won a number of awards including the Micah Award (Los Angeles, USA), Millennium Excellence Award for Women's Empowerment and the Martin Luther King Jnr. award for Social Justice (Ghana). Angela is also a conference speaker, consultant, lecturer and a registered para-professional counsellor with the Ghana Psychological Council. She is a licensed Minister of the International Central Gospel Church. Her interests are young women's leadership development, working with survivors of violence, women's mental health advocacy, Christian Discipleship and Pastoral Care.

JONAH D. KWOTUA is a Pastor of the Assemblies of God, Ghana and passionate about the Kasena culture. He played a key role in the translation of the Kasem Bible, and currently teaches at the Assemblies of God Theological Seminary (Northern Campus) located at Kumbungu in the Northern Region of Ghana. Before his teaching engagement, Rev. Kwotua was pastor among the Talensi and Kasena (both ethnic groups in the Upper East Region of Ghana). Rev. Kwotua holds the MTh (African Christianity) from the Akrofi-Christaller Institute of Theology, Mission and Culture (ACI), Akropong-Akuapem, Ghana; and has enrolled for his Doctoral studies with the Pan African Theological Seminary (PAThS), Lome, Togo (DMin). He has a number of unpublished materials on the Gospel and Culture engagement.

JUDITH A. BAWA is a Senior Research Fellow and one time Deputy Director of the Institute for Distance and Continuing Education at the University for Development Studies (UDS) (2016 to 2019). Trained originally as an Agriculturalist, she holds a Masters Degree in Social Development and Sustainable Livelihoods from the University of Reading in England. Before accepting to work at the UDS, Ms. Bawa served as the National Coordinator for Gender Development programme at the Ghana Institute for Linguistics, Literacy and Bible Translation (GILLBT). Her interest research areas are Gender, Culture and Development and the Environment in which she has a number of publications. Judith has two sons and four grandchildren.

JOSHUA D. SETTLES (PhD) is a Senior Ministry Specialist with InterVarsity – Link, and a Research Fellow at the Akrofi-Christaller Institute of Theology, Mission, and Culture in Ghana. He holds a BSc in Finance, and a MA in Modern European History, both from the University of Tennessee Knoxville, an MA and a PhD in Theology, both from the Akrofi-Christaller Institute. His research interests include Primal Religions, Christian History, Missions, and Black American Christianity.

KEHINDE OLABIMTAN (PhD) holds a Master of Environmental Design degree in architecture from the University of Lagos, Nigeria, and a Doctor of Philosophy in theology from the University of KwaZulu-Natal, South Africa. He is an adjunct lecturer at Akrofi-Christaller Institute of Theology, Mission and Culture in Ghana and taught at Bowen University in Nigeria. His teaching and research works have essentially been on the interactions between Christianity, Islam and African religion in the 19th century. His doctoral thesis Samuel Johnson of Yorubaland, 1846-1901: Identity, Change and the Making of the Mission Agent was published by Peter Lang (Oxford) in 2013 in the Africa in Development Series. He is an associate teaching faculty at St. Stephen's College, Edmonton, Alberta, while working on a Doctor of Ministry in theology and the environment.

SEBLEWENGEL DANIEL (PhD) is the Head of Academic Affairs and lecturer of Practical Theology and Ethiopian Church History at the Ethiopian Graduate School of Theology, Addis Ababa, Ethiopia. She obtained her PhD in Theology at Akrofi-Christaller Institute, Ghana in 2011. Over the years, she has served in several capacities at the Ethiopian Kale Heywet Church. Seblewengel has also been involved in various initiatives which include eradicating harmful traditional practises, especially FGM and the book she co-authored led to the declaration of zero tolerance to FGM by the major ecclesiastical bodies in Ethiopia. She published academic articles and is the author of the book titled Perception and Identity: the relationship between the Ethiopian Orthodox Church and Evangelical Churches in Ethiopia published in 2019.

VELLAH TEMKO NGAINA (PhD) is a Research Fellow at Akrofi-Christaller Institute of Theology, Mission and Culture in Akuapem-Akropong Ghana. She has participated in many training programmes and published academic research-based articles on Bible translation, language and Biblical studies. Her research interests are Biblical studies, New Testament Studies, Bible Translation, Gospel and Culture and Women Advocacy.

VICTOR J.T. ZIZER (PhD) is head of department, for Leadership, at Pentecost University, Accra, Ghana. He served the Presbyterian Church of Sierra Leone as Senior Pastor for fifteen years, eight of which was as Moderator of the Church. During this period, he obtained a Master in Education (Guidance and Counselling) at the Njala University, Freetown and taught part-time at The Evangelical College of Theology and The Reformed Theological School, both in Sierra Leone. He completed his PhD in theology, at the Akrofi-Christaller Institute, Akropong – Ghana, focusing on Christian history, and specifically researching on the Role of the indigenous language education in the expansion of Christianity in Sierra Leone. During this period, he also served as Associate Minister with the Presbyterian Church Ghana. He has written a few articles in his research area, with a recent one on 'Hannah Kilham and Gender Issues: The Place of Females in the Liberated African Villages of Sierra Leone', Ghana Journal of Religion and Theology Vol. 8.1 (2018) 67-95. His continues to pursue interests in Christian history, education, gender and Counselling.

JAMES KWEKU GYEKYE WALTON (PhD) is a Senior Research Fellow at Akrofi-Christaller Institute of Theology, Mission and Culture, from where he received his PhD. He is also a clergyperson of the Methodist Church Ghana, which he has served for several years in both educational and pastoral ministry. He has research interests in Christian History and Contemporary African Christianity and has a number of articles in them to his credit. He is the author of Early Ghana Methodism as well as a contributor to the volume: The 'Golden Pod': Its Religious, Socio-Economic and Political Impact on the Gold Coast and Ghana.

INDEX

A

D

E

F

G

I

J

O

P

Q

R

S

Milton Keynes UK
Ingram Content Group UK Ltd.
UKHW021321181123
432831UK00021B/583

9 789988 334819